has not

LXE

MOVEMENTS IN JUDAISM

PUBLISHED

ZIONISM. By Richard J. H. Gottheil, Ph. D., Professor of Semitic Languages in Columbia University, New York City.

HELLENISM. By Norman Bentwich, author of "Philo-Judaeus of Alexandria," etc.

IN PREPARATION

MYSTICISM. By Joseph H. Hertz, Ph. D., Chief Rabbi of the United Kingdom of Great Britain and Ireland.

RATIONALISM. By Isaac Husik, Ph. D.

REFORM JUDAISM. By Samuel Schulman, D. D., Rabbi of Temple Beth-El, New York City.

MOVEMENTS IN JUDAISM

HELLENISM

HELLENISM

BY

NORMAN BENTWICH

Author of "Philo-Judaeus of Alexandria," etc.

PHILADELPHIA
THE JEWISH PUBLICATION SOCIETY OF AMERICA
1919

COPYRIGHT, 1920,
BY
THE JEWISH PUBLICATION SOCIETY OF AMERICA

TO MY WIFE
HELEN

*Who represents for me the perfect union of
Hebraism and Hellenism
In Love*

*"I remember for thee the kindness of
thy youth, the love of thine espousals;
how thou wentest after me in the
wilderness, in a land that was not sown."*

CONTENTS

		PAGE
	PREFACE	11
I.	INTRODUCTION	15
II.	THE HELLENISTIC CULTURE	51
III.	HELLENISM IN PALESTINE TILL THE DESTRUCTION OF THE TEMPLE	85
IV.	HELLENISM IN THE DIASPORA	126
V.	THE HELLENISTIC-JEWISH LITERATURE	197
VI.	THE RABBIS AND HELLENISM	250
VII.	THE AFTERMATH	297
VIII.	CONCLUSION	331
	NOTES	361
	BIBLIOGRAPHY	377
	INDEX	381

PREFACE

The title of this book should be rather Hellenisticism—if one might coin the word—than Hellenism, since it is concerned not with all the culture which produced the brilliant civilization of classical Hellas, but with its debasement which was spread over the world during the three centuries immediately preceding the Christian era. The Jewish people both in Palestine and the diaspora were constantly in contact with this Hellenistic influence which colored every aspect of their thought. In the first three centuries of the Christian era they were engaged in an incessant struggle with the products of that influence which determined the bent of their future development and the bent of the religious history of the world. The interaction of Judaism and Hellenistic culture is then one of the fundamental struggles in the march of civilization; and Hellenistic Judaism is, after the Bible, the most remarkable contribution of the Jewish genius to the world's thought.

I have tried to show the relation of this development to the idea of Catholic Judaism, and have con-

sidered the Hellenistic Jewish literature and
philosophy from a standpoint of rabbinical tradition. In taking up this position I differ from most
of those who have treated of this epoch. They have
been chiefly interested in the relation to Christianity, and have taken as the criterion of value the
approximation of the teaching which finally broke
away from Judaism. Even Moritz Friedlaender,
who has dealt with the subject in a number of
books, professedly from a Jewish point of view,
fixes his eyes on the Christian Church as the end of
Hellenistic Judaism, and eulogizes the divergences
from the rabbinical tradition with an ecstasy of
which only a faithful convert is capable. It is a
commonplace with this school to contrast the broad
universalism of Hellenistic Judaism with the
narrow legalism of the Pharisees which eventually
prevailed in Palestine. Their view does not com-
mend itself to me. The fusion at which the univer-
salists were aiming was not with the clear Hellenic
reason, but with a lower amalgam of Greek and
Oriental ideas which tended to debase Jewish
monotheism. Nor was it the ethical teaching of
Christianity which came from a Hellenistic development, but its dogmatic and gnostic elements.
The preservation of historic Judaism was the lode-

star of the ancient Rabbis and the sufficient basis
of their opposition to the strange doctrines. I have
often found a parallel between the Jewish circumstances of the present day and those which existed
in the Hellenistic period; and as this book is meant
to be rather a popularized than a scholarly presentation, I have not refrained from pointing out the
lesson. And I hope that the account of the conflict of Judaism with the culture of the ancient
world may have a direct interest for the Jewish
life of our own day.

The literature on the subject is abundant, though
naturally the greater part of it is written from a
Christian point of view. I have set out in the
bibliography the chief works to which I have referred, but there are two works to which I am under particular obligation: Schürer's *History of the
Jewish People in the Time of Jesus,* which, in spite
of its title, covers nearly the whole Hellenistic
period, and Bacher's *Agada der Tannaiten,* and
Agada der Palästinensischen Amoräer, which
form the best guide to rabbinical philosophy and
theology.

I have had to write the book at intervals and in
different places, between legal work, and for the
greater part of the time I have been away from a

good Jewish library. I must ask indulgence therefore for the inaccuracies which I doubt not will be
found. Dr. Solomon Schechter, and my brother-
in-law, Dr. Israel Friedlaender, made many helpful
suggestions, and my debt of gratitude is still fresh
for the more indefinite but more precious guidance
which they have given me to the whole subject.

LONDON, *September,* 1915.

CHAPTER I

INTRODUCTION

In the first of the blessings which Balaam pronounces upon the children of Israel, he exclaims: "Lo, it is a people that shall dwell alone, and shall not be reckoned among the nations." [1] Philo, expounding the passage, adds: "Israel shall be apart not so much by reason of the separation of their homes or the cutting-off of their land, but by reason of the peculiarity of their customs; for they shall not mix with other peoples, so that they may not deviate from their distinctive way of life." [2] The idea of the separation and selection of Israel is the constant theme of the prophets, as it was the dominant motive of the Mosaic legislation. The Law not only contained a rigid prohibition against the paganism of the surrounding peoples and against intermarriage with idolaters, but enacted a way of life affecting the daily conduct of the individual, which had as its object the isolation of the nation in order to fit it for the moral mission. It has been said epigrammatically by a modern French writer that Judaism is not a *religion* (a force which binds

15

men together) but an *abligion* (a force which
keeps them separate). And for three thousand
years it has resisted the pressure of other creeds.

The mass of the people, indeed, did not always
remain loyal to the principles of their teachers
and lawgiver. Many a time " they mingled themselves with the heathen, and learned their works "; [3]
and most of the kings of Israel and Judah, indulg-
ing the more material ambitions for territorial aggrandizement, made alliances with their heathen
neighbours, and imitated their ways, and were
faithless to the ideal of a chosen people. But the
prophets never allowed that ideal to die or to become obscured. While they denounced the idolatry
of the backsliders, and foretold the destruction of
the political power of the kingdom as a punishment
therefor, they declared that, after the people had
been chastened in exile, a remnant would return to
Palestine to form there the centre of a spiritual
supremacy over mankind. " And it shall come to
pass, that he that is left in Zion, and he that
remaineth in Jerusalem, shall be called holy, even
every one that is written unto life in Jerusalem." [4]

At the same time the prophets preached this
idea of a universal Judaism, and already in those
days the " sons of the stranger " were joining
16

themselves to the Lord. Foreseeing the captivity of the nation, they declared that Israel was to be " a light to the nations," and, taught by him, all the families of the earth should come up to do worship upon the mountain of the Lord in Jerusalem. " My house shall be called a house of prayer for all peoples." [5]

The destruction of the political kingdom came about as the prophets had foretold, and Israel and Judah were carried away captive to Assyria and Babylon. With other peoples the loss of political independence and their enforced exile from the national territory have regularly marked the decline, and often the death, of their culture; but with the Jewish people the reverse happened. Aroused to a consciousness of their transgressions by the national disaster, and to a consciousness of their peculiar spiritual heritage by closer contact with the idolatries and superstitions of their Chaldean masters, the exiles were more receptive to the exhortations of the teachers who sought to inspire them. True, a section in Babylon thought that exile meant national extinction and that assimilation was the only course open to them, and exclaimed: " We will be like the heathen, like the families of the coun-

17

tries."[6] "Our bones are dried up, and our hope is lost; we are clean cut off."[7] And the majority, though they remained loyal to the religion, preferred their exile-homes, amid the brilliant material civilization of Babylon, to the return to their ruined land. But a sturdy remnant, cherishing the conviction of a national restoration, resisted the blandishments of their environment, and, when the opportunity came, returned to Palestine to re-establish the cult of their fathers. So, too, of the large body of exiles, who, on the fall of Jerusalem, had gone down to Egypt with the prophet Jeremiah, a number remained loyal, or rather returned to loyalty, to the Mosaic law, and preserved their national way of life. The Aramaic papyri, recently found in Assouan, establish the existence of Judean communities in Upper Egypt from the sixth century, living their own life separate from the rest of the population, worshipping at their own shrine, speaking their own language, observing the Passover, and in close touch with the national centre.[8] Some amount of syncretism colored their beliefs, for they seem occasionally to have paid homage to other deities besides the God of their fathers; but these strange ideas probably disappeared when the

18

whole nationality yielded to Ezra's great reformation.

Without committing oneself to the dogmatic
speculations of the higher critics who are pleased
to assign the composition of the Mosaic code to the
period following the Restoration, it is clear from
the historical narrative of the books of Ezra and
Nehemiah that the religious organization of the
Jewish people was much more thoroughly carried
out after the return to Palestine than before the
captivity. At Babylon, where the exiles had contrived to keep the religion alive without the temple
worship and its ritual, the foundation had been laid
for two new institutions, the house of prayer and
the house of study, the *Bet ha-Keneset* and the *Bet
ha-Midrash*. When the faithful remnant returned,
indeed, they first set about the work of rebuilding
the temple, but they brought with them the habit of
meeting for prayer and study, without ritual and
without sacrifices, in local gatherings. Every village in Judea where a Jewish community was settled and every place in the dispersion where Jewish
life flourished had its religious meeting-place and its
teacher.' While the priests and the Levites were
the hereditary leaders of the cult at the sanctuary,
in the country scribes, distinguished for their

19

knowledge of the law and the traditions, were the leaders of the religious life.

The dedication of the temple, the foundation of the central authority, known as the Men of the Great Synagogue, the definite ordering of the religious life, and the restatement of the whole Law are alike ascribed to Ezra who came to Judea from Persia in the reign of Artaxerxes I (about 450 B. C. E.). Most famous of the scribes, who were the popular teachers, and himself a member of the high-priestly family, Ezra stands out as the supreme influence in the foundation of a Jewish religious democracy. As it is said by the rabbis: "Ezra was worthy to be the bearer of the Law to Israel, had not Moses preceded him." [10] By his work, and the work of the organization which he called into being, the religious ideas and ideals of the prophets and the Mosaic law of holiness were woven into the life of the people, so that it became in very deed "a nation one on the earth," unique in its intense religious earnestness and its high moral standard. Now more than ever the Jews were a theocracy, a people devoted to the single idea of God. Knowledge of God was their conception of wisdom; service of God their conception of virtue; their poetry was the expression of the yearning of the soul for

God; history was a religious drama in which God was the protagonist, judging the nations with righteousness; the conception of God was their philosophy—they did not require any other: their faith in God and their religion were strong enough to satisfy their desire for knowledge. They felt the more deeply for the very limitation of their outlook.

The Judaism of the Mosaic books, as organized by Ezra, was the first example in the history of humanity of a religion which was independent of a cult, and which was the basis of both national and personal morality. The Torah became a law of life to the individual, and the inheritance of the congregation of Jacob was handed down and amplified from generation to generation, and almost the whole intellectual activity was centered upon it. The scribes determined in its main lines the selection of the holy writings which formed the nation's special possession. By the constant teaching and interpretation of these writings in the houses of study the Jews became, in a real sense, " the People of the Book." But the scribes were not merely the guardians of the tradition, they were active teachers who continually sought new themes to inspire the people with love for their faith and for the Law. As Ben Sira writes at a rather later period:

He that giveth his mind to the Law of the Most High,
And is occupied in the meditation thereof,
Will seek out the wisdom of the ancients and be occupied in prophecies;
He will keep the sayings of the renowned men,
And where subtil parables are, he will be there also.[11]

The Wisdom of Ben Sira itself, though dating from the Hellenistic period, is typical of the literary activity of the scribes. The Greek translator recommends it in the prologue because it contained wise sayings, dark sentences and parables, and certain particular ancient godly stories of men that pleased God. Describing the origin of the book, he relates how his grandfather, Jesus ben Sira, " when he had much given himself to the reading of the Law and the Prophets and other books of our fathers, and had gotten therein good judgment, was drawn on also himself to write something pertaining to learning and wisdom, to the intent that those who are desirous to learn and are addicted to these things might profit much more in living according to the Law."

Among the Jews, as among no other people, did the thought of its greatest teachers become a living

influence upon the mass. The words attributed to
the Men of the Great Synagogue at the beginning
of the Sayings of the Fathers: " Make a fence
around the Torah, and raise up many disciples,"
illustrate the spirit which was working during the
two centuries of Persian rule. The observance and
study of the Law were the dominant interests. The
outward conditions of Palestine conduced to the
steady strengthening of the religious consciousness.
For two hundred years the country was free alike
from political complications and from religious in-
tolerance. Simultaneously with the preaching of
the great prophets of Israel, Zarathustra had denounced the paganism of the Persians, and inculcated the principles of a higher religious belief.
Hence the Persians had an inherent sympathy with
Jewish monotheism, and from the time of Cyrus till
the fall of the empire they made no attempt to interfere with the religious observances and beliefs
of their Jewish subjects

The Jews of Babylon and Egypt were under the
same tolerant sway as those in Palestine. In the
book of Esther, it is true, we read of attempted persecution in Persia itself, based on the charge that the
people scattered through the dominions of Ahasuerus had " laws diverse from those of every

people; neither keep they the king's laws"; but the issue shows that the attempt was not successful. It was the outcome of a personal political intrigue and not of permanent popular feeling. On the other hand, the Jews were under no temptation to assimilate the ideas and manners of the Persians, who were mainly concentrated in the eastern parts of the empire, and who did not develop a dominant intellectual culture. The other subjects of the Persian dominions were a mixed multitude, lacking a strong national feeling; but the Jews retained and deepened their individuality, regarding their religious culture as the planks and timbers of which the nation was constructed. While the tolerant sway of the Persian empire preserved Judea from exterior disturbance, the circumstances of the people continued to isolate them from the influence of external culture. The anti-Semites of the first century used to make it a reproach to the Jews that the Greek writers made no mention of them, which proved that they were a mushroom people. Josephus, in refuting the attack, explains the absence of communication with Hellas, in the period that preceded Alexander's conquests, by the self-contained character of the land. " As for ourselves, therefore, we neither inhabit a maritime country, nor do

we delight in commerce, nor in such communication
with other men as arises from it; but the places we
dwell in are remote from the sea, and having a
fruitful country for our habitation, we devote ourselves to its cultivation. Our principal care is this,
to educate our children well, and we think it to be
the most necessary business of our whole life to observe the laws that have been given us, and to keep
those rules of piety which have been handed down
to us. Since, therefore, we have had a peculiar way
of living, we had no occasion in ancient times for
mixing with the Greeks, as they had for mixing with
the Egyptians by their intercourse of exporting and
importing commodities; or as they mixed with the
Phoenicians who lived on the sea-coast, by reason
of their desire for gain in commerce." [12]

Being essentially engaged in agriculture and devoted to their own traditions, the Jewish people in
Palestine were not affected in the fifth and fourth
centuries by the Hellenic civilization which, during
that period, was spreading over the maritime
provinces of Asia Minor. A few stray references
to the Jewish practice of circumcision occur in
Herodotus [13] and Aristophanes. [14] The Bible, on
the other hand, contains references to Javan (the
Hebrew for Ionia) in Ezekiel (27. 13) where it is

mentioned as a mart of the Phoenicians, and in
Isaiah (66. 19) where the prophet speaks of
" Tubal and Javan, and the isles afar off that have
not heard of the fame of God " ; and in Zechariah
(9. 13) who speaks of God stirring up the sons of
Zion against the sons of Javan. Some communication, then, between Hellas and Palestine existed
even in biblical times. As early as Joel,[15] the merchants of Tyre and Sidon are denounced for having
sold the children of Judah and Jerusalem unto the
Greeks. Jewish slaves must have been brought to
Greece, or at least to the greater Greece established
on the Asiatic coast, in the heyday of Greek life.

Nor is it impossible that the monotheistic utterances of the Ionian philosophers Xenophanes and
Heraclitus in the fifth century B. C. E. were in some
indirect fashion influenced by reports of the Jewish
teaching about God. But if a few philosophers
picked up some Jewish lore, there was no general
intercourse or exchange of culture which had any
permanent effect on thought. As Josephus again
points out in his refutations of Apion, who charged
the Jews with aloofness, the Greek city-states in
their prime were equally aloof, and their culture
was exclusively national. Plato ordained for his
ideal Republic that it should not admit foreigners

to intermix with its population, but should keep
itself pure and consist only of such as persevered in
their own laws. And this was the standpoint of the
Hellenes of the classical age who regarded all foreigners as "barbarians." A modern writer, con-
trasting the work of Israel and Hellas, has said:
"Both peoples felt themselves a peculiar people
marked off from the surrounding races by distinc-
tions more ineffaceable than those of blood—by its
possession of intellectual or religious truths which
determined the bent and meaning of history. For
centuries their work went forward at the same time,
but in disparate spheres, each nation unconscious of
the other's existence." [16] Between Greeks and Barbarians, between Israel and the heathen, there could
be no intimacy, no union. Yet this very spirit of
exclusiveness was one of the conditions which enabled each to nurture and bring to maturity the
life-giving germ which it bore within it. "While
the Jews had developed their sublime idea of God,
the Greeks were moved by an impulse for a many-
sided culture. They were achieving in their little
city-states, each with its intense national life, the
art, the literature, the science, and the philosophy
which have ever since been the inspiration of the
civilized world."

It was not until the semi-Hellenized Macedonian prince Philip had destroyed the independence of these city-states, and his son Alexander, who succeeded him to the sovereignty of Hellas, had conquered the Persian empire, that the period of national creation and national exclusiveness gave way to a period of international communication and cosmopolitan culture. Palestine fell into Alexander's possession in 332 B. C. E., Egypt a year later; and from that time the position of the Jewish people was changed. The aim as well as the effect of Alexander's conquests was to link up the East and the West not only politically, but also intellectually. National feeling hardly existed among the eastern peoples, save the Persians and the Jews: it was decaying among the Greeks. Alexander sought to bring about a great fusion of ideas in a cosmopolitan empire, which, by a combination of racial excellences and national cultures in some larger expression of political life than the Greek city-state, should advance the work of humanity and give expansion to the Hellenic spirit. Hellenism was to be dominant, but it was to be brought into contact with Oriental systems. The fusion of cultures was prepared by the physical intermingling of the various elements who were to build up together the new civilization. To this end the conqueror established cities and colonies at the most vital points of his empire, and planted in them groups of his diverse subjects and, among others, of the Jews.

The Talmud " and Josephus ¹⁸ contain several stories of the special regard which Alexander conceived for the Jewish people, but one and all are probably apocryphal. Nevertheless, it is not unlikely that the great conqueror realized the value for his imperial edifice of the one subject people in the Persian empire who had preserved in its purity a national culture; or that the pupil of Aristotle, who possessed a desire for knowledge equal to his master's, had some vague notion of the peculiar philosophic character of the Jewish belief. Plutarch records as one of Alexander's maxims that God was the father of all men, and especially of all the best men; and he held his mission to be the pacification of the whole world. If Josephus may be believed, Aristotle had been brought into touch with a Jew, and had acquired from him some knowledge of his religion. Clearchus, one of his disciples, relates a conversation which the master had with a man who was a Jew by birth, and came from Coele-Syria (the Greek name for Palestine). "These Jews," he continues, re-

porting Aristotle, " are sprung from the Indian
philosophers: they are named by the Indians Καλανοί
and by the Syrians Ἰουδαῖοι ; and they took their
name from the country which they inhabit, Judea :
but the name of their city is hard to pronounce,
for they call it Hierousalem. Now this man being
hospitably treated by the people, and having come
down from the upper country to the places on the
coast, became Hellenized, not only in language but
also in mind; so that when we were in Asia in the
places where he resided, he conversed with us and
the other philosophers and made a trial of our
skill. And as he had much converse with learned
men, he rather communicated the wisdom he himself possessed."

Aristotle, in the cited passage, goes on to tell of
the remarkable temperance of the Jew in his diet
and manner of life. Unfortunately, the book of
Clearchus has not been preserved, and we have no
other record of Aristotle's reflections on the Jewish
people.[19] But from this fragment and from that
of another early Peripatetic philosopher, Theophrastus, it may be inferred that the Jews were regarded in the school as a singular philosophical
people worthy of study. The ideas of the Peripatetics were to some extent the ideas of Alexander;

and therefore the favorable treatment which he
showed a people, materially of little account, may
be partly due to the respect for their moral and cul-
tural individuality. Yet, apart from these considerations, the Jews, on political and economic grounds,
were a valuable element in his civilizing enterprise.
They were already dispersed; settlements of them
were to be found in Mesopotamia, Persia, Egypt,
Syria, and the Caucasian provinces, and the Greek
conqueror was only continuing the policy of the
Persian kings when he carried a number of them
to the city at the Delta of the Nile which he designed
and named after himself.

Be the motives what they may, the effect of Alexander's action in transplanting the Jews from
Palestine to different points of the empire was to
mark a new stage in the extent of the Jewish dispersion and a new epoch in the history of civilization. His action was followed by his successors,
who split up his empire, but preserved his cosmopolitan outlook. The Jewish colonists carried with
them their religious ordering of life and their organization around the place of assembly and study,
henceforth known by the Greek name of *synagogue*
(*i. e.,* assemblage). Recently archæologists have
recovered a monumental record of the founda-

tion of a synagogue at Alexandria in 308 B. C. E.,
and similar inscriptions from the following century
are frequent. Recognized as a separate nationality, the Jews were allotted a special quarter in the
Hellenistic cities, not by way of restriction, but as a
privilege; and they were allowed to exercise their
own autonomous jurisdiction, so that their peculiar
manner of life might not be infringed.[20] Alexander's aim was not to destroy the individual characteristics of his diverse subjects, or to enforce one
uniform culture upon them all, but to bring together
different peoples in order that from the exchange
of their ideas some fruitful union should arise.

The first Ptolemy (Lagus), who secured Egypt
and Palestine in the scramble for empire which followed Alexander's death, increased the numbers of
the Jewish colony at Alexandria, and distributed
thirty thousand soldiers from Judea in Egyptian
garrisons.[21] The dynasty which he founded, and
which for over a century ruled over the territory he
had gained, maintained, with hardly an inter-
ruption, these principles of tolerance, and thereby
secured the loyalty of the Jewish population. If
we are to believe the narrative of the third book
of the Maccabees, towards the end of the third
century B. C. E. occurred a persecution of the

32

Egyptian Jews; but, like the attack of Haman,
the movement was based on temporary political
animosity, and did not result in any permanent
dislike. Again, Seleucus I, who at the beginning
of the third century carved out for himself a
Syrian empire from the eastern portion of Alexander's conquests, settled a number of Jews in his
foundation of Antioch and other less celebrated
colonies. He accorded them civic rights as well as
autonomy for their own concerns, and made no attempt to interfere with their religious liberty.[22]
Even if, as several scholars hold, the royal decrees,
quoted by Josephus, should not be authentic, it is
clear that during the third century the Jewish settlements in Egypt and Syria were steadily growing in
importance, and that their privileges were maintained throughout the shifting domination of their
warring rulers.

The Jews in that period as to-day were dispersed
over the civilized world. Strabo, the famous
geographer, who just before the beginning of the
Christian era wrote a large historical work, says in
a fragment about them: " They have penetrated
already into every state, so that it is difficult to find
a single place in the world in which their tribe has
not been received and become dominant." [23] Strabo

is a careful and accurate writer, and as he was a considerable traveller, he could speak from personal knowledge. There is the less reason to doubt his testimony about the extent of the Jewish dispersion, because it is supported not only by the Jewish authorities, Philo and Josephus, who doubtless are prone to exaggerate the importance of their people, but also by documentary evidence which cannot lie—the inscriptions and epitaphs of the age.

The dispersion had begun seven centuries earlier, when the people of Israel were carried off by the king of Assyria to the banks of the Tigris and Euphrates; and it went on continuously and increasingly, partly by voluntary and partly by forced migrations, whilst the numbers of the Jewish population in the Greek cities were largely augmented by the adhesion of proselytes. The ten tribes of Israel never returned to their national land,[24] but, remaining beyond the Euphrates, may have become the nucleus of a later Jewish settlement in that region. Moreover, only a small section of the Judeans returned with Zerubbabel after the Babylonian captivity to Palestine, when Cyrus granted the restoration of the nation and the temple, and many more remained in the Persian realm. The chief Jewish centres in the far East were Babylon, Seleucia, Nisibis, and Nehardea; but throughout the country they were powerful, and at times they made themselves independent of the civil power. A Babylonian Jew in the first century B. C. E. founded a little kingdom; and some time later two Jews of Nehardea, named Asineus and Anileus, gathered around them a band of daring spirits, and established a robber-principality which defied the Parthian and the Roman governments.[25] About the same period the rulers of Adiabene, a kingdom east of the Tigris, and some of their subjects were converted to Judaism, and threw in their lot with the Jewish nation in their struggle for freedom. In an eastern direction, then, the Jewish dispersion extended as far as and beyond the limits of Greek and Roman expansion, and helped to fix the boundaries of Hellenistic culture and Roman rule. The Jewish population formed a kind of buffer-state between the Graeco-Roman world and the Barbarians, a buffer-state in which Hellenistic culture had a place, but a subordinate place.

The first impulse of the Jewish diaspora which was set up by the Babylonian captivity was toward the East, the second, which was stimulated by Alexander's conquests, was towards Egypt and Syria.

Their part in the foundation of Alexandria has already been noted; and under the almost unbroken favor of the ruling dynasty, their colony continually increased. Philo estimates that in his own day, *i. e.,* at the commencement of the Christian era, there were one million Jews in Egypt, of whom a quarter part were at Alexandria.[26] Two of the five districts into which the city was divided were entirely peopled by them. They largely controlled the important corn trade of the Nile, and the alabarch, whose function it was to regulate the commerce of the Delta, was frequently chosen from their community. Alexandria was the centre of the Jewish community in Egypt and the second Jewish city in the world; but there were considerable settlements stretching up the Nile as far as modern Abyssinia. A special Jewish district was established in the Delta around Leontopolis, where, at the time of the Seleucid persecution, the exiled priest Onias obtained permission to erect a temple to be a new centre of Jewish worship. The temple, which had its special ritual, outlived the sanctuary at Jerusalem by three years, but it never obtained a position to rival the authority of the central shrine. The account in the Talmud of its foundation, according to which one Rabbi held that Onias built it

36

for the glory of God, while another maintained
that it was for the propagation of heresy, indicates
that the sages regarded it with dubious respect.[27]

Inscriptions have revealed the existence of a Jewish community at Arthritis [28] and the dedication of a
synagogue " to the most high God," which points
to a congregation which was sympathetic enough
with Hellenistic ideas to admit subordinate deities.
The Fayyum papyri likewise show records of
a synagogue (Σαββάτιον) of the second century
B. C. E.[29]

Westwards the Jewish settlements stretched
along the African coast. Cyrene, the territory
neighboring to Egypt which had been semi-
Hellenized since the sixth century, had a Jewish
colony that enjoyed equal rights with the Greeks
from the time of Ptolemy Lagus. Strabo divides
the population of the district into four parts: Citizens (i. e., presumably, persons with the full Greek
rights), peasants, metics (resident aliens), and
Jews.[30] Earlier than the colony at Cyrene, earlier
perhaps than the establishment of any other colony,
the Jews must have had a settlement in the
Phoenican city of Carthage. Perhaps some were
taken there as slaves by the merchants of Tyre and
Sidon, for the Septuagint translates *Tarshish* in the

book of Isaiah [31] by the word Καρχηδών (Carthage), and near Carthage, at the coast town of Boricum, a temple was standing in the reign of Justinian, which was said to have been founded by King Solomon. This indicates the tradition of early Jewish settlement in the region; and recently a vast Jewish necropolis has been found near the site of the old city.

In Syria the only Jewish colony of which the foundation is specially marked is that of Antioch.[32] But the early Seleucid emperors, in furtherance of the previous policy, moved the Jews from the plains of Mesopotamia, and encouraged their settlement in all parts of their realm. They flourished especially at the centres of the empire: at Antioch, its capital, Apamea, its military headquarters, and Tarsus, its chief seat of culture.[33] Further they were spread over Asia Minor and the islands off the coast. The letters which, according to the author of the first book of Maccabees, the Roman consul wrote, to the subject-allies and friends of Rome to seal the alliance which the Senate had made with Simon the Maccabee, were sent " to Demetrius (of Syria), to Attalus (of Pergamus) and to Ariarathes (of Cappadocia) and to Arsaces (of Parthia), and unto all the countries, and to Lampsacus (?)

and to the Spartans and unto Delos and unto Myn-
dos and unto Sicyon and unto Caria and unto Samos
and unto Pamphylia, and unto Lycia and unto Hali-
carnassus and unto Rhodes and unto Phaselis and
unto Cos and unto Side, and Gortyna and Cnidus
and Cyprus and Cyrene." [34]

The Roman document (which, if genuine, dates
from 139 B. C. E.), though it does not conclusively
point to the existence of Jewish communities in all
these territories, at least argues that they were
known along the coast of Asia at the time, and also
in the Greek islands.   The journeys of the first
Christian apostles are evidence that two centuries
later synagogues did in fact exist in these places.
Some congregations may have originated with the
Hebrew slaves who were sold in distant countries
from the time of the captivity, but a voluntary
stream of expansion was started by the great national and religious revival which the Maccabean
victories initiated.   The Jews, in fact, took the
place in the Hellenistic and Graeco-Roman world,
which the Phoenicians had occupied in the Myce-
naean and Hellenic ages, as an international people,
with these differences, that they established more
permanent settlements, adopted more thoroughly
the surrounding culture, and at the same time ex-

erted a more profound influence upon their environment. From the islands and from Alexandria they made their way to the mainland of Greece, and the journeys of the apostle Paul prove the extent of their expansion by the first century in this direction, as well as along the Mediterranean shores. He visited congregations at Thessalonica, Beroea, Philippi, Corinth, Athens, and as far west as Illyricum. Jerome, some centuries later, speaks of the Jewish colonies as forming an uninterrupted chain from Mauretania (Morocco) to the Indies.

Scattered though they were over the whole of the Hellenistic world and beyond, the Jewish communities possessed a solidarity lacking to every other people. Their settlements occupied a position which may be contrasted with that of the old Greek colonies along the shores of the Mediterranean Sea. These had been centres of intellectual civilization, whereas the Jewish colonies were centres of distinctive religious and moral life. The bond of unity with the motherland among the Greeks had been mainly sentimental, and often disappeared with conflicting interests; but the Jews of the diaspora were linked together with the centre of the nation and the religion by the existence of a supreme legislative body, the Jerusalem Sanhedrin, and a supreme sanctuary, the Jerusalem temple. The institution of the yearly money-offering for the temple worship and the three yearly pilgrimages to Jerusalem at the time of the festivals not only symbolized, but consolidated the unity of the people. According to Josephus, no less than 2,700,000 males gathered together in the city at the time of these great pilgrimages,[35] of whom by far the larger proportion came from the Jewish colonies. And in view of these immense gatherings of devotees, one can understand the boast of Philo when he calls Jerusalem the capital " not of one nation but all nations." [36] At the same time the cohesion of the Jews in each city was maintained by the institution of the synagogue, and in more important centres by the large measure of local self-government which was secured to them. The synagogues were the meeting-places of Jews and those sympathetic to their ideas, not merely for prayer and learning but for general purposes. They were the centres of Jewish life and culture in the broad sense. Their organization has many points of resemblance with that of the Greek towns, suggesting that they were in themselves little townships. As Renan says, " The Jews had a patriotism aiming not at the formation of great compact states, but of little autonomous communities in the bosom of other states." The exact form of the constitution of their communities is uncertain; it has to be reconstructed from a number of inscriptions, but it appears to have been on the following lines. An indefinite number of archons (rulers) regulated the affairs of the synagogue with or without a deliberative council. Associated, and occasionally identical, with the archons were an indefinite number of religious heads, entitled archisynagogi, whose duty, it is conjectured, was to preach on the sabbath and give instruction in Jewish law. The title without the duties was given to those who had done good service for the congregation, whether born Jews or proselytes. Benefactors of the community might also receive the right of a special seat (προεδρία) ; and sometimes a golden crown, in imitation of the habits of Greek cities, was presented to them.

The Jews then recognized themselves, and were recognized by others, as a separate society; and where they were numerous, or their settlements were of old standing, they occasionally formed an autonomous " ethnos," sometimes living in a separate quarter." The rights of such an ethnic community varied, but in all cases its officers possessed a power of taxation for the purpose of the contribution to the temple and the local needs, and a civil and petty criminal jurisdiction over disputes between Jews and on matters of Jewish law.[38] The Alexandrian community had powers of taxation entirely independent of those of the Greek city. But this position was exceptional. It had also its own Sanhedrin or Bet Din, which administered the Mosaic law. The organization of archons and council was frequently applied to the larger ethnic groups as well as to the single synagogues. Thus, in the time of Philo the affairs of the Alexandrian community were directed by a number of archons and a council, probably of seventy-one members (which was the number of the supreme council of the nation at Jerusalem). Previously one supreme genearch or ethnarch had governed the Jews, and " like the governor of an independent city enforced the fulfilment of the national duties and the observance of the laws." [39] Similarly at Antioch a single archon, and at Damascus a single ethnarch, was responsible for the good order of the community.[40] And at Cyrene, says Strabo, the Jews had their own governor as if an independent polity.

In certain favored towns, where their settlements were of ancient standing, the Jews had the full po-

litical rights of the city as well as their own autonomous rights. They formed a separate tribe or
Phyle, and therefore were relieved from taking a
part in the religious cults which were an important
feature of Hellenistic municipal life. Elsewhere
they had special rights as a separate community, but
were not citizens of the city or the empire (as a
body). Whether full citizens or not, they preserved, by their organization into synagogues and
by the organization of their several synagogues
again within a town, a distinct and separate national-religious existence with a strong sense of cor-
porate life. A powerful religious consciousness
flourished among their groups, and gave them a
solid strength which was proof against envy and
hatred, seduction and force. Jewish separatism
was the source of the dislike which the natives, and
especially the Greeks, felt toward them; but it was
the foundation of their strength; it was not so much
a barrier against the admission of Gentiles to their
community, as a wall of protection against the introduction of pagan ideas into their life. They
contrived to maintain national life in an international diaspora. When other peoples were losing
their individual stamp through a characterless
amalgamation of cultures, they preserved intact the

distinctive moral and social outlook of Judaism;
and when the city-state was ceasing to foster any
high ideal of life, they established a new form of
association which provided a powerful motive of
conduct for thousands who had not been born in
their nation. The synagogal organization of the
diaspora not only gave Judaism the necessary mould
for resistance against foreign ideas, but fitted it to
become a centre of universal idealism amid the de-
nationalized mass of humanity.

While, on the one hand, the Jews were dispersed
by their settlements among the Hellenistic peoples,
it was part of the plan of Alexander, which was
faithfully maintained by his successors, to introduce
the Greek people into all parts of the empire.
Lower Syria, especially, as one of the strategic centres, received a large Hellenic population. Instead
of uprooting the population of the subject countries,
as Eastern conquerors had done, the Greeks took
their own country to them. Alexander is said to
have planted Macedonian colonies at Samaria, at
Scythopolis (the old Beth-shean), at the east end
of the plain of Esdraelon where the high road to
Damascus descended to the Jordan valley, and also
at Neapolis (Schechem), the old centre of the kingdom of Israel. The Ptolemies went further, and

subsequently surrounded the Judean plateau with Greek cities.

Many anthropologists regard the ancient Philistines as immigrants into Palestine from Crete, who brought the culture of the Aegean Islands to the East, and in their struggles with the Hebrews marked the first clashing of East and West.[41] The new Philistia was more certainly peopled by the Greek settlers. Within a century all along the Palestinian coast, and likewise in the country east and north-east of Jordan, a string of Greek cities were organized as semi-independent city-states, and beset Judea, as it were, with a wall of Hellenistic culture. On the coast were Gaza, Ascalon, Azotus (Ashdod), Joppa (the modern Jaffa), Apollonia, Doris, Sycamina Polis (on the site of the modern Haifa), and Ptolemais or Acco (the modern Acre); while in the trans-Jordan districts of Peraea, then one of the most fertile parts of Asia, a league of ten Greek cities, known as the Decapolis, comprised Damascus, Gadara, Gerasa, Dium, Philadelphia, Pella, Raphia, Scythopolis, Hippo, and Canetha.[42]

To this day no part of the eastern world can show so many and such striking Greek ruins as the country east of the Jordan. The plateau of Judea alone remained free from Greek settlements: its soil was

not fertile enough to attract Macedonian colonists.
But the whole of Galilee, which already in the days
of Isaiah was known as Galilee of the Gentiles,⁴³
was inhabited by a mixed population in which the
Jews were at first a minority. The provinces of
Gaulanitis, Batanea, Trachonitis, and Auranitis, to
the east of Palestine proper, had likewise Hellenized, and for the most part non-Jewish, inhabitants.
In fact, South Judea alone possessed a compact
Jewish population during the third and the greater
part of the second century. The Greek cities displayed, superficially, a complete establishment of
Greek institutions and customs—magnificent temples to the Greek gods and goddesses, local myths
about the Greek heroes and heroines, gymnasia,
public baths, annual celebrations of games, and in
many cases philosophical schools and academies.
Archaeology proves the rapid growth of Greek art
and Greek ideas in the country, and one of the most
splendid monuments of Hellenistic sculpture, the
so-called Sarcophagus of Alexander, is from Sidon.
The Stoic teachers of Ascalon were famous, as were
its grammarians and historians; while Gadara, on
the east of the lake of Galilee, produced in the second century a distinguished Epicurean philosopher,
Philodemus, and a distinguished epigrammatic

poet, Meleager. Greek was the common language throughout the Hellenized districts around Judea, and indeed through all the Hellenized kingdoms from Macedonia to India—not the pure classical idiom of Athens, but a conventionalized dialect known as the κοινή, *i. e.,* the common tongue or *lingua franca.* Thus, by the middle of the third century, when the Hellenizing process had firmly impressed the vast territory that Alexander had brought under his dominion, Judea and the Jews were, in large measure, isolated. The central community in Palestine and the scattered congregations in the dispersion were alike surrounded by a Hellenized environment, speaking a common language, participating in common cults, sharing a common way of life, and professing common cosmopolitan ideals. A certain national feeling still survived in the home of Greek culture, a few remnants of it in Egypt; but, for the rest, save in the Jewish communities without as well as within Judea, there was an utter decay of national patriotism, a rush to a glittering, soulless cosmopolitanism, a divesting of national traditions, and a superficial adoption of a new culture.

It was impossible that the Jews, living in the midst of such a disintegrated society, and forming part of a "melting-pot empire," should not be affected by the denationalizing tendencies. They were encompassed by an influence as subtle as the atmosphere. Little or no attempt was made to compel them to uniformity, but the very absence of external pressure made the resistance to the surrounding ideas the harder. Persecution, as all history has shown, is calculated to strengthen the individuality of the persecuted, and assimilation is most difficult to combat when there is toleration of the differences of a minority by a dominant majority. It was only the profound working of the synagogue and the religious law upon the mass of the people, and the consciousness of being a chosen people entrusted with a spiritual heritage, that preserved the Jews from absorption in the stream of Hellenism which dissolved every other form of culture. Some amount of assimilation and imitation inevitably took place. When it came into contact with triumphant Hellenism, the Jewish life lacked all that elegance and refinement, the beauty of form, and the ministration to the æsthetic senses which the Greeks had strikingly developed in their national life and carried far and wide in their dispersion. Moreover, Jewish thought lacked that systematic expression of intellectual ideas, the searching out of

49

nature, and the inquiry into ultimate causes which represented the deeper note of the Hellenic spirit, and now, to an extent, became the common property of the cultured world. Greek manners, Greek words, Greek ideas, were introduced into Judea: the Greek language and Greek culture made their way more thoroughly into the communities of the diaspora. The two advances of Hellenization, which progressed under different conditions for the two main parts of the Jewish people, must be examined separately; the outcome in each was different, but the struggle in both cases centered around the same point: the national religion. The essential conflict between Hebraism and Hellenism in the ancient world was a conflict between monotheism and paganism. But in order to appreciate the nature of the struggle and its importance in the history of human development, it is necessary to consider the character of the Hellenism with which, in the third and second centuries before the Christian era, Judaism was brought face to face.

CHAPTER II

THE HELLENISTIC CULTURE

The late Professor Butcher, in a lecture on Hebraism and Hellenism, quotes a verse of some ancient poet:

> Thus the sharp contrast of the sculptor's plan
> Showed the two primal paths our race has trod.
> Hellas, the nurse of man complete as man,
> Judea, pregnant with the living God.

This antithesis between Hellenism and Hebraism was impressed somewhat differently upon the English people by a teacher of the last century, who had a remarkable power of fixing general ideas in pointed phrases and establishing epigrammatic judgments upon the history of civilization. Matthew Arnold laid down, with an insistence which almost repels question, that " the uppermost idea with Hellenism is to see things as they really are, the uppermost idea with Hebraism is conduct and obedience." The ruling principle in the one case is spontaneity of consciousness; in the other strictness of conscience. The Greeks were objective,

the Hebrews subjective in their outlook. Now the
contrast between the Hebrew people, concentrating
their thought on God and morality, and the
Hellenic people, developing to their highest excellence the human faculties and especially the
power of reason, is broadly true. While their
independent city-states flourished from the eighth
to the third century, the Greeks, or Hellenes, as they
are more properly called,[1] developed a literary, a
plastic, and a dramatic art, such as no other people
at any epoch has equalled; they evolved a system of
social and political life more harmonious and more
beautiful than any subsequent development of the
state; and, lastly, they fostered a freedom of
thought and an intellectual searching into the nature
of things which have been an inspiration to every
enlightened age. On the other hand, the people of
Israel and Judah had produced but little of special
excellence in any of these directions, save a body of
laws, which they held to be divinely revealed, and a
collection of writings dealing with God's relation to
the individual man and to the nation and with the
individual and national conception of God. But
they had organized a system of life based upon
these laws and writings, which embodied the lofty
conceptions of their sages, and made the daily con-

duct of the mass an expression of the national philosophy. There had been no such thorough impregnation of the Hellenic national life with the thought of the philosophers. While the cultivation and appreciation of beauty were a common possession, the search for truth and the acquisition of knowledge had been throughout, even in the most brilliant periods of culture, the pursuit of the few. The mass of the people retained the primitive notions about the nature of the divinity and the rudimentary ideas of morality, of which the deeper thinkers had exposed the falseness.

Thus, side by side with the most finely-trained sense of physical excellence and literary form, a crude polytheism and dark superstitious practices existed in Hellas. In the heyday of Greek life the high standard of public morality which was evoked by the sense of the individual's duty to the state, checked the lower instincts of paganism. But with the decay of patriotism in the city-state, which finally led to the conquest of Hellas by the semi-civilized Macedonian power, the sanction of public morality passed away, and a moral decline was bound to follow. "The Greek state," said the late Professor Caird, " and the ethical harmony of life realized in it, could be regarded only as the creation of a people of artists, who by a combination of skill and good fortune had for once moulded the untoward matter of human existence into a political work of art." But neither the state, nor the ethical harmony of life realized in it was capable of transplantation to the Greater Greece which was constituted by the conquests of Alexander the Great. The Hellenistic culture which was spread over Alexander's empire was very different from the Hellenic culture which had flourished in the communities acquired by Philip of Macedon. The outward show of the life of the city-state could be reproduced—the temples with their columns and ornaments, the splendid public places of meeting and amusement, the gymnasia with their contests, the festal processions with their music and dancing, the civic theatres with their mythological dramas, and the academies with their teachers and scholars—all these were multiplied over vast kingdoms. But the ideal spirit of struggle for human perfection, which had given to Hellenic culture its distinctive excellence, was lacking in the imitation, and the defect deprived it of the old ennobling influence. Just as in the Hellenistic age the creative power in art died away, so also the freedom of thought and the intellectual eagerness were wanting. " Hellen-

ism properly so-called never passed over into Asia
. . . . Its living force, productive genius, self-
organizing power, and active spirit of political communion were stifled and gradually died out. All
that passed was a faint and partial resemblance of
it, carrying the superficial marks of the original." '
We may think, by way of comparison, of the
Frenchified civilization of the Levant in our own
time, which is a poor imitation of the genuine
French culture.

It was then, for the most part, a soulless culture
which the half-Hellenized Macedonians and the
degenerate offspring of the Hellenic city-state
brought to the East. Its religious teaching did not
form an organic element in the life of the citizen,
and was either an intellectual diversion, or a way of
salvation for souls weary of the world. And when
it was mingled with Oriental ideas, it degenerated
into an altogether bastard growth of sensuality and
rationalism. The Hellenistic city-state which was
spread over Alexander's empire, missed the intellectual and spiritual excellence of its model. The
mixed population which inhabited it had a varnish,
as it were, of high culture; but below the varnish a
motley mixture of primitive superstitions, barbarous
fears and feelings, coarse passions, and crude ideas

and beliefs, springing out of the old eastern cults, marred the Hellenic conception of life.

The two deeper influences which the Hellenistic civilization conveyed over the Oriental world were: 1) the religious cults; 2) the philosophical systems; the first designed for the masses, the second for the select band of intellectuals. Both soon showed a remarkable degradation from the spirit of Hellenism in its home. Lacking a mould of resistance to outside influences such as Hebraism possessed in its sacred law and its organization in synagogues, Hellenism received from its new environment many impurities. In order to appreciate its decadence in the diaspora, we may briefly consider the Hellenic religion of the classical age.

The Olympian hierarchy was primarily an interpretation of nature. The elements, the celestial bodies, and the native forces, which formed the raw material of polytheism among every people, were invested by the fertile and beautiful fancy of the Hellenes with a full personality, and reproduced in the heavens all the " passions and pleasures, the wishes and quarrels, of the human family." [3] In order that man should be at home in the world and preserved from fear of the unseen powers about him, " all that is unintelligible, all that is alien to

him, has been drawn, as it were, from its dark re-
treat, clothed in radiant form, and presented to the
mind as a glorified image of itself." ʻ While the
Hebraic seer soared straight to the idea of one,
supreme, transcendental Ruler, ordaining all things
in heaven and earth, removed above all human
qualities, yet in close communion with man through
the law of righteousness which He revealed to them,
the Hellenic poet transformed every phenomenon
of nature, black night and rosy-fingered dawn, earth
and sun, winds and rivers, sleep and death, into
separate divine and conscious agents, to be propiti-
ated by prayer, interpreted by divination, comprehended by passions and desires identical with those
which stir and control mankind. The human passions and faculties themselves, which, though part
of man, seemed to possess him from without, were
invested by the mythological and plastic mind of
the Hellene with divine personality. Converting
nature-powers which his ancestors had brought
from the East to new spiritual values, he incarnated
in Aphrodite the passion of love, in Ares the lust of
war, in Athene wisdom, and in Apollo the arts.

But as Hellenic life found its highest expression
in the city, the Hellenic theodicy was closely associated with the community. The gods and the divine

heroes were the founders and the sustainers of civil society; and not only the community as a whole, but its separate minor organs were under the protection of patron deities. The state's relation to the gods was expressed in ritual and art, in the festal games, the dramatic performances, the splendid processions, the majestic temples, the idealized statues, of which the record and the relics have aroused the admiration of every succeeding age. And together the Olympian gods were the protectors and guardians of Hellenic national life, preserving it from contamination by the inferior barbarian peoples, and animating it with the consciousness of a common origin and common beliefs.

Now in the prime of Hellas this religious system, created by the poetic fancy and the harmonizing spirit of the people, had satisfied their minds and had given a real inspiration to life. But when philosophers began to reflect and speculate about the nature of reality, its lack of truth and seriousness and its weakness as a moral influence became apparent. The two dominating principles of Hellenism, the desire to know the truth of things and the desire to harmonize life, were in conflict. Hence the greatest poets and philosophers of the golden age of Hellenism in the fifth and fourth centuries protested against the popular religion. Aristophanes genially ridicules it; Euripides dramatically impugns its anthropomorphism; finally Plato in his ideal Republic proposes to root it out, and substitute in its place the idea that " God is a being of perfect simplicity and truth, both in deed and in word, and neither changes in himself, nor imposes upon others either by apparitions or by words, or by sending signs, whether in dreams or in waking moments." *

The Greek sages attained to a lofty conception of God, and were fully conscious of the falseness and also of the demoralizing influence of the current paganism; and the most splendid of them formulated a conception of the divine goodness and unity which does not fall far short of the Hebraic monotheism. They identified God, indeed, with some abstract or metaphysical term, and did not invest Him with life and personality; and conceived Him rather as a final than an efficient active cause—that toward which all existence moves, more than that from which all being comes. Yet they did clear away from the idea of the divinity the crude material mythology, and associated it with morality. But whereas the prophets and the scribes and the Men of the Great Synagogue not only swept away the vestiges of idolatry, but made the belief in one universal God and the observance of the law of righteousness part of the life of the Jewish people, the Hellenic philosophers and poets did not affect the ideas of the main body of their fellows. The saying that Hellenism paid regard to beauty and Judaism to conduct has this amount of truth: in Hellas it was the feeling for beauty, in Judea the law of righteousness which impregnated the mass and determined the distinctive character of the people. And when Judaism and Hellenism expanded outside their national boundaries, these were the contrasted ideas which they carried with them into the diaspora.

The Homeric mythology remained the basis of the state religion in the Hellenistic empires, but, with the spread of rationalism, its hollowness was thinly veiled. The religion of the Greeks, which had become the amusement of their scepticism, now decayed into an empty ceremonial. The priests tried to satisfy the people with fine shows, but made no attempt to influence conduct. Even the shows, after a time, lost their attraction, and it is significant that the word which originally meant consecration came to imply careless performance.

If the philosophers failed to raise the people to their higher conceptions, the sophists who were the popular lecturers, and, as it were, the journalists of the day, did succeed in spreading a cheap and crude scepticism which undermined such faith in the old divine hierarchy as remained. Rationalism is the stamp of the first two centuries of Hellenistic culture. But the common people will always require some object of worship, and the Hellenistic age saw the growth of a number of new cults which closely reflect its character. In the confusion which accompanied the incessant wars of Alexander's successors, the power that seemed to control things was fortune or chance; and to this deity—the Greek Τύχη—the most constant court was paid. Pliny, in a well-known passage reproducing a Hellenistic source, writes:[6] " Throughout the whole world at every hour and place, by every voice, Fortune alone is invoked, and her name spoken: she is the one defendant, the one culprit, the one thought in men's minds, the one object of praise, the one cause. . . . . We are so much at the mercy of Chance, that Chance is our God." More ominous than the worship of Fortune was the growing cult of the stars and planets.

Certain dark fears and forebodings, a substratum of primitive superstitions, had always lurked beneath the outward brightness of Hellenic life. This *Hinterland* of thought came into prominence when the Greeks met eastern civilization. The religious systems of Assyria and Chaldea frequently conceived of the gods as evil spirits which are to be placated; and as, in the general interchange of thought, the elements of their civilization penetrated the Hellenic world, the superstitious seeds which were already there were nourished, and produced a rank harvest. Scepticism and superstition are closely allied, and the step was inevitable from disbelief in the state gods to gross terror of the heavenly powers that seemed " to fix man's destiny without regard to human will and human fears." One may find a parallel in modern America, where the decay of the old faiths has led on to the spread of the so-called Christian Science. The faith in astrology, spreading from Babylon westwards, became an obsession of the age; the Jewish sages opposed it, and continually denounced it, but many of the people devoutly believed in it. The stars were regarded as the absolute rulers of the world—had not Aristotle taught that they were divine beings?—and the influence of the seven planets on human life was a commonplace of thought. The Jewish good-wish is still " Mazzol-Tov "—*May your planet be good*—and our planet-week still bears witness to the popularity of the idea. " Astrology fell upon the Hellenistic mind as a new disease falls upon some remote island people; and the religion of later antiquity was overpoweringly absorbed in plans of escape from the prison of the Seven Planets." '

From the fusion of eastern ideas with the old Hellenic mystical teaching known as Orphism (which probably itself had an Oriental origin) all kinds of strange cults arose, ranging from the monastic spirituality of the neo-Pythagorean brotherhood to the wildest sensualities of the votaries of Bacchus and Isis. Men sought desperately for some union with the divine power, either through " ecstasy "—the release of the soul from the body—or through " enthusiasm "—the possession of the soul by the god. " People have lost their soul," said Dr. Johnson in the eighteenth century, " out of their body, and now turn hither and thither in search of it "; and his words exactly describe the condition of society in the Hellenistic period. To recover their souls some people ate their god or drank his blood, others swallowed his

name, others sanctified themselves by wild dances.
At the same time the belief in the immortality of
the soul, which in the flush of national life had not
been widespread, was strengthened, and the " mysteries " were largely concerned with the purification
of the soul for the future life. The idea of a personal redemption through union with the divine
spirit lay at the heart of all that was vital in the
religious thought of the Hellenistic age.

It was a common feature of these mystical cults
to place a mediator between the devotee and the
god whom he seeks.   Man could not soar up to the
abstract godhead direct, so he peopled the celestial
sphere with manifold spirits and demons who would
interpose their influence on his behalf, if supplicated
aright.   In order to bring the deity nearer to the
earth, the figure of man was projected into the godhead.   Under the influence of the Egyptian worship of Isis and Osiris, the conception of the primal
man gained a footing in philosophy and religion.
He was distributed through all things, and played
an important part in the origin of the universe; he
was even resolved into one of the fundamental ideas
of the Stoic philosophy.   The influence of eastern
ideas again was responsible for the deification of
kings, living and dead.   True Hellenism by its

instinctive moderation apprehended the difference
between man and God. Though the gods were
conceived in a human likeness, a definite line of de-
marcation was fixed between their world and human
beings. But the megalomania and likewise the self-
debasement of the Oriental were greater; on the
one hand divine rights were demanded, on the other
conceded to the rulers. Kings had been worshipped
in Egypt from the oldest times as the highest gods
incarnate; and the Hellenistic sovereigns, adopting
the Egyptian prerogative, established their worship
throughout their kingdoms. Hence the idea of the
incarnation of the divine power was popularized in
the lands of the East. The marvellous career of
Alexander gave him some claim to be regarded as
a God-man; but the honor which was given to him
after death was accorded, without the same justification, to the Ptolemies and the Seleucids and their
spouses in their lives. The Savior, the Benefac-
tor, the God-manifest, are the titles by which the
rulers of Egypt and Syria loved to be known to their
subjects; and most of their subjects were not loth
to placate them. The Jewish moralists alone
raised their voices against this degradation of religion. From Egypt, too, came the notion of
trinities of divine powers, which was innate in the

ancient hieratic religion. The mystical connection of Isis, Osiris, and Horus is the prototype of a vast development of Hellenistic theology. Egypt is the hearth of materialistic theology, of the notions of the immaculate conception, the divine incarnation, the various chambers of the after-world; and Hellenistic theology is marked by a gradual surrender of Greek to Egyptian thought.

At Alexandria, then, and throughout the Hellenistic kingdoms, Greek religion lost its ideal element, and became a mixture of universal scepticism and empty show, of gross superstitious beliefs in magic and astrology, and of Oriental mysticism and human abasement. It lacked for the most part a moral law, a sincere faith in divine help, a simple explanation of the origin of the world, a consolation in trouble and death. These were the very things which Judaism offered to a weary and jaded humanity. Is it surprising that it should have become conscious of its superiority, and have not only resisted the assimilation of the surrounding cults, but emerged as a vigorous missionary faith?

The decay of philosophy runs parallel with the degeneration of Hellenic religion. Philosophy at Athens represented the most splendid efforts of the human mind to know the truth, to see things as they

really are. It is true that a Socrates was condemned and put to death by his countrymen for his
" atheism " and for leading men astray by his dialectics; but his treatment was exceptional, and pro-
voked by a peculiar crisis in Athenian public life.
Each man was ordinarily left free to think out as
he chose the problems of the universe and to form
schools of any who wished to follow his teaching.
Aristotle opens his history of philosophy by a statement that all men desire to know about things; and
his standpoint is characteristic of the Hellene. Elsewhere he expresses very strikingly the love of
knowledge as it was conceived by the Hellenic
mind: [8] " Let us not listen to those who tell us that,
as men and mortals, we should mind only the things
of mortality. But so far as we may, we should
bear ourselves as immortals, and do all that in us
lies to live in accord with the sovereign principle of
Reason, which is our true self, and which is supreme
in capacity and dignity."

With this expression of Greek passion for
knowledge we may compare the standpoint of the
Jewish sages, that man should only seek to know
the things of this world, as it is said: " The heavens
are the heavens of the Lord; but the earth hath He
given to the children of men "; [9] and again: " For

67

My thoughts are not your thoughts, neither are your ways My ways ";[10] or in the words of Ben Sira: " Seek not things that are too hard for thee, and search not out things that are above thy strength."[11]

From the sixth to the fourth century, a number of philosophical schools flourished in Hellas and Ionia, and besides the philosophers proper, the sophists, who claimed to know all that there was to know or all that was worth knowing, purveyed a general culture. The intellectual activity and the spirit of inquiry culminated in the teaching of Plato and Aristotle. The two supreme figures of ancient philosophy, the one the master of those who think, the other of those who know, gathered the finest thought of Hellas on the nature of being and on the pursuit of the good, on the state and the individual, on poetry and fine art, on logic and rhetoric, on physics and mathematics. The Hellenic mind searched into every aspect of human life, and sought the truth about it. Ethics and theology were always an important part of their philosophical systems, and from the time of Socrates they were the chief concern; but they were studied without any religious preconception. The philosophers were conscious of the hollowness of the popular polytheism, and their object was to provide inquiring minds with an account of the universe which should be more satisfying than the poetic mythology. Both Plato and Aristotle, indeed, attained by reflective reason to a conception of the single government of the universe. For Plato the ultimate principle is the Idea of the Good working through a number of subordinate spiritual existences or Ideas which are in part ethically conceived. There was an idea of justice, of beauty, of truth, and human excellence. Aristotle likewise derives the Cosmos from one supreme principle, the Primum Mobile of the scholastic philosophy, which has as its ministering agencies the divine powers that dwell in the stars. The Hellenic genius thus gradually worked its way from the multiplicity of causes and deities to the idea of one Moving Cause, which was at first materially but in the end spiritually conceived. But it never reached the notion of a personal God; its supreme deity remained a creation of the reflective reason, abstract and impersonal, cold and aloof from humanity.

The teachings of Plato and Aristotle were handed down, respectively, in the Academic and Peripatetic schools. But the spirit of the masters did not survive them. Greek philosophy like

Greek art and Greek religion, was the offspring of
Greek political life, and with the subjection of the
city-state the eager search for truth no less than the
harmony of life was irretrievably lost. Men had no
stimulus and little leisure for the pursuit of
knowledge for its own sake during the ceaseless wars
which followed on the death of Alexander the
Great; they required practical guidance in life, and
a certain answer to their questions about the nature
of reality. Thought became dogmatic, and philosophy practical. These characteristics mark the
two post-Aristotelian schools, the Stoics and the
Epicureans, which soon became the most prominent
over the Hellenistic world. Ethics rather than
the discovery of truth was the chief consideration
in both; and the aim was to devise a plan of the good
life for the individual so that he should be independent of outward circumstances. To satisfy the
speculative bent of the Greek people, which still
insisted on some rational explanation of the universe, a system of logic and of physics was attached
to the ethical doctrine. But, consciously or uncon-
sciously, the true centre of interest changed. The
logical and physical teachings of the Stoics and the
Epicureans were a dogmatic framework designed
to fit their ethical tenets. The new science, like the

old mythology, was an attempt to make the world intelligible and comfortable. Happiness, not truth, was the end.

Stoicism was the most characteristic, as it was also the most powerful, intellectual expression of Hellenistic culture. It had its origin in the greater Hellas, of which Syria and Palestine formed a part, and its founders came from the Hellenized Orient: Zeno from Citium in Cyprus, Cleanthes from Assos in Asia Minor, while later some of its most famous exponents were sprung from Ascalon, Tarsus, and Alexandria. Probably it possessed an original infusion of Semitic thought, and it professed from the beginning a cosmopolitan ideal in which national differences were to be swept away, and all men were to be bound together by brotherly love and one common faith. The cosmopolitan tendency was one of the features of the time; philosophers proclaimed themselves citizens of the world, and in place of the old Hellenic exclusiveness advocated the fusion of all cultures. The Jews alone held fast to a national way of life.

Unity and simplicity were the leading motives of the Stoic system, but they were attained by the merging of higher and lower conceptions. The Stoics conceived the world as the manifestation of one principle which was variously described—materially as fire, spiritually as reason. This principle permeated and comprehended all things:

> All are but parts of one stupendous whole
> Whose body Nature is, and God the soul.

The religious creed of pantheism finds its finest expression in the hymn of Cleanthes to Zeus. The writer proclaims the divine element in man: " For our race is of Thee; we alone of all the mortal things that live and creep on the earth have obtained a reflection of speech. To Thee all this universe, which revolves around the earth, hearkeneth obediently, wheresoever Thou directest it, and willingly acknowledgeth Thy sway. . . . Thou canst make the odd even, and bring order into chaos, and what is unlovely may be lovely to Thee."

Similarly the Stoic ethical doctrine was summed up in the single rule that man should follow nature, *i. e.,* the spirit of the whole cosmos, and live according to reason. Negatively he was to eschew all emotion, and root out all the passions which carried him away from the rational life. He must be independent and self-reliant, needing neither divine nor human help. Positively he must try to discover the law of nature, and live according to it in harmony with the world-process.

In practice, however, the Stoics who aimed at a universal religion and almost at a universal church, made terms with the popular polytheism, and sought to adapt their pantheism to it. They had a power of assimilation and adaptation which rendered them the most successful missionaries of the ancient world, the lineal predecessors of the Roman Catholic Church. Pantheism can find room for a number of gods: it has only to distribute its collective deity among the various powers it wishes to absorb. This is what the Stoics did, and thus became the champions of Hellenic polytheism against a higher conception of God. They distinguished between the universal divine power, working as a unity in the world, and its individual parts. The stars were deified, the air was peopled with demons and unseen powers, and the Olympian hierarchy received a fresh lease of life as the retinue of the supreme divine principle. Among the chief devices by which their philosophy was adapted to the popular ideas was the allegorical interpretation of the Greek epic poems. Homer was venerated by the Greeks of the Hellenistic age almost as much as the Bible by the Jews; and in the desire to show that he had anticipated their doctrines, the Stoics sought beneath the letter of his verse for hidden

73

meanings, and prospected with great skill in ety-
mologies. The motive that prompted them is
simply stated by one Heraclitus, a famous exponent
of the allegorist's art: " If Homer used no allegories, he committed all impieties."

Characteristically of the new spirit of the age,
philosophers were impelled to find authority for
their teaching in the works of the national poets, or
at least they felt the necessity of reconciling the
ancient poetry with their doctrine. Socrates and
Plato had not scrupled to attack Homer and
Hesiod; but the Stoics and the other schools did not
dare to take that bold step, and explained away
what they could not accept. They were led then to
find deeper significance in all manner of things on
which people set store: in Homer and Hesiod words
and numbers, visions and dreams. Clearness and
directness of thought had passed away in the decay
of intellectual freedom. While according to their
strict theory they required that life should be led
absolutely according to reason, in practice the
Stoics accommodated their moral doctrine to
human weakness, and fostered crude superstitions.
They became the professors of astrology, of divination, and of soothsaying; and, upholding, as they
did, a complete determinism, they laid great stress

on the exposition of celestial influences and the interpretation of dreams and visions. At the same time, while they made their more vulgar and irrational concessions to popular ideas, they did undoubtedly exercise a bracing moral influence by opposing the sensuality, the self-indulgence, and the luxury of a decadent age. Their numerous preachers spread a kind of ethical culture for the masses, not very different from the Ethical Culture of our own day; and the Cynics, who were an extreme band of the school, went about like the mediæval friars or the modern apostles of the simple life, exhorting the people to self-restraint and continence, insisting that virtue was the only happiness, and themselves providing an example of reducing material wants to their lowest terms.

Between the Stoics and the Jews there was something in common, but more of antipathy. Alike they stood for a certain Puritanism, and for the moral ordering of life; alike they derived the Cosmos from one principle, and believed in the existence of a universal law of conduct, by observing which man could attain happiness; but there the likeness ended. The Stoics' creed was a materialistic pantheism; the Jews maintained a transcendental monotheism. The Stoics, instead of set-

ting themselves against popular superstition, allowed their teaching to be contaminated by it,
became the champions of the pagan deities, and,
by a system of allegorical interpretation, contrived
to shelter the many gods under the pantheistic principle.   The Jews were rigidly opposed to paganism
and all its ways, and refused to whittle away their
pure conception of God by any concession to lower
ideas.   The Stoics were determinists and rational-
ists, and held that man must stand by his own
strength; the Jews believed that man had freedom
of will and that the individual could have communion with God, and through God's grace alone
attain to blessedness.   The Stoics denied the immortality of the soul; the Jews upheld resurrection.
The Stoics taught that the universal law of conduct
was to be found in the study of nature, but they
never positively formulated it; the Jewish law was
contained in a revealed code and an ordered way of
life which was taught to all the people.   The
Stoics stood for a cosmopolitan civilization which,
while it was tricked out with fine phrases about the
brotherhood of man, meant in reality the impure
amalgamation of all kinds of creeds and cultures.
The Jews held fast to their national traditions, and
fiercely resisted the attempt to fuse their creed.

The physical struggle which the Jews waged with
the Hellenistic peoples was reflected by the intellectual contest between Judaism and Stoicism.
Nevertheless a section of the Jewish-Hellenistic
people was much influenced by the Stoic doctrine,
and Jewish-Hellenistic philosophy adopted part of
the Stoic teaching and Stoic phraseology.

The hostility of Judaism toward the other great
post-Aristotelian system, the philosophy of Epicurus, was more obvious and more glaring. The
name Epicurus became a synonym in the rabbinical
literature of Judaism for a heretic or a renegade.
Epicureanism has come to be associated with the
low ideal of pleasure-seeking as the end of life; but
in its purer form its aim was contentment, and in
some aspects its teaching was higher than that of
the more blatantly moral Stoicism. Epicurus and
his followers opposed the popular superstitions:
they maintained that the gods had no concern with
the affairs of this world, but formed a happy society
of their own, and man had neither anything to obtain nor anything to fear from them. Man's happiness was to be found in the pursuit of the right
kind of pleasure, and he must accept all that befell
him with equanimity. The Epicurean creed in its

highest expression is contained in a Greek couplet
which runs thus:

> There is nothing to fear in God,
> There is nothing to feel in death:
> That which man desires can be obtained,
> That which man dreads can be endured.

But Epicureanism was one of those systems which,
though they spring from lofty conceptions and
profess a not ignoble aim, are so disposed toward
human weaknesses that they are inevitably debased in practice, and become the buttress of a degenerate and degraded outlook. The denial of
divine interference in the world was converted to
atheism; the wise pursuit of pleasure, which it regarded as the human end, to unrestrained self-indulgence; its thorough-going materialism in thought
to thorough-going materialism in life. Hence,
naturally enough, to the Jew the Epicurus, the follower of hedonism, was a type of what was low and
godless, what was essentially and fundamentally
antipathetic to Judaism.

Besides the two new schools of Stoics and Epicureans and the two older schools of Academics and
Peripatetics, other systems of philosophy which had
an influence on the Jews of the diaspora flourished

in the Hellenistic era. Against the dogmatism of the other schools, the Sceptics maintained an altogether critical standpoint. They questioned the basis of knowledge through the senses (which was the Epicurean criterion) or through the reason (which was the Stoic standard). They conducted a negative polemic both against the popular religious polytheism and the quasi-philosophical theology of the schools, and advocated for themselves a position of agnosticism. Thus they performed part of the destructive work of undermining paganism, which was to prepare the way for a purer religious teaching.

On the other hand, the desire for a deeper religious life than was provided by the state cults found a philosophical expression in what is known as the neo-Pythagorean school. Pythagoras, among the early sages of Greece, had most clearly been stimulated by eastern influences, and he had grafted the eastern longing for the supernatural on the Greek longing for knowledge. He travelled in Egypt, and, according to the Jewish and Christian apologists of an uncritical and inaccurate age, sojourned in Palestine and learnt wisdom from Elijah. But, putting such myths aside, the fact remains that he approached in his teaching of God the Hebraic con-

ception of monotheism, and in his practical ethics
the Hebraic discipline of life by a system of law
and the regulation of daily conduct. The Pythagorean school achieved no great prominence during
the classical period, though their doctrines entered
as an element into the various Socratic systems. But
when in the Hellenistic age the scientific ardor di-
minished and the stimulus of eastern ideas was
increased, the severe discipline and the mystical
yearnings which the brotherhood fostered immediately responded to man's wants. The more earnest spirits, sick of material luxury in the Oriental-
ized Greek cities and without faith in the attainment
of rational knowledge, attached themselves to a
school which preached pure ethics and the simple
life and held out the hope of communion with a
supernatural, transcendental power. The Pythagoreans intensified the dualism between body and
soul, which was characteristic of Greek moral philosophy from the beginning. According to their
tenets, the soul existed in heaven before its incarnation, and the body was its prison from which release
could only be won by a rigorous training. The true
aim of man was thus to free his soul by ascetic exercises, and in a mystical ecstasy to attain to spiritual
bliss. In another part of their teaching they laid

stress upon the powers of numbers and words; the
elements of language were well-nigh universally
regarded as a link between the divine and human,
and numbers, it was believed, not only symbolized
but exercized wonderful virtues.

The first century before the Christian era has
been termed the most unphilosophical age of ancient
times; and if the positive dogmatism of the Stoics
and Epicureans was the typical teaching of the first
period of Hellenistic culture, the religious mysticism
of the neo-Pythagoreanism was the typical product
of its second stage. Many of its ideas were
adapted by the other schools, and new combinations
were made with the religious systems of the Oriental peoples. It will be shown how Judea did
not escape the influence, and in the sect of the
Essenes we have probably a mingling of Jewish and
Pythagorean ideas. But though in ethical standpoint and religious yearning the teachings of
Pythagoras—both the genuine and the apocryphal
—reveal something akin to Judaism, even this development of Hellenistic philosophy was antagonistic to the Jewish spirit. Its monotheism was
tainted with foreign ideas; the dualism between
body and soul led to a rigorous asceticism which
contrasted with the sanity and moderation of the

Jewish way of life; lastly, its outlook on society was anti-national and anti-social, since it advocated flight from the world and the abandonment of civic duty as the way of virtue.

Moral philosophy was part of the fashionable equipment of the Hellenistic age; and just as Marie Antoinette and her court liked to play at the simple life amid the pomp and luxury of Versailles, so, amid the dissolute and luxurious haunts of Alexandria and Antioch, jaded men and women loved to listen to eulogies on virtue and diatribes on the vanity of riches. The Stoic and Cynic missionary in his thread-bare cloak at the street-corners preached the self-sufficiency of virtue; the eclectic lecturer on moral welfare culled the most attractive ideas from all the sages of Hellas and the East, and displayed them to an admiring audience. Rhetoric indeed was the supreme and most popular art of the Hellenistic civilization, and impregnated every other form of literature. Poetry, drama, history, and philosophy became rhetorical. The lecture-hall took the place of the market-place and the theatre as the centre of intellectual intercourse, and the tract and the oratorical exercise became a standard form of writing. The new generation of sophists gave their audiences a superficial acquaint-

ance with Hellenic ideas which passed for philosophy. An appearance of philosophical knowledge
and fluency in the up-to-date theologies were required of every man claiming to be enlightened.
The schools only affected a comparatively small
part of the population, but the sophists and rhetors
gave a smattering of the serious side of Hellenism
to the whole of the upper and intellectual classes.
The philosophy which was thus hawked around
was as poor an image of the thought of the genuine
Hellas as the Hellenic cults which were set up in
the cities of Egypt and Syria were a poor reflection
of the national religion of Athens and Sparta.   In
estimating the attitude of the Jewish people toward
Greek culture, we have then to remember that the
civilization they encountered was a second-rate and
second-hand Hellenism, which had indeed a treasure of artistic and intellectual achievement to attract
and inspire, but lacked altogether the eager spirit
that had created that treasure, and at the same time
was mingled with all manner of foreign cults and
cultures—Chaldean astrology, Phrygian mysticism,
and Egyptian theophanies—in such a way that its
own inherent weaknesses were emphasized and exaggerated, and its nobler aspects were hopelessly
obscured. We must beware of regarding the

struggle between Hebraism and Hellenism in the Hellenistic age as a struggle between a narrow and intolerant monotheism, on the one hand, and a broad enlightenment and intellectual activity, on the other. Rather was it a struggle between an established national-religious culture, with a high moral standard and large human aspirations, and a confused amalgam of cultures, with a low moral standard, declining intellectual grasp, and vague cosmopolitan professions.

CHAPTER III

HELLENISM IN PALESTINE TILL THE DESTRUCTION OF THE TEMPLE

Judea was surrounded by Alexander the Great and his successors with a girdle of Greek cities. Along the coast-lands of ancient Philistia on the west, and on the further side of the Jordan on the east, these cities formed a close and well-knit chain; while to the north, in the country of the Samaritans and in Galilee, Samaria, Sepphoris, Neapolis, and Scythopolis were inhabited by a mixed multitude, which was not slow to adopt the manners and cults of the dominant Hellene. On the south, where the desert ended, lay the Hellenized kingdom of Egypt with which Judea was in constant contact. Thus the little Jewish territory was as a rock around which there beat the waves of the Hellenistic sea. Politically it formed part of a Hellenistic kingdom from the time that it fell into Alexander's possession in 332 B. C. E. till the final victory of the Maccabeans, nearly two hundred years later.

After the death of Alexander, says the Hebrew
chronicler, " his servants bare rule, every one in his
place . . . . and evils were multiplied on
the earth." ¹   Palestine fell to Ptolemy, the ruler
of Egypt; his dynasty had frequently to fight for it
with the Seleucid rulers of Syria, but they kept possession for one hundred years.   Of the inner history
of the Jewish people in Palestine during the period
we know scarcely anything directly.   Josephus
fails us for this time, and we must perforce be content with conjecture and inference.   The coast-
road, which ran from Egypt to Syria along the
plain of Sharon and across the vale of Jezreel or
Esdraelon, was the great highway of the Greek
armies; and the plain itself was one of the great
battlefields.   Hence the Jewish people as a whole
must have come into frequent touch with Greek
soldiery and merchants.   At the same time the
upper classes assimilated more deliberately the
culture of the surrounding cities.   The way to
success in public life lay through imitation of Greek
manners, and the temptation to conformity was
exceedingly powerful.   When the darkness is
illuminated by the record of the Maccabean
struggle, told soberly and sincerely in the First Book
of the Maccabees, and oratorically in the epitome

of the history of Jason, which is known as the
Second Book, we are brought face to face with the
nation ranged into two parties: an advanced Hellenizing section of aristocrats, and a stubborn core of
the people, bitterly opposed to Hellenism, and sincerely loyal to the Jewish law.

The Hellenistic influence had found its way
gradually from the outward activities of national
life to its fundamental ideas. As early as 300
B. C. E., Hecataeus, a Greek historian, speaks of
Jews who, by mingling with the Persians and Macedonians, had fallen away from their traditional
wisdom.[2] The Olympian gods and the myths
about them were rapidly acclimatized in the Greek
cities. The story of Perseus and Andromeda was
located at Joppa, and Heracles, who had a Phoenician origin and preserved in the Greek mythology
the reputation of a great traveller, found a new
kingdom in the East. At Tyre and at Philadelphia
(the old Rabbath Ammon, east of the Jordan) he
was worshipped as the chief deity, and games were
instituted in his honor. The Samaritans contrived
to associate him with the Bible story and to prove
his derivation from Esau;[3] and the Second Book of
the Maccabees narrates how the Graecizing high
priest Jason sent a deputation to Tyre from Jerusa-

lem with an offering for the quinquennial games of the Greek god. The worship of Astarte was centred at Anthedon, near Gaza; Dionysus was the patron deity of Scythopolis, which was called Nysa after him, and Pan of the city of Panias, erected by the sources of the Jordan. The Greek cities issued coins on which were stamped the figure of their protecting god or some religious symbol connected with the town; and as these coins were the only currency of Palestine, the Jews acquired some acquaintance by their agency with Greek religious ideas.

Palestinian commerce, also, passed largely through the Greek coast cities. The Phoenicians of old by their trading journeys had brought the ideas and the inventions of the East to the knowledge of the Hellenes in the West, and now the elegant manners and material civilization of the West were brought to the knowledge of the Jews by the Greek merchants. The large Greek vocabulary which passed into the Jewish speech, and found a permanent place there, contains a number of words of commerce, of the common objects of trade and of apparel, of furniture and decoration, and of administration and law. Commerce brought with it an introduction of the arts into the country.

88

After the Restoration from Babylon the Jewish way of life had been solemn and sober, lacking in grace and refined pleasures; but under the influence of the new civilization, the arts of building and music made their way into Judea. To the plastic arts, however, because of their association with pagan mythology, and to the games and athletic contests, which were made the occasion for the lower pagan ceremonies, the Jewish consciousness offered constant resistance. It was marked as a special outrage of the Hellenizing party in the time of Antiochus Epiphanes that the priests set up a gymnasium and theatre in Jerusalem.[4]

The book of Ben Sira, which is an invaluable record of Jewish social life in the third and beginning of the second centuries, illustrates the introduction of a more elegant life and a growing appreciation of art. Thus the writer praises music: " Pour not out words when there is a musician, and show not forth wisdom out of time; a concert of music at a banquet of wine is as a signet of carbuncle set in gold. As a signet of emerald set in gold, so is the melody of music with pleasant wine." [5] The book of Daniel, again, which dates from the second century B. C. E., mentions a number of musical instruments, unknown in other parts of the Bible: the cornet, sackbut, and psaltery, and two of them with Greek names.[6]

Ben Sira's moralizing about the honor due to the physician points to the existence in his day of a regular medical profession. It was still necessary to recommend the use of skilled service; and there were doubtless those who looked with suspicion on the introduction of science for the healing of disease, lest it should impair faith. The Jewish moralist seeks to conciliate the two outlooks:[7] " Honour a physician," he says, " with the honour due to him, for the uses which ye may have of him. For the Lord hath created; for of the Most High cometh healing, and he shall receive honour of the king. The skill of the physician shall lift up his head, in the sight of the great men he shall be admired. The Lord hath created medicines out of the earth, and he that is wise will not abhor them. . . . My son, in thy sickness be not negligent, but pray unto the Lord, and He will make thee whole. Leave off from sin, and order thine hands aright and cleanse thy heart from all wickedness. . . . Then give place to the physician, for the Lord hath created him."

It is a moot question whether the Palestinian literature of the third century bears traces of the infusion of the deeper side of Hellenism. Some scholars have detected it in the two books of the Canon which are supposed to have been written at this period, Ecclesiastes and the Song of Solomon.[8] A passage in the latter bears a remarkable correspondence with a verse in one of the Idylls of Theocritus, the most distinguished of the Alexandrian poets, and some see in its wealth of sensuous imagery a non-Hebraic influence. But the correspondence with Theocritus may be due to an Oriental source common to the two poets, and the lack of any clear order in the thought and the luscious imagery of the Hebrew song are alien to the Hellenic spirit. As regards the book of the Preacher, some have seen a reproduction of Greek words and phrases in certain novel Hebrew forms; while the well-known passage: "Two are better than one. . . . For if they fall, the one will lift up his fellow," [9] corresponds with a maxim of Homer. The sceptical attitude, which runs through the whole book, and the intellectual standpoint of its author more notably reflect intercourse with outside culture and the indefinite influence of the Greek atmosphere. That Palestinian Jews were acquainted with the Greek literature of the time does not depend on mere probability, but is vouched by several pieces of direct testimony. The books of the Maccabees state that some of the loyal Hassideans could write as well as read Greek; and the Hellenistic historian Eupolemus, who must have lived during the second century, speaks of the Greek version of the Scriptures as well known to his countrymen.

The legends which recount the making of the Septuagint Version by seventy sages sent by the high priest in Jerusalem to Ptolemy in Alexandria are certainly apocryphal; but it is significant that pseudo-Aristeas, who probably wrote not later than at the beginning of the first century B. C. E., should have conceived such a story, and that the Talmud also recounts the sending of sages to write the Law in Greek. The first Palestinian Jew recorded as bearing a Greek name is Antigonus of Soco, who appears in the Ethics of the Fathers [10] as the immediate successor of Simon the Just (*i. e.*, about 250), in the headship of the Great Synagogue. In the saying ascribed to him, " Be not as servants who minister to their masters for the sake of reward," Greek influence has been traced.[11] The introduction of the knowledge of Greek was not, however, the danger which aroused the people to bitter resistance against Greek aggression. Probably the scribes and the strict followers of the Law, known as the Hasidim (the Pious Ones) and afterwards as Perushim (the Separatists), were from the outset antagonistic to the Greek language and Greek ideas; but the gradual process of blending the foreign culture with the Jewish outlook might have gone on for long, and might in the end have sapped Jewish individuality, had it not been for the attempt to force a cruder and more vulgar Hellenism on the masses of the people.

Posterity loves to pillory an individual for an evil of gradual growth; and the individual upon whom the odium of this attempt is regularly cast is Antiochus Epiphanes, the Seleucid emperor who reigned from 175-166 B. C. E. Yet he was less the promoter than the instrument of the policy which had its roots in the corruption of a part of the Jewish people. Nations, it has been said, always touch at their summits; and the aristocracies of all countries have a tendency to share common hopes and a common outlook. More especially when there is one dominant civilization, the ruling classes of smaller nationalities are prone to desert their own culture for that of the larger world. The

7

tendency asserted itself in the priestly caste of the
Jewish people, who, if no longer the popular leaders, were the hereditary holders of power under the
Ptolemies.   The high-priesthood had descended to
the family of Onias, and a branch of their family,
the Tobiades, sought by ingratiating themselves
with the Egyptian sovereign to carve out for themselves a Hellenistic principate in Palestine.   They
built palaces in the Greek style, and they fostered
Greek influences, until finally, over-reaching themselves, they tried to foist Greek religious cults on the
community.   We may refer to them the words
in Daniel: " The children of the violent among thy
people shall lift themselves up to establish the
vision." [12]   In the time of Antiochus, the faithful
high priest Onias III drove them out of Jerusalem
because of their Graecizing ways, and then matters
hurried to a crisis.[13]

The Ptolemies had observed the tradition of not
interfering with the religion of their various subjects; but when Palestine passed at the end of the
second century B. C. E. into the power of the
Seleucids, the statecraft was soon changed.   The
conqueror of the country, Antiochus III, maintained the former liberty, and, according to Josephus,[14] he even extended fresh privileges to the

Jewish community at his capital at Antioch. But
his son Antiochus, surnamed Epiphanes, usurping
the throne which belonged aright to his nephew,
manifested a different temperament. The Seleucid empire was tottering from the blows which
it had received in disastrous wars with Rome, and
Antiochus conceived the idea of strengthening it
by increasing its homogeneity. The Jews were
the one element among his subjects who resisted
the assimilation of Hellenistic culture; their country lay on the outposts of his empire, and he deemed
it desirable to make them like the remainder.
The aspirations of the Hellenizing Jewish aristocracy coincided with his plans. One of the
priestly family, Jason, to satisfy his private ambitions, led the king to believe that the Hellenizing
process might be carried through without difficulty,
and received the appointment of high priest in place
of the loyal Onias III, who had resisted the dese-
cration of the temple. The king gave him authority
" to set up a place for exercise for the training of
the youth in the fashion of the heathen, and to write
them of Jerusalem by the name of Antiochians." [15]

A section of the priests was ready enough to follow his lead; they neglected the temple worship,
and took part in the sports of the gymnasium; " they

made themselves uncircumcised, and were sold to do mischief." [16] The Greek hat—the petasos— was seen about the streets, and Antiochus himself visited the renovated Antioch Hierosolyma, as Jerusalem was to be called, and was splendidly received by his liege. Envoys were sent to Tyre to contribute to the sacrifices to Heracles, but they had scruples on the way, and diverted the money to the less idolatrous purpose of providing ships of war.[17] The loyal party among the priests went into exile in Egypt; and Onias III was murdered, according to some accounts at Antioch, and according to others at Jerusalem.

The insolence of the Hellenizers was not yet complete; and a baser priest than Jason was found, one Menelaus, who, outbidding his rival in promises of evil-doing, received the royal support in his place, and proceeded to stamp out, as he thought, the embers of Judaism. The sanctuary at Jerusalem was converted into a temple of Zeus Olympios, and the Samaritan temple on mount Gerizim, with the approval of the inhabitants of the place, became a temple of Zeus Xenios. All manner of abominations were set up in the sanctuary; the observance of the sabbath and festivals were forbidden, the people were brought by constraint to eat of the sacrifices on the birthday of the king, who had proclaimed his own divinity, and on the day of the feast of Bacchus they were compelled to go in procession carrying branches of ivy.[18] Throughout the country the Jews were compelled to adopt paganism and partake of heathen sacrifices, and the penalty of death was prescribed for men, women, or children who refused. The way had been prepared by Hellenizing Jews and conciliating pagans who, by a bastard kind of comparative religious science, identified the Jewish God with Dionysus Sabazius or with Zeus. But both the Hellenizing Jews and the royal inquisitor had miscalculated the spirit of the Jewish people. In reply to persecution the Hassideans showed a temper which up to that time had no parallel either in their own or in any other history: they were willing to die for their religious beliefs, and to submit to any torture rather than be disloyal to their traditional Law. The readiness to give up life for a faith, for something spiritual and immaterial, was a thing of which the Greeks had not dreamt. It marked the triumph of the Hebraic principle, and it was the measure of the advance of the Hellenizers.

The heroic struggles of the Maccabean brothers converted the passive resistance of the Hasidim into the rising of a people in defence of its national and religious existence. By his exertions Judas saved his country from tyranny, and by his example he saved civilization from submersion by a second-rate Hellenism. In fact, the Maccabean victories mark a turning-point in the history of culture; it ushers in, as it were, a reversal of the movement begun by the victory of the Greeks over the Persians at Marathon and Salamis. Hitherto Greek influence on the East had been dominant and aggressive; now a people of the Orient began to impose its ideas on the West. The Jews had been confronted violently with Hellenism in its decadence; they had realized its degradation without having experience of its finer aspects; they had measured their strength with it, and found it wanting. Henceforth they were aggressive and militant, more fully conscious of their mission as a chosen people, and determined not only to resist the encroachment of foreign ideas, but to spread their loftier doctrine for the uplifting of humanity.

The Maccabean triumph was followed by both a political and spiritual awakening of the nation: the brothers redeemed for a century not only Judea, but almost the whole of Palestine from the Hellenic dominance. Judas, Jonathan, and Simon in turn,

and after them John Hyrcanus and Alexander
Jannæus, carried the war against paganism to the
east of Jordan and to the north of Samaria: the
Idumeans, the Itureans, and the Galileans were
compelled to adopt the victorious creed; the Greek
cities were in many cases subjugated, in all deprived
of their power. Israel conquered anew the Holy
Land; and it is related with special pride that
Simon " captured Joppa for an haven, and made an
entrance to the isles of the sea, and enlarged the
bounds of his nation." ⁱ⁹ From this first Jewish
port Jewish traders went out to carry Jewish teaching even to the strongholds and the cradle of
Hellenism. The danger of the domination of the
vulgar idolatry of the Hellenized peoples over
monotheism was once for all removed; and the nation, exultant in their strength, confirmed in their
devotion to the Law; and burning with a desire to
spread their teaching, became sovereign over the
Holy Land and powerful beyond it.

Spiritually, one of the immediate effects of the
Maccabean deliverance was to stimulate the proselytizing activity of the Jews wherever they were
settled. We shall deal in the next chapter with the
missionary movement in the diaspora, but the same
feeling was manifested, though less strongly, in

Palestine. Palestinian literature of the first century B. C. E., such as it is, has traces of the missionary ardor; and the universalisitc consciousness appears repeatedly in the apocalyptic books, which at this period of seething hopes and fears gave expression to popular wishes. Of the Messiah it is said in the Psalms of Solomon: " He shall make the peoples and the Gentiles serve him under his yoke, he shall glorify the Lord by submission of all the earth " ; and in the Testaments of the Twelve Patriarchs, the writer speaks of " the light of the Law which was given to lighten every man." [20] We read in the Book of Tobit: " All nations shall turn and fear the Lord truly, leaving their idols "; and the fourth oracle of the Sibyl, which many scholars think to have sprung from Palestine, foretells the coming world-wide triumph of Israel: " Every land and every sea shall be full of them." The Gospel of Matthew, in a later epoch, speaks of the Pharisees who " scour sea and land to make a proselyte." [21]

Moreover, the scanty rabbinic records of the times bear witness to the accession of converts; Shemaiah and Abtalion, the heads of the schools at the end of the second century, were such; and Schürer identifies them with the Sameas and

Pollion mentioned by Josephus.[22] Many of the sayings of Hillel, who was the head of the Sanhedrin after them, have reference to proselytes: his famous summary of the Law in the golden rule was evoked by the question of a would-be convert. The arrangement of the temple—the central shrine of the whole people—bore witness to the large hopes and the universal outlook of the Jews. The expectation that the prophecy of Isaiah would be realized, and all the nations would come up to pray on the mount of Jerusalem, was symbolized by the court of the Gentiles, which formed the outermost area of the sanctuary. Josephus says that the altar was holy to all Greeks and barbarians as well as to Jews;[23] and offerings were received from proselytes who were allowed to come up to the great festivals![24] While in some aspects the temple worship was national and exclusive, in others it was cosmopolitan and universal. Inscriptions and directions in the Greek language were called for by the presence at the festivals of embassies from the Jewish communities in the diaspora, for whom Greek was the native tongue. The seals presented to donors of the offerings were inscribed in the popular Aramaic; but the chests for the money contributions were marked in Greek, because only the officials who were conversant with the general language of civilization were concerned with them.[25]

Yet, if one outcome of the national victory was to foster the missionary spirit, and thus indirectly to bring Palestinian Jewry into close touch with the Hellenistic peoples, a more direct result was to strengthen the popular feeling against the infusion of Hellenistic culture. The struggle had been essentially one of conflicting civilizations, and Judaism had proved its inward force. After the establishment of the Maccabean dynasty, the Jewish people in Palestine were divided into three sects, or, one should rather say, two sections and one sect: The Pharisees, the Sadducees, and the Essenes. The Essenes are a sect properly speaking, that is, a community separated from the main body of the people, with a way of life and traditions peculiar to itself. The Sadducees and Pharisees are half political and half religious parties. The Pharisees, who were known among themselves as חברים or associates—one may compare the name Friends by which the members of the Quaker community know each other—were the successors of the Hasidim who had formed the backbone of the resistance to the Greek persecution. They represented politically the party of the people which desired the Jewish rulers to refrain from interference in foreign affairs, and spiritually the Hebraic principle, which stood for the development of Jewish tradition on its own lines and for separation from all denationalizing influence. Positively they were the upholders and expanders of the tradition. and negatively they were the opponents of alien ideas. They formulated a progressive and Catholic Judaism, rooted in the observance of the Law, and continually developing to meet new needs and new thought, but keeping itself pure from admixture with non-Jewish conceptions.

Over against them the Sadducees, so called probably after the priestly house of the Zadokites, were the aristocratic party, which politically cherished ambitions to play a part in the affairs of the East, and spiritually was for narrowing Judaism to a fixed creed contained in the Bible and to a rigid conservative Law. According to Josephus, they were the party of the rich,[26] and it is likely that they are the " proud Jews " attacked in the Wisdom of Solomon.[27] They included a large part of the priestly caste, and they inherited, to a certain degree, the outlook of the former Hellenists. The analogy which Josephus draws between

Pharisees and Stoics is shallow and fallacious; in truth, from what we know of their opinions, the Sadducees may more reasonably be compared with that Greek school. They were essentially materialists: they did not share the Messianic hope of the people, and put their trust in reason; their self-reliance, their rigidity in enforcing the letter of the rabbinical law, and their denial of the resurrection [28] reflect the spirit of the Stoic. The Jewish aristocracy in the Maccabean kingdom continued to imbibe the outside culture of the day, and thus became estranged from the general populace, till, finally, it lost touch with the national feeling. From a party the Sadducees became a sect, and eventually a name of reproach. With the destruction of the temple they disappeared as a political force; and the Sadducees referred to in later rabbinical writings are identical with Gnostics and other heretical groups. [29]

The traces of Hellenistic influence on the Essenes are clearer, though the influence was derived from that development of the Greek spirit which was in some ways akin to Hebraism. The Philonic author of the tract " That every good man is free " associates their name with the Greek Hosios (pious); [30] but with more probability its

104

origin is to be sought in the Syriac root חסא (pious). Kohler,[31] on the other hand, connects the word with the Hebrew חשאים (the silent ones), who appear in the Mishnah as a body of secret saints.[32] The derivation is fathered by a wish to support his theory that the Essenes may be identified with the saints, the strictest of the Pharisees of whom we hear much in rabbinic literature. But our only direct authorities for the Essene tenets [33]—Josephus and " Philo " among Jews, and Hippolytus and Eusebius among Christians—consistently describe them as a sect forming an isolated branch of Jewry, and playing no part in the national life. Josephus says that they were excluded from the temple service, and had secret books of their own. It is therefore open to doubt whether they can be regarded as the successors of the pre-Maccabean Hasidim, and identified with the most pious of the Jewish people. They are more likely " the saints who waste the world " referred to in the Talmud, who practised austerities to the extent of not taking part in the duties of social life. The statements as to their numbers point to a small community, segregated from the general population; " Philo " speaks of four thou-

sand living in Syria and Palestine,[34] and Josephus
gives similar testimony.[35]

They were a body of devotees, living either in
the wilderness or in special villages, under very
strict and peculiar discipline; they rejected blood
sacrifices, fostered a high moral standard, and
eschewed sensual pleasures to the point of asceticism. In their ascetic practices, as " Philo " did
not fail to see, they were false to the teachings of
Judaism. Their doctrine was distinguished by a
pronounced dualism of body and soul. They
taught that bodies are corruptible, and that the
matter of which they are made is not permanent.
But the souls are immortal, and endure forever.
They are formed of the most subtle air, and are
enclosed in bodies as in prisons, into which they
are drawn by a certain material enticement; when
they are set free from the flesh, they rejoice at the
release from a long bondage, and mount upwards.[36]

The Christian Hippolytus adds an account of
their doctrine of resurrection, on which they laid
particular emphasis.[37] They believe that the flesh
will rise again and be immortal like the soul, which,
separated from the body, enters a place of fragrant
air and radiant light there to enjoy rest. Hippolytus is at pains to point out that the notions of

resurrection were original with the Essenes, and together with other doctrines were appropriated from them by the Greeks; he asserts also that their ascetic life is older than that of any other nation, and that Pythagoras and the Stoics borrowed from them. The Christian standpoint was that all good ideas which were championed by the Church were adopted by the Greeks; but it is suggestive that both he and Josephus connect the Essene teachings with those of Greek schools.

Unfortunately, no extant work can be definitely attributed to an Essene; some have so ascribed the book of Jubilees, others the Testament of Job, others the greater part of the apocalyptic literature; but all this is guess-work. Yet, from the descriptions of the Christian historians and the Jewish apologists, the influence of foreign thought on their doctrines is manifest, and the first Jew of modern times who studied Hellenistic-Jewish literature, Azariah dei Rossi, said they were Greek-speaking Jews.[38] The probable conclusion is that the dualism of the Essenes is due to an interchange of thought with the neo-Pythagorean school, which was actively missionary in the second and first centuries B. C. E. It may be that other foreign influences from Persia and even from India entered into their system, and that they represent an early example of a large religious syncretism. But the correspondence with the Hellenistic Puritans, who acknowledged Pythagoras as their master, stands out prominently. The Essenes share with them not only the dualistic doctrine of body and soul, but the striving for bodily purity, the practice of ablutions, the rejection of blood offerings, the encouragement of celibacy, the belief in prophetic powers, the striving after ecstacies and mystical visions, and, lastly, the divorce of religion from national and social life. At the same time the Jewish character is manifested in their close attachment to the Mosaic law, and notably in their strict observance of the sabbath and of the feast of Pentecost, to which they attributed peculiar holiness.

It is likely that they were a body which sprang up under Greek influence in the second century, during the bitter days before the strength of the Jewish revival against Hellenism had asserted itself, having as their object the realization of an ascetic idea of life and importing the pessimistic Greek religiosity into Palestine. They bear witness to the possibility of combining Hellenism and Hebraism in an intense religious spirit, while their remoteness from the mass of the people throws light on the general aversion toward such movements. They reached the height of their development in the first century B. C. E., when from their midst sprang a preacher of singular piety, John the Baptist, and they passed out of Jewish history a little later to exert a large influence on the history of the Church. The Ebionites, who were the Jewish element in early Christendom, were their successors in Palestine, and took over many of their ceremonies and customs and doctrines.[30]

While Hellenistic rationalism affected the ideas of the Sadducees, and Hellenistic dualism, with its corollary of the ascetic life, characterized the ideas of the Essenes, another Hellenistic influence may be traced in a peculiar Jewish literature of the period, which flourished inside as well as outside Palestine. The apocalyptic and pseudepigraphic books reflect many characteristics of Hellenistic religion. They were very numerous: the passage in the fourth book of Ezra (the second book of Esdras in the Protestant Apocrypha) counts the sacred writings as ninety-four, or, according to one variant reading, as two hundred and four. Of this total, twenty-four are in our Hebrew Canon, which leaves at least seventy apocryphal works. Some of these were certainly Christian productions, but a large number were of Jewish authorship; and while the majority had their origin among the Greek-speaking communities of the diaspora, several that are extant bear the marks of Palestinian birth.   Not one has completely survived in its original Hebrew form.   They never received the sanction of the Rabbis, and at the crisis of the national religious life they were cast out of Jewish tradition as of dubious value or mischievous. They have been preserved by Christians in Syriac, Greek, Armenian, Slavonic, Coptic, or Latin translations, in which they could influence the writers of the Church, but could not exercise any hold over the congregation of Israel.   The heads of the Jewish schools, in their struggle to preserve Judaism intact after the loss of national independence, perceived the danger of this literature, and banned it not only from the Canon of Scripture but from the house of study.   But in the time preceding the national catastrophe the books enjoyed a certain amount of popularity.

The pseudepigraphic literature falls into three classes: Apocalypses, or revelations of the unknown world; Testaments, which are largely summaries of universal history in the form of prophecies; and haggadistic or legendary elaborations of the Bible record. They are all of the genus of religious fiction. Typical of the first class is the book of Enoch, of the second the Testaments of the twelve Patriarchs, of the third the Book of Jubilees. The three were probably written by Palestinian Jews in Hebrew. They have this in common that they contain much fantastic and imaginative speculation about the Messiah and angels and the future world, and profess to reveal a secret or inner knowledge which is not contained in scriptural history. The motive which underlies their composition is that, besides the knowledge of God and the history which is revealed in the Bible, a deeper and more recondite wisdom exists which may be divulged to the saints. This conception of a twofold wisdom—one for the mass of the people, and the other for the sage—was part of Hellenistic, especially Pythagorean thought, which distinguished between the esoteric and exoteric doctrines of the philosophers. From the Hellenistic world it made its way into Judaism. But the secret speculation was early felt to be alien to the true spirit of the religion. An ingenious suggestion of Krochmal refers the last warning of Ecclesiastes against the making of many books to the secret doctrines;[40]

111

and Ben Sira more clearly utters the warning: "
" Reflect on that which is permitted, but busy not
thyself with secret things. Rebel not against that
which is beyond thee: too great for thee is the
vision; for many are the thoughts of man, and false
imaginations lead astray. A presumptuous man
shall have an evil end, and he who loves visions of
good shall be carried away by them."

The content of the secret literature was likewise
somewhat alien to the spirit of Judaism: it was
mainly concerned with heaven and the life to come,
and the general outlook was pessimistic about the
affairs of this world. It is true that visions about
the celestial kingdom are to be found in Ezekiel
and several of the later prophets, as well as in
Daniel, whose book is the one fully-developed
example of apocalypse in the Hebrew Canon; but
these very examples illustrate the semi-foreign
character of such speculations, since they arose
from the mixture of Babylonian and Persian with
Hebrew beliefs. The teachings about angels,
the topography of the heavenly world, and the
pseudo-prophetic visions of past events had begun to
find their way into Jewish thought before the large
syncretism of the Hellenistic age had taken place.
But a great impulse in this direction was given by

the new conditions which followed on the foundation of a cosmopolitan culture.

The contact of Hellenistic thought with eastern civilization had the effect of emphasizing the gloomy and mystical elements which underlay the rational thought of classical Greece, and of bringing into light the undergrowth of primitive beliefs and speculations which had come down from Oriental sources. In the horror of death which seized on men after the city-state was broken up, a demand grew up for knowledge of the after-world; and in the distrust of human reason, which was consequent on the decay of intellectual activity, crude and wild imaginings were eagerly accepted. The Hebraic and Hellenistic-Jewish Apocalypses display the same temper, and are the outcome of the same spirit as prompted the Hermetic writings of Egypt, the neo-Pythagorean Cosmogonies, and the Visions and Testaments of Apollonius of Tyana."

It was rather a Graeco-Egyptian or Graeco-Syrian than a Hellenic influence which in this secret teaching modified Jewish monotheism and the religion of the Torah. The Pharisees, and through them the Synagogue, were alive to the dangers of such syncretism for the religion of Israel, and

113

hence, prolific as was the literature even in Palestine, it did not vitally affect the thought of the main body of the Jewish people. It is probable that it appealed particularly to the Galilean 'Am ha-Arez, the common populace of the north, and to the mixed population of the Hellenistic cities which had been only partially converted to Judaism.

The national consciousness nourished by the Torah had an instinctive aversion to whatever was not true to the cardinal points of Judaism; and therefore the doctrines of mediating angels and heavenly journeys, and the other theosophical speculations of the Testaments and Apocalypses and Assumptions were never organically united to Catholic Judaism. They were " external " things, an Oriental leaven which played a large part in the composition of Christianity, but left only a small impress on rabbinic theology, and that in a sifted and expurgated form. Palestinian Judaism, for the most part, kept itself aloof from those mixed beliefs as well as from the more vulgar form of polytheism and paganism; but in Alexandria, Antioch, and Tarsus, and other centres of the Hellenistic diaspora, they became subversive of a pure monotheism and a temptation to the abandonment of the Torah.

114

But although the main body of the Jewish people
rejected Hellenism and its ways, intercourse with
the Greek peoples and the use of the Greek
language was by no means eschewed. At this
period the Palestinian teachers regarded the Greek
translation of the Scriptures with favor, as an instrument for carrying the truth to the Gentiles,[43]
and it was even said that Greek was the only
language into which the Bible could be properly
translated,[44] and again that the Aramaic Targum
was made from the Greek.[45] Greek translations of
parts of the Bible seem to have been made in Palestine itself; for if the preface to the Septuagint
version of Esther is to be believed, that book was
done into Greek in Jerusalem by Lysimachus, son
of Ptolemy, and brought into Egypt by one
Dositheus in the fourth year of Ptolemy and Cleopatra.   The date has been generally identified with
114 B. C. E.   Supposing the statement true,
Lysimachus may have been an Egyptian, and therefore a Hellenistic Jew sojourning in Palestine.
That there was a constant coming and going between the Jewish community under the Ptolemies
and the independent Jewish kingdom during the
whole period of national existence is shown by
many circumstances.   The dispossessed high priest

Onias IV flees to Egypt from the Seleucid persecution, and nearly a hundred years later the leaders of the Pharisees likewise flee to the same refuge from the persecution of Alexander Jannaeus. In the time of Herod, again, the Alexandrian family of Boethus became high priests. Aristobulus, one of the earliest Alexandrian-Jewish philosophers, according to the book ascribed to him, came from Palestine, and the grandson of Ben Sira, whose statements are above suspicion, went down to Egypt when Euergetes was king (*i. e.,* 132 B. C. E.), and continued there some time, and found " a book of no small learning." This means probably that he found a book of the same kind as his grandsire's in vogue among the community, which may be the book we know as the Wisdom of Solomon. " Therefore I thought it necessary for me to bestow some diligence and to interpret it (*i. e.,* the work of his grandfather) and set it forth for them also which in a strange country are willing to learn, being prepared before to live according to the Law."

In the opinion of Zunz,⁴⁵ likewise the Greek original of the first apocryphal book of Esdras, which is a kind of Targum and Midrash of the biblical books of Ezra and Chronicles, is derived from Palestine. The Palestinian literature of the second and first centuries before the Christian era has come down to us almost entirely in Greek translations from the Hebrew, and, on the other hand, Hellenistic ideas have been traced in the earliest rabbinic records.

The political independence of the Jewish kingdom involved acquaintance with the paramount cosmopolitan culture no less than the former subjection to a Greek empire. One of the qualifications for membership of the Sanhedrin was a knowledge of languages, including Greek;" and the influence of Greek law has been traced in the Jewish legal system. Diplomatic intercourse was carried on through Greek, and the Jews had friendly relations with some of the Greek peoples. Almost all the terms of public life and government which are found in the Talmud are Greek transliterations, and the institutions of the religious life likewise were clothed in a new dress. The Hellenistic term Συνέδριον (Sanhedrin) supplanted the Hebrew כנסת הגדולה; and though in Palestine the house of prayer and assembly still preserved its Hebrew name Bet ha-Keneset, the Hellenistic "synagogue" replaced it in the language of the Graeco-Roman world.

117

It is striking, too, that the officer of the Synagogue, who is still called Parnass, owes his name to a Greek word (Πρόνους " man of foresight "), and that the raised platform where the prayers were read is called in Talmud the *Bima,* from a Greek word; and the ark is *Tik* from the Greek θήκη, and in the Aramaic Targum, which represents the popular speech, the word *tsitsith* is translated *Kraspedin* from the Greek word [48] for fringes.

Language then provides many indications of the Hellenistic influence on the Jewish ritual. A less permanent memorial of that influence is to be found in the coins of the Maccabean dynasty, which from the beginning of the first century often bear a Greek legend. The gathering at Jerusalem, on the three yearly festivals, of deputations from all the Hellenistic and Greek-speaking communities must have made Greek a familiar language in the Jewish metropolis. At the beginning of the Christian era there was a synagogue at Jerusalem for the Greek-speaking Jews, the Libertines, *i. e.,* the Jews of Rome who were *libertini* or freedmen, the Cyrenians, the Alexandrians, and those of Cilicia and Asia.[49] Possibly there was one large synagogue for these communities, divided up into various chapels, after the manner of the old

118

Sephardic synagogues in the East, and the Talmud contains a reference to the synagogue of the Alexandrians at Jerusalem.[50] The community of Hellenistic Jews living at Jerusalem in the first century were to some extent divided from the general body. They had Greek names such as Stephen and Philip, and many of them doubtless were converts. Nicolaus, one of the seven appointed to dispense charity among the Greek community, is described as a proselyte of Antioch.[51]

The development of the Christian heresy shows that these Graecized Jews and Judaized proselytes were prone to follow Hellenistic teachings which derogated from pure monotheism. Greek influences, however, no longer exercised a disintegrating influence as in the days before the Maccabees. Various attempts from without were made to foster a Hellenistic revival in Palestine, but they failed. After his conquest of Syria and Asia in 60 B. C. E., Pompeius tried to restore to power and independence the Greek city-states in Palestine, as a means of weakening Jewish national solidarity; he succeeded in re-establishing in some degree their material prosperity, but their culture made little or no impression on the Jewish people. The sages met the attack by strengthening the command

against participation in heathen festivals and assemblies. When a little later the semi-Judaized,
semi-barbarian Herod tried, in the manner of
Antiochus Epiphanes, to set himself up as the patron
and champion of Hellenism, he gained the good-
will of the Roman Cæsars, but alienated the
sympathy of his people. He founded splendid
Greek cities,[52] such as Sebaste on the site of the old
Samaria, Capernaum and Tiberias by the sea of
Galilee, Cæsarea and Antipatris on the coast; and
settled in them a mixed population of Greeks and
Jews; he endowed lavishly Greek gymnasiums and
temples, he instituted Greek games at Jerusalem, he
sent magnificent embassies to Greek festivals at
Athens and Olympia—in fact he was more Hellenist than the Hellene. But his actions had little
effect on the Jewish national life, and were not the
expression of any tendency of the Jewish people.

The mass of the nation was solidly welded together by its religion and its law. Did a section,
such as the Sadducees and the Essenes, modify its
ideas through the blending of Hellenistic notions,
it gradually dropped out of the national life. Did
a king seek to foster, or a Roman conqueror seek to
impose, a more vulgar Hellenism, the people found
strength and consolation in their schools and their

synagogues, and in cryptic prophecies denounced
the coming vengeance upon the wrong-doers, and
the ultimate universal triumph of the Jewish law.
Did Hellenistic notions find their way into the
Palestinian schools, they were transformed by the
Jewish spirit, or, if they could not be so digested,
they were rejected. The national religious
consciousness was proof against the temptation to
assimilate, no less than against the pressure of
armed force. Hence, while the upper classes were
conversant with Greek, while Jerusalem was, in
many ways, one of the most cosmopolitan cities of
the world, and the temple was one of the seats of
the world's worship, still Hellenism only colored, without undermining Palestinian Judaism, and
Greek as a language never ousted the native
Aramaic as the speech of the people, or Hebrew
as the vehicle of literature. Paul is compelled to
speak Hebrew in Jerusalem, and Titus summons
the people to surrender in Aramaic.[53] The extent
to which Greek was a foreign language even to the
cultivated Jew of Palestine is illustrated by the example of Josephus. The most famous of the
Palestinian Hellenists, who was born in 37 C. E.
of a priestly family of Jerusalem, and therefore
belonged to the upper classes, admits that he could

not speak Greek with sufficient exactness, though he had taken great pains to obtain the learning of the Greeks and understand the elements of the Greek language. "For," says he, "our nation does not encourage those that learn the languages of many nations, and so adorn their discourse with the smoothness of their periods; because they look upon this sort of accomplishment as common not only to all sorts of freemen, but to such servants as care to learn them. But they give him the reputation of being a wise man, who is fully acquainted with our laws and is able to interpret their meaning."[84] He wrote his first work, on the Wars of the Jews, originally "in the language of our own writing," *i. e.,* Hebrew or Aramaic, and sent it thus to the "Upper Barbarians"—as he so calls the Jews in Parthia and Babylonia who presumably did not understand Greek. For the benefit of the Gentiles and the Greek-speaking communities he translated the books into the common language of culture;[85] but he did not acquire the command of that language till after he had been brought as a prisoner to Alexandria by Vespasian.

It would be rash to infer from the autobiographical remarks of Josephus that the habit of Greek speech was unknown to the Palestinian community; and circumstances point against such a conclusion. But other facts corroborate his statement that the command of Greek was rare among the people and not prized by them. The Palestinian culture therefore was in its main lines essentially and exclusively national. From the time of the Maccabees the definite individual stamp which had distinguished it ever since the Restoration from Babylon is emphasized. The introduction of Greek ideas, which had at first made headway among a section of the people, was stoutly and successfully resisted; attempts at fusion and syncretism were distrusted by the sages of the Sanhedrin and the leaders of the Synagogue, and merely affected small sections which were converted into sectaries. Between Judaism and paganism there was open war, and in Palestine the Jews were the aggressors. Outside Palestine indeed the Hellenistic theology made large inroads into Jewish doctrines, and considerably modified the Jewish monotheism, but in Palestine it was almost as rigidly excluded as idolatry. The universalistic standpoint, which was common to the Jews in their own land and those in the diaspora, cannot fairly be ascribed to Hellenistic influence. It is splendidly and repeatedly proclaimed by the

prophets of Israel, and must be accounted as part
of the Hebraic genius. The ideal, as the greatest
teachers understood it, was to be attained not by
the abandonment of national life and tradition, but
by their expansion. According to Hillel—the outstanding interpreter of the Law before the loss
of national independence—" the kingdom of righteousness would be established not by merging
Judaism in a broad humanitarianism, but by making Judaism itself an embodiment of the principles
of humanity." [56]

Palestine, then, was the cradle of an intense
Hebrew life, which, amid the ever-increasing
welter of civilizations and cultures in the Graeco-
Roman world, maintained a pure and distinct
national character. And it preserved Judaism
and the national life of the Jews, not only for its
own community, but for the people all the world
over. The congregations of the diaspora could
be allowed to assimilate more freely the Hellenistic
culture, because at the centre the clear standard
was upheld and the Hebraic outlook was undefiled.
Lastly, during the two hundred years, in which
Judaism was continually expanding and consoli-
dating its teaching on its own soil, the individuality
of the people was so confirmed that, when the centre

was violently broken up, and the political forms of national existence were taken away, the spirit remained strong and enabled the national religious life to hold out both against internal disintegration and outward compulsion.

CHAPTER IV

HELLENISM IN THE DIASPORA

The influence of Hellenistic thought on the Jewish communities of the diaspora was naturally larger and more direct than on Palestinian Jewry; for in the dispersion the Jews were not merely surrounded by, but living in the midst of, a Greek-speaking cosmopolitan population. And they lacked the solidarity and the power of resistance to foreign ideas which is the outcome of a concentrated national life in a separate territory. The centrifugal tendency was bound, therefore, to be more pronounced, and to grow as their identification with the life of the country in which they were settled became more complete. Strong as was their consciousness of being a peculiar people, they rapidly assimilated Greek thought. The process can be best studied at Alexandria, because the literary records of Alexandrian Jewry are the fullest. The first and the fundamental step toward the introduction of the outside culture was the adoption by the Jews of the Greek language as their mother-tongue; and, accordingly, the first sign of Hellenism

and the basis of its influence was the translation
of the Scriptures into Greek. The translation
probably had two motives: a desire of the Jews to
make their holy books known to the people about
them, and the substitution of Greek for Hebrew
or Aramaic as the language of reading the
Scriptures in the synagogue, which was rendered
necessary by the growing Hellenization of the
community.

Legend soon gathered itself about an event
fraught with such importance to the destinies of
the Jewish people and to the whole of civilization.
The Hellenistic writers, Aristeas, Joscphus, and
Philo, and likewise the Talmud,[1] recount a story
of seventy-two sages sent by the high priest from
Judea to Alexandria at the request of King
Ptolemy Philadelphus (about 250 B. C. E.) and
lodged in the island of Pharos opposite Alexandria,
each in a separate cell, till they had completed the
translation of the five books. Each of the
versions, it is said, agreed word for word, which
proved the divine inspiration of the translation and
its authoritative character. The story bears the
impress of *tendenz* fiction, no less than another
legend recorded in the Talmud—which originated
some centuries later, when bitter experience had

given a new significance to the event—that while
the translation was being made, a plague of darkness hung over Palestine.[2]   The one story reflects
the remarkable attachment which the Greek-
speaking Jews showed to the version for three
centuries; the other the misgivings, which were
engendered later among the Rabbis, of the
Hellenizing movement that started from it.   Internal and external evidence, indeed, point to the
conclusion that the first two books of the Pentateuch were translated at Alexandria about the era
of Ptolemy Philadelphus, to whose instigation the
legend ascribed the origin of the whole work.   This
early section of the translation is written in the
common Greek dialect of the Hellenistic era, but is
full of Hebraisms and is innocent of literary artifice
or style.   In time the other books of Moses, the
historical books, the books of the Prophets, and the
Holy Writings were translated—in the case of the
last-named, with certain haggadic additions which
do not appear in the Hebrew Canon, but which are
parallelled in the Aramaic Targum.

The first literary work of the Hellenistic Jews
was the translation, the next the expansion, of their
Scriptures.   From references in the fragments of
Hellenistic-Jewish historians preserved in the col-

lection of Alexander Polyhistor (flourished about
80 B. C. E.) it is certain that the greater part of
the translation had been completed by the beginning of the first century before the civil era. The
form is a little less crude in the later parts, but the
version of the prophetic books shows little literary
sense or Greek literary influence. Still less does it
exhibit the impress of the knowledge of Greek
philosophy, though ingenious critics, with theories
to prove, have made it a favorite hunting-ground
for traces of Stoic and Platonic teaching. Nevertheless, if the Septuagint itself does not manifest any
considerable modification of Hebraic ideas, the
effect of studying the Scriptures in Greek, and of
not studying them in Hebrew, was momentous for
the Judaism of the diaspora. Gradually but
surely the Jews began to assimilate the religious
ideas of the people about them, and to look on
the Scriptures under the influence of those ideas.
Words stand rooted in a national soil; and if the
terms of Greek theology came with a new meaning
to the Jewish mind which impressed them with its
own stamp, on the other hand, as the Greek translator of Ben Sira recognized, " things originally
spoken in Hebrew have no longer the same force
when they are translated into another tongue; and

not only these (the maxims of his grandfather),
but the Torah, the Prophets, and the other Books
of the Bible have no small difference when they
are spoken in their original language."

The Greek version could not convey just the
same conception of monotheism as the Hebrew
Bible, and there was, moreover, a conscious avoid-
ance of anthropomorphism. Thus, when the Hebrew text says that Moses saw God on His throne,
the Septuagint renders it that he saw the place which
God inhabits.³ God speaks to Moses not " face to
face," as in the original, but in a vision.⁴ Again, a
desire to glorify and justify the Jewish people led
to the insertion of additions to some of the later
books (Esther, Daniel, etc.). On the other hand,
the desire to conceal what might be made a reproach
by their enemies led to the omission of a few
passages, such as the story of Judah and Tamar.
The Talmud ⁵ mentions that thirteen passages were
altered in the Septuagint translation for the sake of
King Ptolemy; and the process of making altera-
tions to suit Greek taste was practised on a large
scale by the later commentators and adapters of the
Greek Bible. Hence, partly by the unconscious influence of a change of language, partly by deliberate modification, the seeds of an impure Judaism

were sown in the Bible and the Synagogue of the diaspora.

We have but sparse records of the development of the Alexandrian or any other Hellenistic community between the beginning of the third and the middle of the second centuries. Our main sources of knowledge are inscriptions and fragments of pagan historians, and we have to infer the internal development from our fuller knowledge of the subsequent period. The anti-Jewish chronicles of Manetho, an Egyptian historian of the second century B. C. E., argue the existence of a passive enmity between the semi-Hellenized Egyptians and the Jews; but the exalted positions filled by Jews at the court of the Ptolemies prove that the governing powers did not share the prejudice. Moreover, the writings of the worthier Hellenistic historians indicate that the monotheism of the Synagogue won the respect of the philosophical classes. The knowledge and command of Greek were doubtless gaining steadily among the Jews, and the elimination of Hebrew from the religious service must have been slowly going on. At the same time the earlier Hellenistic-Jewish literature affords scant suggestion of the introduction of foreign ideas.

After the Septuagint, the Chronicles of
Demetrius are the oldest historical work of the
diaspora of which we can judge, and they are
faithful in substance to the Scripture narrative.
Again the story of the Seleucid persecution and the
Maccabean struggle written by Jason of Cyrene,
of which an epitome exists in the Second Book of
the Maccabees, if less reliable than the record of
the Hebrew book, is impregnated by the same spirit
of loyalty to the religion, and by an equal national
pride.⁶ The prefatory letters which introduce the
epitome, as also the preface of the translator of
Ecclesiasticus, reveal the close kinship of feeling
between the Palestinian and Alexandrian communities. Nor is it without significance that the loyal
members of the priesthood, when they fled for
refuge from the tyranny of Antiochus Epiphanes
and the Hellenizers, and a little later Onias IV,
when he failed to be elected high priest of Jerusalem, turned to Egypt, and established a new
sanctuary. Political considerations of the enmity
of the Ptolemies to the Seleucids doubtless influenced them; but in Egypt they could find a staunch
body of their brethren devoted to the temple
service.

That the cruder side of Hellenism, the religious cults, affected a section of Jewry in the diaspora as in Palestine is but natural: in every age and place there are Jews who desire to drop their individuality. One monument records a contribution of money by a Carian Jew, Jason, towards the festival of Dionysus, another, found in a temple of Pan in Upper Egypt, records the thanks of two Jews to the Greek god for their deliverance,' another from Delphi an offering of an emancipated Jewish slave to Apollo. These, however, are but isolated examples, and the anti-Jewish scribblers are never wearied of reproaching the Jews with misanthropy and " atheism " because of their aloofness and religious Puritanism in a period of free exchange of divinities. The mass of the people rigidly maintained their separateness and their resistance to paganism. Whereas to-day the charge is made that the Jews are cosmopolitan in a national society, then the current complaint was that they were national in a cosmopolitan society.

Nevertheless, the more intellectual and more refined Hellenism, contained in the philosophical thought of the Greek masters, gradually affected a section of the people. The two alleged pre-Maccabean writings which exemplify such an influ-

ence are demonstrably later forgeries.   Both the
Letter of Aristeas and the fragments of the " Exegesis " of Aristobulus, which have been preserved
by various Church fathers, do not date before the
first century; and the exact harmony of Jewish and
Greek thought ascribed to these early Hellenistic-
Jewish worthies represents the notions of a later
age.³   But there is no reason to doubt that Aristeas
and Aristobulus were early exponents of a Hellenistic-Jewish reconciliation between the rational
ethics of Greece and the revealed moral law of
Israel: the pioneers of a Jewish moral philosophy.

The Maccabean triumph marks a turning-point
in the history alike of Hellenistic and Palestinian
Judaism. The vindication of Jewish independence prompted in the dispersed Jewish community
a feeling of pride in their special culture, and an
intense desire to impart it to the nations; and
henceforth they are essentially an active rather
than a passive factor in the Hellenistic world.
Their apologists teach the defensive, and adopt the
offensive by attacks on paganism. The consciousness of a religious mission to the world, which had
been aroused in the crisis of the first captivity, was
revived with redoubled force by the crisis through
which the people passed; and the prophecy that

Israel should be a light among the nations could now be made a living and practical ideal. What had been a vision to the prophets was now a mission to the people. Two conditions favored the expansive movement in the diaspora. The Jews were in close contact with the Hellenistic world, and by the assimilation of the general culture of the age could express their message in an intelligible form. Moreover, the Hellenistic welter of peoples, owing to the decay of their religion and the growing disbelief in pagan polytheism, were groping for some religious teaching which should afford a sanction for morality and give to life a purpose and a hope. The day had come of which the prophet Amos⁹ had spoken, when there should be " a famine in the land, not a famine of bread, nor a thirst for water, but a famine for hearing the words of the Lord." Hellenism, which had lost its freshness as soon as it was transplanted, was more and more obscured by Oriental elements; philosophy did not satisfy the masses, and the Greek paganism, which for a time attracted the world by its beauty, was found lacking upon the moral and spiritual side of religion for which the East has always felt a longing.

At Alexandria especially a great burst of Jewish literary activity was directed toward the pagan masses; and a Jewish ethical literature was forecast which had as its purpose the propagation of Hebrew monotheism in the educated Gentile society and the glorification of the Jewish law as a form of natural and rational religion. Much of the literature has disappeared, but enough has survived to give us an adequate idea of its tone and character. The propagandist writings which were intended to recommend Judaism to the masses were of two kinds: Hellenized versions of the Bible-stories, tricked out in the rhetorical style of the day and embroidered with numerous falsifications; and moral exhortations to the heathen disguised behind the mask of famous Greek sages and poets. Of the first some improve the stories of Genesis and Exodus in prose; others in verse. Artapanus, a historical romancer, seeks to magnify the greatness and the miraculous power of the patriarchs, of Joseph and of Moses, ascribing to them with reckless bravado the invention of the Egyptian arts and sciences. One Ezekiel, who is called by the Church fathers the "poet of Jewish tragedies," among other poetic works composed a drama in iambic trimeters on the Exodus, in which he seems to have contented himself with paraphrasing the biblical narrative in verse, and arranging dramatically the incidents of Moses' life. His work was probably intended for reading and not for action, seeing that the Jews altogether eschewed the theatre. It is possible, however, that religious plays were given at the Jewish festivals for the benefit of the prose-lytes. Another writer named Philo composed a narrative poem in hexameter verse about the his-tory and beauties of Jerusalem. The fragments of it show that his ignorance of the laws of scansion is equalled by his love for the Holy City. But he drew more on his imagination than on knowledge. Describing the water-supply of Jerusalem, he writes of some mysterious spring: [10]

> For flashing from on high, the joyous stream,
> Flooded by rain and snow, rolls swiftly on
> Beneath the neighboring towers; and spreading o'er
> The dry and dusty ground far shining, shows
> The blessings of that wonder-working fount.

And, depicting the high priest's fountain:

> A headlong stream, by channels underground,
> The pipes pour forth.

The Letter of Aristeas, more prosaically but not less imaginatively, describes the wonders of Jerusa-lem which must have been a commonplace of Alex-

andrian-Jewish heroics.   With a different kind of
inventiveness the anonymous author of the history
of Jannes and Jambres compiled a fictitious account
of the magical powers of Moses, which were pitted
triumphantly against   the   arts   of   the   famous
Egyptian wizards.   A regular battle of false books
raged in Egypt; the enemies of the Jews composing
scandalous and grotesque accounts of their origin
and practices, the Jews retorting with this spurious
aggrandizement of their ancestors.

The popular recommendation of the one God
and the moral law to the pagan, though carried on
under false colors, had a higher motive.   To
bring the teachings of the Bible to the knowledge
of the populace, who required something more
attractive than the bald narrative of the Septuagint
or the rhetorical chronicles of the historian, some
bolder spirits foisted monotheistic verses on pre-
historic pagan seers, such as Musæus and Orpheus,
and above all on the Sibyl, who described herself as
a divine prophetess of the orders and counsels of
the gods concerning the fates of cities and king-
doms.¹¹   Others   interpolated   passages   into   the
maxims of the ancient moralist Phocylides and the
" dark   philosopher "   Heraclitus,   and   into   the
tragedies of Sophocles and Euripides and the

comedies of Menander. The popular Jewish writers in Palestine ascribed their books to the pre-historic fathers of Israel; but the Jewish writers of Alexandria ascribed their poems to the misty prophets of Hellas, who were already used as the vehicle of religious and ethical teaching by Greek philosophical schools.

To-day, when the distinction between fiction and history has been considerably developed, literary forgeries may appear not only contemptible but immoral. That distinction was unrecognized in the Alexandrian age; and when people cared little about the true authorship, provided the appearance of age was given, they were adopted as a vehicle of every reforming movement which aimed at moral teaching. By the side of the Jewish Sibyllines may be placed the spurious poems which the neo-Pythagoreans ascribed to the founder of their school, and the spurious dialogues which the Platonists added to their master's works. The feeling for truth and exactitude altogether was weak. Spurious literature was a habit of the time, similar in design and conception to our historical and religious novel, by which the doctrines of a later epoch are put into the mouth of historical characters, not so much with a view of deceiving the people about their origin, as with the hope of winning a greater acceptance for them by the seductive association. The purpose of these writings was less to convert the Gentiles than to prepare their minds for a favorable reception of the Jewish teaching which was delivered in the synagogues by word of mouth. They must have been intended for the less intellectual part of the Greek reading population. Although the critical standard of the age was low, it cannot be imagined that men who had received a literary training were deceived about the origin of this literature; but didactic hexameter verse was the form of writing which would appeal to the half-educated and half-Hellenized natives among whom Jewish activities were largely exercised. Spurious literature only has an influence when the ideas to which it seeks to give authority are in accord with the demands of the people; and to this extent it reflects more certainly the popular opinion than the works of aristocratic literary circles. As Ossian met the demand of the eighteenth century for more naturalism in poetry, so the false Sibyl met the demand of the Hellenistic world for more spirituality in religion, and her oracles were a kind of Tracts for the Times.

140

It is commonly accepted that the earliest of these Sibylline oracles extant is the third, part of which is dated in the second century. In an introduction, which forms a prologue to the series of Jewish Sibyllines, the writer denounces the heathen, and proclaims the unity of God: " Ah, mortal men, creatures of flesh, how full are ye of self-importance, and reck not that your life must end? Neither do ye tremble at the God who rules over you, the supreme God who knows, sees, and understands all things. He is the Creator who preserves all, and sent His sweet spirit into every being and made it rule over all men. There is one God alone. He is very great, omnipotent, unbegotten, invisible. He sees everything, but cannot be seen by any mortal. For what flesh can behold with his eyes the heavenly and immortal Being, since mortal man cannot even bear to gaze on the beams of the sun? Give worship unto Him, the only God, the Ruler of the universe, who exists alone from everlasting to everlasting." Throughout the passage no Hellenic influence appears save in the form of the poetry: the thought is undiluted, unmodified Hebraism; even the phrase about " sending the spirit " is merely a reproduction of a verse in the Psalms,[12] and so through-

10   141

out the oracle the spirit is everywhere Hebraic. Pointing the lesson that righteousness exalteth the nation, the writer menaces with doom the Greek kingdoms, unless they put aside their idolatry and their wickedness.[12] An obvious similarity exists between his outlook and that of the author of the Hebrew apocalypses; but whereas the latter offered encouragement and consolation to his own people, the Greek writer preached to the Gentiles. The popular Hellenistic-Jewish literature is directed outwards, not inwards. "The Jewish religion," says Gibbon,[13] "was admirably fitted for defence, but was never designed for conquest, and it seems probable that the number of proselytes was never much superior to that of apostates. . . . . The Jews eschewed missionary activity, and were flattered by the opinion that they were alone the heirs of the covenant; and they were apprehensive of diminishing the value of their inheritance by sharing it too easily with the strangers of the earth." The statement of this historian expresses the exact reverse of the truth as regards the Hellenistic era of Judaism. For two hundred years and more, from the time of the Maccabees till the loss of national independence, the Jews were preeminently a missionary people. Not only their own historians Philo and Josephus, but the classical authors of the period record the striking success of their mission. Jewish practices were spread wherever there was a Jewish community, and the synagogues attracted thousands and hundreds of thousands of converts,[15] being, as Philo describes them, " schools of prudence, justice, piety, holiness, and in short, of all virtues by which things human and divine are well-ordered." [16]

For a considerable time the admission of proselytes did not have the effect of weakening the religion or the national cohesion; before the Gentiles were received as full members of the congregation, they had to adopt the national way of life. Some of the staunchest Jews were not born in the faith. But in the end the missionary activity exposed its dangerous side in weakening the hold of the Torah. In order to win over the Gentiles, the Jewish preachers tended to lay stress on the inner as against the literal meaning of the law, to color Judaism with the current ethical notions, and to explain away what might appear tribal or exclusive; and naturally the newcomers, for the most part, had not the same feeling for the tradition as those who had for generations lived under it. They were prone also to interpret the doctrine they

learnt in the light of ideas strange to it, and to de-
judaize the fundamental conceptions of the religion.
Many of them did not become full members of the
congregation, but remained on the outskirts of the
Synagogue, and were known as " the fearers of the
Lord," accepting the beliefs but not the law of
Judaism.

The infusion of Greek ideas into Jewish teaching is signally illustrated by the development of
the mission of a higher intellectual order, which
was addressed to the cultured classes, unsatisfied
with the philosophical systems. Already in the
second century attempts were made to reconcile
Jewish belief and Jewish law with Greek theology
and Greek ethics, and to recommend Judaism as a
philosophical religion. But it was not till the first
century before the common era that that movement
took on large proportions. The ethical schools of
the Stoics and the Epicureans were effete and in
decay, losing their individuality in a floating
eclecticism, and seeking some consolation in the
weariness of existence. On the other hand, the
school of Pythagorean thinkers was groping its
way toward a religious philosophy, and seeking to
satisfy men's spiritual and intellectual wants by a
system of mystical idealism. The Jews, with their

144

sincere conviction of a divine unity and their possession of a divinely revealed law, began to develop a philosophy of their own, which they offered to the Hellenistic world as a better and an older explanation of the universe than that of any Greek thinker, and a surer guide to happiness than any other system. The motive of their philosophical writing was thus, in part, missionary ardor. The mastery of Greek doctrines and the mastery of Greek literary artifices were steadily increasing. But they did not merely assimilate the intellectual culture of their environment; their Jewish spirit was paramount, and their appeal to the Gentiles retained a distinctive literary form.

Two anonymous books which have survived from this semi-philosophical Jewish literature, the Wisdom of Solomon and the so-called Fourth Book of the Maccabees, both probably date from the beginning of the first century B. C. E., and spring from Alexandria. In the Wisdom the ideas of the Greek philosophers only appear incidentally. Its main theme is a warning against ungodliness, and in form it has a certain correspondence with Proverbs and Ben Sira and the other Hebrew examples of the Wisdom literature. But throughout the book images and concepts show the influence of Hellenistic culture. It is indeed half a polemic against the idolatry and materialized ethics of paganism, half a panegyric of Wisdom, which is advanced to a new power by the blending of philosophical ideas with the religious conception of the Bible. The author vividly describes the creed of the so-called Epicureans who say: " Short and sorrowful is our life; and there is no healing when a man comes to his end. By mere chance were we born, and hereafter we shall be as though we had never been. . . . . Come therefore, let us enjoy the good things that are present, and let us use the creation with all our soul as youth's right. . . . . Let us fill ourselves with costly wine and ointments, and let no flower of the spring pass us by. Let us crown ourselves with rosebuds before they be withered. Let none of us go without his share in the revelry. Let us leave tokens of our joyfulness in every place." "

Against this creed he sets up the Hebraic view of life. " God created man to be immortal, and made him to be an image of His own eternity. The souls of the righteous are in the hands of God, and there shall no torment touch them. . . . . For even if in the sight of men they be punished, their hope is full of immortality; and having borne a little chastening, they shall receive a great good." [18]

He speaks here with a certainty of the reward of the righteous, of which Job and the Preacher had been in doubt. Later he attacks the idolatrous paganism which corresponds with materialism in thought. " Surely vain are all who are ignorant of God, and could not out of the good things that are seen know the true Being. Neither by considering the works did they acknowledge the artificer, but deemed either fire, or wind, or the swift air, or the circle of the stars, or violent water, or the lights of heaven, to be the gods which govern the world." [19] And expanding the images of Isaiah, he denounced those " who call them gods which are the work of the man's hands; gold and silver to show art in, and resemblances of beasts, or a stone good for nothing, the work of an ancient hand. But Thou, O Lord, art gracious and true, long-suffering, and in mercy ordered all things. For to know Thee in perfect righteousness, yea, to know Thy power is the root of immortality." [20] The assurance of immortality as the basis of the theodicy is a striking feature of the Wisdom of Solomon, and distinguishes it from the Wisdom books of the Bible. It has often been pointed out that the Hebrew Scriptures are silent

147

upon such a hope. A few passages indeed suggest
a conviction of the reward of the righteous after
death, as when the Psalmist utters his personal
faith: [21]

Thou wilt not abandon my soul to the nether-world ...
Thou makest me to know the path of life;

which contrasts with the verse: [22]

For in death there is no remembrance of Thee;
In the nether-world who will give Thee thanks?

Or again: [23]

As for me, I shall behold Thy face in righteousness;
I shall be satisfied, when I awake, with Thy likeness.

But the belief in a retribution in after-life seems
to have played no part in the popular faith. Even
the later books of the Bible do not breathe any trust
in personal immortality, but rather question it.
" If a man die," says Job, " may he live again? " [24]
And Ecclesiastes proclaims on the vanity of human
life: " The wise man, his eyes are in his head; but
the fool walketh in darkness. And I also perceived
that one event happeneth to them all." [25] Ben Sira
maintains the biblical outlook: " Who shall give
praise to the Most High in Hades, in place of them
that live and return thanks? Thanksgiving perish-
eth from the dead as from one that is not. All men

148

are earth and ashes." [26] The doctrine of reward in after-life is plainly stated indeed by Daniel: " And many of them that sleep in the dust of the earth shall awake, some to everlasting life, and some to reproaches and everlasting abhorrence. And they that are wise shall shine as the brightness of the firmament; and they that turn the many to righteousness as the stars for ever and ever." [27] Since, however, the date of Daniel is within the Hellenistic era, the passage is no index of the Hebraic attitude before that period, but only goes to prove that in the second century the Palestinian as well as the Alexandrian Jews accepted the doctrine of the immortality of the soul.

The doctrine of individual immortality is foreshadowed rather than realized in the Bible. But in the Hellenistic literature it is definite and prominent; and if not wholly derived from Hellenistic influence, it was certainly nourished by it. It is likely that Persian thought influenced both the Hebrew and Greek teaching of immortality, and the circumstances of the age made the foreign seed productive. In the Hellenic city-state and in the Hebraic kingdom the sufficient reward for a man's work was found in the survival of the nation, and the life of the individual was merged in the community. But when the close national life was broken up, and the dispersion of the Jews and Greeks was accomplished, the individual assumed a new importance, and the salvation of his soul became the special care of religion and reflective thought.[28] Thus the promise or rejection of immortality is a matter of supreme concern in Hellenistic philosophy. The Epicureans and Stoics denied it, the Pythagoreans affirmed it; and the Mysteries, which played an important part in the religious life of the time, inculcated the belief by an elaborate ritual.

For the Jews, during the crisis of the struggle for independence, the teaching of immortality became a new stronghold of the religious consciousness against the attacks of materialism and rationalism. In Palestine, where it was established during the second century, it took the distinctive form of a belief in resurrection of the body. The acceptance or rejection of that belief was one of the main points of contention between the Pharisees and Sadducees. Whether the Sadducees altogether denied the immortality of the soul, or merely rejected resurrection, is not certain.[29] But it is significant that, even when the idea of individual im-

mortality was established, the Hebrew intuition of
the unity of body and soul persisted in the teaching
of a second life for the body as well as for the soul.
In the diaspora, however, and more especially at
Alexandria, where Jews and Greeks were brought
into contact with the ancient eschatological teaching of Egypt, the antithesis between body and soul
was accepted, and the doctrine that appears in the
Jewish Hellenists is of the soul's after-life. The
writer of the Wisdom of Solomon describes the
soul as existing before it is placed in the body, which
is but an earthly tabernacle for the heavenly Nous,
and must restore the soul like a loan. His doctrine
is still somewhat vague and tentative, as though he
were preaching something that was not generally
accepted. Yet he develops the foreshadowing of
the Psalmist to a clearer belief.

In the later Hellenistic literature, such as the
apocalyptic Book of Enoch, to be dated probably
at the end of the first century B. C. E., a vulgariza-
tion comes with greater certitude, and the details
of the future life are depicted with an assurance
which is in marked contrast with the reserve of
the pseudo-Solomon. The distinction which the
Rabbis drew between the visions of Isaiah and the

visions of Ezekiel may be applied to the different
conceptions of the next life in the Hellenistic age.
The author of the apocryphal book speaks as a
metropolitan resident, the author of the apocalypse
speaks as a villager.

The ethics and the teaching of immortality
which are found in the Wisdom of Solomon manifest the Hebraic consciousness of God and the seriousness of the Hebraic outlook upon life, unim-
paired and strengthened and deepened by the
knowledge of outside culture and the larger intellectual experience. But what may be called the
lyrical theology of the book, which describes God's
relation with the world, blends the ideas of
philosophy with the Hebraic images, so as to form
conceptions that mark a new direction of Hellenistic Judaism. The Wisdom books of the Old
Testament, outlining the primitive reflection of the
Hebrews on the nature of the divine, pictured
Wisdom as a link between God and man. Wisdom
in her perfection is alone with God,[30] and exists
with Him before the creation. She is the divine
purpose, the divine scheme of human life, and
man's goal is to seek the apprehension of the divine
ideal.

> The Lord made me as the beginning of His way,
> The first of His works of old.
> I was set up from everlasting, from the beginning,
> Or ever the world was.
> . . . .
> Then I was by Him, as a nursling;
> And I was daily all delight,
> Playing always before Him.[31]

The conception of Wisdom is somewhat expanded in the book of Ben Sira, but essentially it remains true to the biblical character. The author proclaims her divine origin in the opening chapter of the book: " All wisdom cometh from the Lord, and is with Him for ever. Wisdom hath been created before all things, and the understanding of prudence from everlasting." [32] And later, in another lyrical hymn, he personifies her, and makes her speak thus:[33]

> Wisdom shall prove herself,
> And shall glory in the midst of her people:
> I came out of the mouth of the Most High,
> And covered the earth as a cloud.
> I dwelt in high places,
> And my throne is in the pillar of cloud.
> . . . .
> He created me from the beginning before the world,
> And I shall never fail.
> In the holy tabernacle I served before Him,
> And so was I established in Zion.

The personification may be more elaborate
than in the Bible, and the faint suggestion of
metaphysics is creeping into Hebraic fancy, but the
root of the conception is the Wisdom of Proverbs
and Job. And the identification of the Law with
Wisdom is preserved. He that hath possession of
the law shall obtain wisdom.[34]

A further development from poetry to theology
is made in the Alexandrian literature. The Hellenistic Jews, through their acquaintance with the
Greek philosophers, began to be conscious of the
problem raised by the transcendence and perfection
of God, on the one hand, and His immanence in
the world, His constant control of human affairs,
and the existence of evil, on the other. They
found in the Greek schools spiritual doctrines about
the divine Reason and the divine Wisdom which
governed and ordered all things, and detected in
them a close relation with the Bible teaching of the
Wisdom and Word of God. Desiring to display
Judaism as a philosophical faith, they were naturally
led to associate the Hellenistic attributes of Sophia
and Logos with the images of Hokmah and the
Dabar. The Wisdom of Solomon exhibits the
first stage of this philosophical-religious syncretism:
" Wisdom reacheth from one end of the world to

the other with strength, and ordereth all things graciously. . . . . She is the artificer of all things; more mobile than any motion she pervadeth and penetrateth all things. For she is a breath of the power of God, and a clear effluence of His glory. Therefore can no defiled thing fall into her. For she is the brightness of the everlasting light, the unspotted mirror of the power of God, and the image of His goodness. And she, being one, hath power to do all things, and remaining in herself, reneweth all things. And in all ages entering into holy souls, she maketh them friends of God and prophets." [35]

Elsewhere, she is depicted as manifest in the pillars of fire and cloud. The author of Proverbs had indeed personified Wisdom " building her house," [36] but the imagery of the Alexandrian author is different in kind as well as degree. He attributes to " Sophia " the properties which the Greek philosophers attached to the monistic impersonal principle that they held to govern the universe. Consciously he applies the intellectual ideas of Hellenism to the poetical ideas of Hebraism, and fuses the two. So, again, when he pictures the Logos or Word executing judgment upon the Egyptians, though his imagery is here Hebraic, the personified conception of a divine instrument marks an advance from primitive theology toward the philosophical teaching which became the distinctive feature of the Alexandrian school. " Thine almighty Word leaped from Heaven, out of Thy royal throne, as a fierce man of war into the midst of destruction, and brought Thy unfeigned commandment as a sharp sword, and standing filled all things with death, and it touched the heaven, but it stood upon the earth." �("³⁷ "⁾ He associates the word by which God made all things with the Wisdom. The one like the other is the divine instrument, and is on its way to being treated as a separate being.

Contact with Greek philosophy has tended to deepen the Hebrew consciousness of the author of the Wisdom, nor does he feel the necessity to explain or allegorize away anything in the Scriptures. Among a considerable section of Hellenistic Jewry, however, the influence of Greek culture did tend to the neglect of the Torah, and to exclusive attention to the hidden meanings. The need was felt for conciliating religion with philosophy; and in order to effect this object, the Bible was made the pretext for all kinds of fancies and speculations, and the obligation of the Law was rejected. The

Alexandrian Jews believed that all wisdom was contained in Israel's divine revelation. Therefore the philosophical tenets which they had been wont to admire must be hidden there and must have originated in the Bible. Allegorical interpretation which aimed at extracting doctrines from the text that were not to be found in its literal sense was the distinctive literary product of Alexandrian Judaism. The master of this interpretation and the chief figure of Hellenistic-Jewish philosophy is Philo-Judæus, who is likewise the highest type of Jewish missionary. Philo, indeed, who lived from about 40 B. C. E. to 40 C. E., sums up Hellenistic Judaism, representing both its strength and its weakness, its splendid aims and its latent dangers, its groundwork of Hebraism and its unconscious adoption of incompatible Hellenistic conceptions.

Allegorical interpretation is an art peculiarly fitted to flourish in a society which is harmonizing the cultures of different ages and different peoples, since its purport is to trace a more abstract and a profounder doctrine beneath a simple record. Allegory is a literary device by which some ulterior purpose is conveyed in the form of a story; allegorical interpretation is the converse method, by which a secondary meaning is read into a story.

Allegory has been a regular habit of thought among the Oriental peoples, and the Bible shows not a few traces of it; but the philosophical interpretation of ancient records as allegory is essentially the product of a sophisticated community. The allegorist is an apologist seeking to bring out an agreement between his ancient traditions and the culture of his environment. There must be a conscious cleavage between the two, and a conscious desire to bridge it, before allegorism can flourish.[33] Its pursuit was stimulated at Alexandria by the advance of Greek thought; but it is not perhaps altogether fanciful to suggest that the influence of the Egyptian monuments favored the habit of allegorical interpretations in the Egyptian community. It is the principle of ancient Egyptian thought that all ideas are represented by a material symbol or hieroglyph; and to those living amongst the wonders of Egypt it became natural to regard the concrete as the symbol of the abstract.

Alexandrian Jews acquired from their Hellenistic environments not only the intellectual culture which they desired to harmonize, but also the machinery of conciliation. The Stoics applied allegorical exegesis to Homer and Hesiod in order to deduce their philosophical tenets from the

poems. The neo-Pythagoreans likewise, who had
their chief seat at Alexandria, were prone to allegory. From these Greek models Philo and his
predecessors learnt the art of reading philosophy
into the books of Moses. Allegorical interpretation of the Bible was not, however, the exclusive
pursuit of the Alexandrian Jews; it may well be
that, while they derived their methods from their
pagan contemporaries, they inherited the seeds
of the habit from their fathers. The oldest
halakic Midrashim, such as Sifre and Mekilta,
make mention several times of a certain school
of interpreters called דורשי רשומות ;[39] and the interpretations quoted in their name are regularly
allegorical or rather symbolical. The meaning
of *Reshumot* appears to be signs or symbols, and
the peculiar method of the *Dorshe Reshumot* was
to see in the words of the Scriptures symbols which
should be taken in a figurative sense, not in their
plain and literal meaning. The method is also
known as *Mashal*. Such interpretations of
Scripture go back to the prophets of the Bible themselves. Thus Hosea[40] says of Jacob's struggle with
the angel that it was a struggle in prayer; and Micah
(7. 20) takes the patriarchs as types or symbols,
Abraham of kindness, Jacob of truth.

It is from these simple beginnings that the *Dorshe Hamurot* seem to have developed. When they found a passage in the Bible that in its literal meaning conveyed anthropomorphic ideas, or when they could point some higher moral teaching by taking the concrete words of the Bible as tokens of something spiritual, they introduced allegorical interpretations. They explained the verse in Exodus: " And they went three days in the wilderness, and found no water," [41] to mean that the Israelites did not find the words of the Law, which are symbolized by water, as it is said, " Ho, every one that thirsteth, come ye for water." [42] So, too, in the Exodus verse which follows: " And the Lord showed him a tree, and he cast it into the waters," [43] they interpreted " tree " as the Torah; as it is written: " She (the Torah) is a tree of life to them that lay hold upon her." [44] It is noteworthy that Philo, interpreting the same verse, [45] explains the tree as a medicine for the soul, causing it to love labor; and several times in his allegories he expounds water as a symbol for the divine Word or Logos. [46]

Palestinian and Alexandrian allegorists alike sought for symbolical values in the proper names of the Bible, and were not unwilling to make a change in the word of the text if they might thereby extract a lesson from it. The *Dorshe Reshumot* interpreted Rephidim (the place where Amalek fought with Israel) as רפיון ידים [47], the weakness of the hands. The passage then suggests that Amalek attacked Israel because of their neglect of the Law. And in the Ethics of the Fathers [48] the names of two stages in the journeying of the Israel-ites [49] וממתנה נחליאל ומנחליאל במות are given a symbolic value: " Whosoever labors in the Torah, behold, he shall be exalted; as it is said: ' From the gift of the Law man attains to the heritage of God, and by that heritage he reaches heaven.' " Philo regularly finds a significance in biblical names; and as he traces it from the Hebrew form of the word, he must be drawing upon a Hebrew and Palestinian source for this part of his allegorizing. Israel is " the man who sees God "; [50] Reuben " the son of insight "; [51] Jerusalem " the sight or threshold of peace." [52]

The primitive allegorical system, then, from which the development at Alexandria appears to have sprung, was the interpretation of the words of the Torah as symbols. Whether the Palestinian school devised certain rules for the allegorical commentary which were handed down to

the Alexandrians is less certain; but some canons
are undoubtedly common to them and to Philo.
Yet while allegorical interpretation of the Bible
had its counterpart in the Palestinian schools, the
dangers of its excessive use were recognized there,
and its progress was checked. *Mashal,* indeed, is
included among the methods of haggadic interpretation in the rules composed by Rabbi Eliezer; but
it is added that the method is only to be used in interpreting passages which do not state a law or
commandment. Allegorical skill was not to
whittle away the Torah, however laudable it was
in relation to other parts of the Bible. According
to the author of the treatise, ascribed to Philo,
" That every good man is free," the Essenes were
distinguished by their habit of treating the words
of the Law as symbols; but in this, as in other re-
spects, they betrayed the influence of foreign
standards, and were not true to the principles of
Palestinian Judaism. The stress remained in
Palestine on the literal sense of the Hebraic tradition; in Alexandria a new emphasis was laid on the
allegory and the spiritual interpretation of the Law.
The fact that a large part of the Mosaic civil and
criminal law was not practically operative in the

diaspora doubtless assisted the tendency to look for moral philosophy beneath the legislation.

Philo is the only Alexandrian-Jewish writer who has left a systematic allegorical commentary on the Bible; but he refers frequently to predecessors who composed moralizing interpretations of ritual commands, and who considered the utterance of the Law to be the " manifest symbols of things invisible, and hints of things inexpressible." [53] Several scholars of recent times held that he was merely the culminating point of an Alexandrian-Jewish school of philosophers; but later research has caused a modification of this idea. Of definitely philosophical writers there is no trace before Philo; but, on the other hand, a large floating body of allegorical teaching existed, in the form of an Alexandrian Midrash, as it may be called, which he worked into his system. This Midrash may have sprung from the interpretations of preachers in the synagogue sounding the spiritual and ethical depths of the biblical reading of the week; and Philo's achievement was to weld these occasional utterances and scattered traditions into a philosophical doctrine. His work is certainly not very systematic; it is largely a collection of homiletical addresses, united in the form of a continuous allegorical com-

mentary on the books of Moses; but it is the nearest
approach which a Jewish writer made in the ancient
world to an ordered philosophy of Judaism. It
is fortunate, then, that a considerable part of it
remains—greater in volume indeed than the rest
of the Hellenistic-Jewish literature together—so
that we can form a fairly complete idea of his
teaching and of the outlook of the society for which
he wrote.

Philo was one of the most distinguished Greek
writers of his time. He commanded the whole of
the classical literature, and he gathered ideas from
every philosophical school. Born of an aristocratic
Jewish family at Alexandria—his brother was
ethnarch of the community—from his youth upwards he was devoted to study; and in his desire to
perfect himself and attain to the knowledge of
God, he appears to have joined for a time one of
those ascetic brotherhoods of Therapeutae or
devotees, who, following Pythagorean examples,
eschewed all civil concerns, and sought to obtain
bliss by sublimating the soul in ecstasy. " I
feasted," he says in characteristic prose-poetry,
" with the truly blessed mind which is the object of
all desire, communing continually in joy with the
Divine Word and Doctrine." Philo's understand-

ing of philosophy was to acquire the knowledge of
God for himself and to spread it among his fellows. He was true in purpose to the Hebraic
spirit which regards the knowledge of God as the
end of wisdom, but in his mental equipment and in
the form of his thought he was some way removed from the type of Jewish sage. He must have
received the Greek secular education (ἡ ἐγκύκλιος
παιδεία) which included Greek literature and the
sciences;⁵⁴ and he passed on to the study of Greek
philosophy. While it is probable that he knew
some Hebrew, it is certain that it was at best a
foreign language to him. He never wrote in it,
and he habitually studied the Scriptures in the
Greek. He knew the traditional teachings of his
people, likewise, which had been gathered around
the Scriptures, through their Greek version, and
thus the Hebraic inheritance, which formed the
groundwork of his system, was moulded by Hellenistic association. Occasionally, even, he contrasts
the Hellenic (Alexandrian) Jews with the barbarian Hebrews, i. e., the Palestinians.⁵⁵ Doubtless in such passages he is addressing pagans, but
the distinction is none the less significant. Yet the
literary form of his works corresponds with the
Jewish Midrash and not with the Greek philo-

sophical treatise; save for one or two minor writings in the form of Greek dialogues, his allegories are all strung on biblical texts.

Unfortunately, the best of the Hellenistic culture of Alexandria in Philo's time was decadent and confused. The purity of the Hellenic thought no less than of the Hellenic language, despite the influence of the great Museum of Alexandria, had been irreparably lost in Egypt through the admixture of Egyptian and Oriental elements, which contrived to veil in mystery what they could not explain by reason. The moral sublimity of the Hebraic imagination was paramount in Philo's system, so that he prevailed to a great extent over the intellectual debasement of his environment, and welded his ideas into a remarkable philosophy of monotheism. Yet dangerous leanings toward theosophy lurked in his expression and in his outlook. These leanings, derived from contact with the surrounding culture, had already led many of his contemporaries away from a pure and simple Judaism, and they were so exaggerated by the generations that followed him that his works became the buttress of heresy. Thus he represents the acme of the Hellenistic development of Judaism; but, as is the fate both of nature's work and human creation, the mature fruit conceals the seeds of decay.

Philo's work has two aspects. On the one hand, he formulates a Jewish system of philosophy for those Hellenistic Jews who were attracted by the intellectual ideas of the Greek teachers and who tended to reject Judaism because it seemed to lack an equally high doctrine. On the other hand, he presents Judaism to the Greek-speaking world as a philosophical system of religion, in order that he may attract to it the earnest spirits who were discontented alike with the religion and the philosophy of the time. Two principal motives again underlay his allegorical habit. He desired, in the first place, to explain away the biblical passages where anthropomorphic expressions were applied to God, and to find a universal value in such passages as, in their literal meaning, described the details of a tribal history or the minutiae of a ritual; in the second, to draw from the Holy Scriptures doctrines of ethics and psychology and theology such as the Greek schools had elaborated. Some Alexandrian Jews sought rather for physical and astronomical wisdom; but Philo opposes them, and substitutes for their explanations a more spiritual exegesis.⁵⁶

167

He describes three diverse attitudes toward the Law, which were held at Alexandria in his day. Some regarded it as merely traditional custom and the Bible as a literary record which constituted the " mythology " of the Hebrews. Others despised the positive Law as such, and derived from it a purely spiritual cult and from the biblical narrative purely spiritual teaching. Finally there were those who combined respect for the positive Law and the spiritual cult, observing the commandments, but seeking by means of the allegorical method an inner and profounder sense.[57] Elsewhere he associates the first class with the Ammonites, the second with the Moabites, and the third with the pious sage Melchizedek.[58] Philo attacks the first class, the extreme literalists who attend only to externals, and actually derive polytheism from the Holy Scriptures. They included those who took the anthropomorphic expressions about God to justify pagan worship. Such perhaps also were the Alexandrian conciliators, who tried to impress the Hellenized Egyptian by ascribing to Joseph and Moses the exploits and attributes of the Greek heroes. Philo attacks likewise the second class who anticipated the antinomian outlook of the Christians, and menaced, as he clearly saw, the in-

tegrity and purity of the Jewish religion. In a
famous passage he thus speaks of them:[59] " Such
men I would blame for the shallowness of their
mind. For they ought to give good heed to both—
to the accurate investigation of the unseen meaning,
but also to the blameless observance of the visible
letter. But now, as if they were living by themselves
in a desert, and were souls without bodies, and
knew nothing of city or village or house or intercourse with men, they despise all that seems valuable to the many, and search for bare and naked
truth as it is in itself. Such people the sacred Scripture teaches to give good heed to a good reputation,
and to abolish none of those customs which greater
and more inspired men than we instituted in the
past. For because the seventh day teaches us sym-
bolically concerning the power of the uncreated
God, and the inactivity of the creature, we must not
therefore abolish its ordinances, so as to light a fire,
or till the ground, or bear a burden, or prosecute a
lawsuit, or demand the restoration of a deposit, or
exact the repayment of a loan, or do any other
thing, which on week-days is allowed. Because
the festivals are symbols of spiritual joy and of our
gratitude to God, we must not therefore give up the
fixed assemblies at the proper seasons of the year.

Nor because circumcision symbolizes the excision of all lusts and passions, and the destruction of the impious opinion according to which the mind imagines that it is itself capable of production, must we therefore abolish the law of fleshly circumcision. We should have to neglect the service of the temple, and a thousand other things, if we were to restrict ourselves only to the allegorical or symbolic sense. That sense resembles the soul, the other sense the body. Just as we must be careful of the body, as the house of the soul, so must we give heed to the letter of the written laws." Elsewhere he says in reference to the commandments: " *Thou shalt not add thereto (the Law), nor diminish from it.*" If we add anything great or small to piety, the queen of virtues, or take anything away from it, we mar it and change its form. Addition will engender superstition, and diminution impiety, and true piety will disappear. . . . . Further Moses lays down another command: *Thou shalt not remove the boundary-stone of thy neighbour's landmark, which thy ancestors have set up.*" This, methinks, does not refer merely to inheritances and the boundaries of land, but it is ordained with a view to the preservation of old customs. For customs are unwritten laws, the decrees of men of old . . . . engraved upon the soul of the generations who through the ages maintain the chosen community." [62]

Philo foresees the chaos that the innovators in religion and those who break from tradition will produce. Chaos in fact already loomed and pointed to an internal disease. The Jewish sects that existed in Palestine had their counterpart in Alexandria, with this distinction that the influence of Greek philosophy upon them was stronger and more direct. Among Philo's apologetic works was a treatise on the Essenes, of which Eusebius, the Church historian, has preserved a few fragments. Another treatise has come down to us in his name, under the title " On the Contemplative Life," which describes the life and doctrines of a peculiar Alexandrian offshoot, the Therapeutae. Several scholars claim that they were a Christian sect, but the better opinion is that they were a local development of the Essenes. The book describes the observances of a monastic community which lived on the shores of Lake Mareotis, near Alexandria. Many authorities are of opinion that it belongs to a later date than the time of Philo, and strong philological grounds militate against his authorship. But there is no reason to doubt that a Jewish sect of the nature described flourished in Egypt during the first century of the Christian era. Their way of life resembled that of the Essenes, but was carried to a further degree of contemplation. They share with the Essenes the dualistic view of body and soul and the affection for the secret doctrine which underlies the literal word of the Scriptures. The author, after describing how they pray twice a day, speaks thus of their learning: "The interval between morning and evening they devote wholly to the contemplation and practice of virtue; they take up the sacred writings, and philosophize about them, investigating the allegories of their national wisdom; for they look upon the literal expressions as symbols of some secret meanings of nature which are intended to be conveyed in these figurative forms. They have also writings of ancient sages who, having instituted this or that doctrine, have left behind them many records of the allegorical interpretations. These they take as a model and imitate the general fashion of their teaching. They do not, however, occupy themselves solely in contemplation, but compose psalms and hymns to God in every possible kind of metre and melody. Thus during six days each of the members, retiring into solitude, philoso-

phizes by himself in one of their so-called retreats,
never going, never even looking outside the threshold of the outer court." At the sacred assembly on
the sabbath—" the day of perfect holiness and the
most complete festival "—one of the elders interpreted with profound care the meaning of the laws.
Our author recounts also the nature of their com-
munions, and especially the rites with which they
celebrated the feast of Pentecost which, because of
its association with the number 50, was treated with
particular veneration.

The Therapeutae, like the Essenes, left no
permanent trace on Jewish life, while, on the other
hand, their semi-monastic communities were the
prototype of a large development in the Christian
Church. The emphasis on individual salvation and
the breaking away from the national life and the
national law, which are their predominant characteristics, and are the resultant of the fusion of
Hellenistic ethics with Jewish religion, cut off these
sects from the Jewish people, and led to their absorption into the anti-national Christian body, so
soon as it had made itself distinct.

In passages which are undoubtedly genuine,
Philo reproaches the ascetics " for their savage enthusiasm." [63] " Truth," he says, " will properly

blame those who without discrimination shun all concern with the life of the State." [64] Disapproving both of excess of spirituality and of excess of religious exercise, he was the champion of those who were conservative in the observance of the national law, and at the same time were anxious to extract from Holy Writ philosophical and mystical doctrines, who prized both the literal and allegorical sense. He aspired to universalize the Jewish law by showing that its individual precepts embody the highest ethical teaching, and in their entirety constitute the law of nature, and to universalize the Hebrew Scriptures by showing that the historical narrative of the Mosaic books enshrines a sublime philosophy.

Philo gave a new bent to the Greek philosophy which he assimilated. His purpose was not to make an intellectual analysis of things or a scientific investigation of nature, but to bring about a union of the human soul with God. True to the cardinal principle of Jewish monotheism, he regards God as the one reality, the one cause, the one goal. All thought and all being are His direct creation: the universe is brought into existence by His will; the human soul is an emanation from His spirit; human knowledge is an inspiration from His power. " Through God, God is known, for He is His own light ";[65] and as man's soul and knowledge are from God, so man's final good is to be joined with God. Man could attain this state in superhuman ecstasy. The Hebraic doctrine of the Shekinah, the divine Presence, which possessed the saint, is clothed by Philo with a Greek dress. " When the divine light shines upon the mortal soul, the mortal light sinks; our reason is driven out at the approach of the divine spirit."[66] The various aspects of Greek thought which form the material of his system are transformed into a religious philosophy by this root idea of God and His relation to man. At the same time the Hebraic principles of his theology are largely modified through the influence of Greek conceptions. He contrives to show how the transcendental God who is utterly spiritual and incorporeal comes into relation with the physical world and the human soul, and hence his whole system depends on, or rather develops into, a doctrine about the divine nature.

The seeds of a formal theology, which are contained in the Wisdom books of the Bible, and fructified in Alexandrian soil, come to full fruition in his mind. His outstanding conception is the Word or the Logos, which is the instrument of

175

God's activity and His immanent manifestation in
the universe. It is impossible to pick out any clear
and definite conception of the Logos and say:
" This is Philo's notion of it." It is described in
endless metaphors and associated with a number of
attributes, now as the Creator of the universe, now
as its noetic model, now as its soul; as the seat of
the Ideas or immaterial patterns after which all
material things are created, and as the law of
Nature binding all things together through its
various forces; as the universal rule of conduct, the
revealed Torah, which guides the whole of humanity; as the divine effluence in the soul, which it is
man's highest function to cultivate, and as the principle of conscience which is placed in us to guide,
to warn, and to reprove. In other passages it is
personified as the high priest, the heavenly man,
the intercessor, the offspring of God, and His
wisdom, in others it is identified with Melchizedek
and the Manna. The presentation combines
Hebraic and Hellenic concepts and, in addition, a
number of floating ideas of divine intermediaries
which were derived from the ancient Egyptian
religion and were current in Alexandria.

Philo indeed constantly asserts the perfect unity
of God. Monotheism is the key-note of his

philosophy; but in his desire to provide stages in the upward march of the human soul to the knowledge of the Godhead, and under the influence of the culture around him, he elaborated this half-poetic, half-philosophical development of the divine instrument. The Platonic system of philosophy forms the dominant element in his syncretism. It was said about a century later: " Either Philo Platonizes or Plato Philonizes "; and there is in truth a profound sympathy between the Greek and the Jewish philosopher. " The aim of Plato's philosophy," said Macaulay, " is to exalt man into a God "; the aim of Philo's theology is to bring man into perfect communion with the one God. The greatest philosophical genius of the Hellenes possessed in a remarkable degree the Hebraic spirit which is zealous for God and makes for righteousness. The religious and spiritual aspects of Plato's teaching had, however, been neglected for three centuries; they were made fruitful by the contact of the Hebrew mind. As in nature a plant is fertilized by pollen brought from a strange flower, so in human culture a thought of one people is often made fruitful by the infusion of the ideas of another.

The cosmology of Philo is based on the Platonic idealism, *i. e.*, the doctrine that between the supreme Being and the material world a kingdom exists of spiritual archetypes, eternal, incorporeal, recognized by mind alone, which preceded the creation of the material world.[67] He who denies their existence is impious and godless. Sometimes Philo declares that the whole of this ideal world is contained in the divine Logos which orders all things;[68] sometimes he equates it with the angels in the Bible. He associates with the Platonic Ideas, which are embraced altogether in the Word, features taken from the pantheistic system of the Stoics. By the school of the Porch the divine substance was presented as the Logos or reason: and syncretizing this with the Hebrew *dabar,* he attributed to the divine power some of the material qualities which the Stoics attached to their pantheistic principle. He speaks of it as most mobile and fiery, stretched through the universe and using an intense motion; in one or two places he describes it as the seed-bearing Logos. These expressions are of course metaphorical, but they illustrate his tendency to adopt images and doctrines from schools to whose general outlook he was fundamentally antagonistic. From the Stoics, too, he

178

adopted a distinction between the thought in the mind and its expression in words, the first being known as the stored-up Logos; the second as the enunciated Logos. Elaborating this idea, he was led to personify the Logos as God's first-born son. The change of the patriarch's name from Abram—exalted father—to Abraham [69]—father of sound, suggests this allegory: " If we are to explain accurately, it is plain that the mind is the natural father of the uttered word, because it is the property of the father to beget, and the word is begotten from the mind." From this analysis of speech, it was a natural step to speak of the creative word of God as the divine offspring. The passage exemplifies the poetic and personifying character of Philo's allegorical interpretations which had its dangerous aspect. Max Müller's theory that language has created all theology is to-day somewhat discredited. But in an age when thought was as loose and mysticism as rampant as in the first century of the Christian era, language most certainly nourished theology.

The current philosophy of Alexandria was full of ideas derived from Egyptian and Oriental sources which engendered various divine genealogies and baffling theories of mediation. The Di-

vine Wisdom, the Ideal Man, the immaculate
conception of the virtues, the mediation of
Hermes—the interpreter between man and the
Absolute—these were the floating beliefs, begotten
of the union of decadent mythology and decadent
philosophy, which left their impress on Philo's
doctrine of the Divine Powers. Thus in one place
he makes the Divine Wisdom the mother of the
Logos; [70] and in another he writes: " The Creator
who has made this universe is the Father of the
creation; and its mother is the Wisdom of the
Creator. God uniting Himself to her has sown
becoming not in human fashion; she having received the divine seed, has in perfect travail given
birth to His son, sensible, only-begotten, and be-
loved—this visible world." [71] And, again, he
speaks of God's union with the truly virgin Wisdom. [72] The notion of an ideal man appears
several times in his allegories of the story of the
creation. God, he conceives, first created a Man
who is immaterial intelligence, the type of perfection; and from this ideal being the terrestrial
man came into existence. Developing Hebraic
ideas in the books of Ezekiel and Enoch, which
represent Adam as the perfect type of humanity,
he separates the heavenly archetype from its ter-

restrial copy, and sets the two in contrast. This mystical conception received great prominence in the mediæval system of Jewish mysticism in the form of the *Adam Kadmon*.

It would be out of place to dwell on the details of Philo's doctrine of intermediary powers, or of an ideal creation midway between God and the material world, or of his resolution of the angels into single words or ideas. We can but note the element of un-Jewish ideas and foreign gnosticism which crept into his philosophical allegories. It does not indeed supplant loyalty to the Law, and it is subordinate to his deeply spiritual and truly religious nature, which makes him humble before God and preserves much of the simple Jewish relation to the Deity; but with others such doctrines were to become subversive of the cardinal principles of Judaism.

Philo in a sense represents the high-water mark of Hellenistic influence upon the Jewish-Alexandrian culture. No other Jewish writer achieved so thorough a combination of Jewish and Greek wisdom, or developed an elaborate system of allegorical commentary. Yet he stands out as the conservative champion of Judaism against several schools, which went much further in the adoption of

Greek ideas and the Greek standpoint. On one
side were the thorough-going materialists. Over
and over again he attacks the followers of a philosophy which deifies the human reason and yet pre-
tends to honor God.¹³ These extreme Hellenizers
assumed the attitude that man was the measure of
all things, and that he must stand by his reason
alone. On the other side were the thorough-going
spiritualists, those who carried to its extreme consequence the allegorical interpretation of the Law,
and used it as a justification for abandoning practical observance. Claiming to be spiritual, they were
really antinomian: professing a rational religion,
they tended to gnosticism. Philo calls them the
children of Cain, who was the symbol of impious
pride; and it may be that he is attacking the prototype of a Cainite sect which in the second century
of the Christian era held gnostic doctrines. Any-
how, by the opening of the Christian era Hellenistic
philosophy had planted the seeds of gnostic heresy
in the Alexandrian community. Sectarianism in
the general community is apt to produce a sectarian
development among the Jews. The Muslim sects
of the Arabs and Persians, in the tenth century, had
their counterpart in Jewry, and the uncounted religious groups among the Graæco-Romans, in the

first and second centuries, were matched by a
medley of tenets sprung from Hellenistic Judaism.

Philo endeavoured to maintain a Judaism which,
while liberal and free in thought, was catholic in
practice; to formulate a mystical philosophy of
Judaism which, adopting many of the ideas of the
Greek sages, should still be true to the fundamental
points of Jewish monotheism. But mysticism always runs to excess. The balance was unstable in
his day, and it could not be fairly maintained a
little later. His was a sophistical rather than a
philosophical age, lacking the sense for the beauty
of the simple; and his own harmony of Hebraism
and Hellenism was not established on a sure basis.
The notions derived from Greek philosophy of intermediary beings between the supreme God and
man, though in passing through the mintage of his
mind stamped with a wholly spiritual character,
were, nevertheless, hardly consistent with the Jewish faith; and the syncretism which had been characteristic of Alexandrian culture throughout its
development, though designed by him to serve a
sublime purpose, led away to confused theosophies,
on the one hand, and to the division of the Godhead,
on the other. Both the Gnostics and the early
Christian theologians look to him as their chief

guide, and the poetical metaphors of his allegories
become with them hard dogmas. The offspring of
Hellenistic Judaism was heresy and the rejection
of the Torah.

Philo, as we have seen, was aiming at the very
opposite: he hoped, by demonstrating Judaism to
be philosophical, to make it a universal religion.
His deeper philosophy and his profounder allegorical interpretations were reserved for a small
circle, and in his day were not divulged to the mass.
It is the Christian scholars who vulgarized them.
The larger part of his work, however, is designed as
an exposition of the Law for the Hellenistic world.
The five books of Moses were not a collection of
the myths, the tribal chronicles, and the particu-
larist laws of one people: they were the divine
revelation for all mankind of moral and ethical
truth. The history of the creation was an ideal
cosmology; the lives of the patriarchs were concrete representations of the highest way of life; the
Mosaic legislation embodied the law of nature
which it was the wise man's aim to attain. More
particularly, Philo's Life of Moses with the appended treatises on Bravery, Humanity, and Repentance, was a missionary work, presenting Judaism
for all cultured people as a rule of reason and phil-

anthropy. It is an ethical interpretation of the
Pentateuch for the Greek-speaking, Greek-educated
world. The philosophical schools had each their
ideal type, Socrates, Diogenes, Epicurus, Pythagoras; but Philo places above them all Moses
" according to some (*i. e.*, the Gentiles) the lawgiver of the Jews, but as the others (*i. e.*, the Jews)
hold the interpreter of the divine laws and the
greatest and most perfect man in every way." " In
reply to the anti-Semitic agitators who charged the
Jewish laws with being tribal and inhumane, he
declares that " they are reflections and copies of
the divine virtues, of which the archetypes were
stamped by God on the soul of the lawgiver." And
the proof of their divine origin and excellence is
their wide sway and their immutability. " The
laws of the Greek legislators were subject continually to change; the laws of Moses alone remained steady, unmoved, unshaken, stamped, as it
were, with the seal of nature herself, from the day
when they were written to the present day, and
will so remain for all time, so long as the world
endures. Not only the Jews, but all other peoples
who care for righteousness adopt them. This
privilege they have which distinguishes them from
every other code. Every other nation has its own

185

laws, and will not accept the laws of another; but the Jewish law attracts and links together all peoples, barbarians and Greeks, those who live on the mainland, and those who live on the Islands."

The Stoics conceived a law of nature providing a rule of conduct for all peoples, but they were unable to specify its provisions. They contented themselves with the assertion of general phrases, to the effect that man should deny pleasure and follow virtue. Philo, identifying revealed and natural religion, the Greek Logos with the divine Word, proclaims the Mosaic legislation as the universal law of the one God, which was designed for the cosmopolis. The five books of Moses begin with the account of the creation, " in order to establish two great lessons: first, that He who is the Father and Creator of the world is also its Legislator, and secondly, that He who obeys those laws will follow the path of nature and will live in accordance with the order of the universe, so that there will be true harmony between theory and practice." Philo interprets the specific enactments of the Jewish law universally; he points a moral lesson as well as a historical value in each festival and each national observance; and in each enactment of the civil law he elucidates an ethical principle which gives it a

186

claim to the obedience of humanity. So far from being narrow and prescribing exclusiveness, the Jewish law in its every detail and its whole outlook enjoins the love of one's neighbor. The service of God is carried out by the service of humanity; in particular slavery is discouraged, and its conditions are constantly mitigated by the law. This belief in the ultimate acceptance of Judaism is thus expressed: " This is the supreme aim of the inspired prophet throughout his legislation, to ensure concord and good understanding and the harmony of different characters, so that families and entire nations and countries, and indeed the whole race of mankind, might advance to perfect happiness. Up to the present time, indeed, this is only a hope, but that it will come to pass I am firmly convinced, and facts show irrefutably, for God increases the harvest of virtue year by year."

That the Jewish mission at that time was an immense force in the diaspora is proved by the testimony of Jew and Gentile. " There is not any city of the Greeks," says Josephus [75]—doubtless with some rhetorical exaggeration, but, yet with a kernel of truth—, " nor any of the barbarians, nor any nation whatsoever to which our habit of resting on the seventh day has not been intro-

duced, and by whom our fasts and our prohibitions
as to food are not observed. As God Himself pervadeth the universe, so hath our law passed
through the world." And Seneca, the Roman
philosopher, spoke of subject Judea having taken
victorious Rome captive.

The outward expansion of Hellenistic Judaism
was greater than its inward cohesion, and became in time a danger. In order to appeal to the
Gentile peoples, Jewish law and Jewish belief were
re-interpreted in terms of Greek thought. The
idea of God was obscured with notions, derived
from Hellenistic theology, of His division into
several powers which were interposed between Him
and the world. The direct relation between God
and man, which was the goal of Jewish piety, was
transformed into mystical progressions through
attributes to the Godhead; speculation about the
immanence of God led on to the acceptance of the
Hellenistic notion of incarnation; and the Messianic hope of a world-wide kingdom of God was
exchanged for the individual ideal of personal redemption in union with the Son of God. The New
Testament illustrates the part which Hellenistic
Jews throughout the diaspora played in the earliest
disruptive development of the Christian teaching.

188

Even at Jerusalem one of the "Grecian Jews," Stephen, proclaimed that the Law and all outward ceremonies were ordained to last but for a time," and thereby roused the resentment of the other disciples. Jews of Cyprus and Cyrene were the first disciples at Antioch to preach to the Greeks, and to constitute the followers of the teachings of Jesus a separate sect." At Ephesus the Alexandrian Apollos turned from preaching Judaism to preaching the new Gospel to the Gentiles. Lastly, the mission of Paul marks the radical conversion of the ethical Hebraic teaching of Jesus into a new Hellenistic religion, in which the theology of the advanced Alexandrian reformers takes the place of the life according to the Jewish law as the basis of union. "The letter which is the law kills and leads to death. The spirit which is the Lord gives life and leads Godwards."

The elements of a new religious system were contained in the Hellenistic communities. The use of Hebrew disappeared, and with it much of the Hebraic spirit. The observance of the Torah, which was the spontaneous expression of the national-religious life in Palestine, came to be regarded, under the influence of Greek ethics, as an obstacle to the spiritual life. The Judaism of the diaspora

was colder and less happy than that of Judea.[78]
Instead of welcoming the Torah with joy, the
Hellenistic Jew invented theories, and sought to
justify his religion. Something of the same contrast exists to-day between the Judaism of the
ghetto and the Judaism of the emancipated Jew-
ries of the West. The interpretation of the Scriptures was raised to a kind of philosophy by allegorizing away the historical meaning and the literal
precept, and by substituting for them eclectic doctrines of Greek schools and Oriental speculations.
Lastly, the belief in the arising of a national Messiah of the house of David was displaced by the
idea of the incarnation of a divine Power who
should judge men at the end of days. Allegorical
development and its destructive effects did not stop
with Philo. Within a century of his death, the
unity of Alexandrian Judaism was irretrievably
marred, and sectarianism was dissolving the Jewish communities of the West.

Of the three great bonds of the Jewish people,
which hitherto had held them together in the diaspora, two had been broken, and the other was
seriously weakened. The triple cord consisted of
the language, and the land, and the law. The substitution of Greek as the language of prayer and

biblical study involved a growing estrangement of thought between Hellenistic and Palestinian Judaism. And though outside Egypt there is little direct evidence that Greek had replaced Hebrew in the synagogue (Mommsen's suggestion that Greek was a compulsory language has been refuted), the rapid growth of Christian heresy at Antioch and other Jewish centres shows that the synagogue there had lost its national character and its national strength. The love of Palestine and the regard for the sanctuary at Jerusalem as the centre of the religious nationality remained an influence of supreme importance so long as the nation preserved its autonomy. Philo bears witness to the deep affection of the Alexandrian community for the temple service,[79] and those pilgrimages to Jerusalem at the great festivals, when deputations came up to worship together from Parthia, Media, and Babylonia, Mesopotamia, Cappadocia and Asia, Phrygia and Pamphylia, Egypt and Cyrene, Greece and Rome,[80] were a powerful means of strengthening the unity of the house of Israel. When Jerusalem and the temple were razed by Titus, with the possible purpose of destroying the bond of cohesion, Hellenistic Judaism lost one of its great bulwarks against disintegration. In Pales-

tine the strengthening of the Law more than coun-
terbalanced the loss of national independence and
of a national centre.   But in the diaspora the hold
of the Law was already threatened, and the weakening of the centripetal forces assisted the encroachment of gnostic and antinomian ideas from
the environment.   Christianity in its Palestinian
origin had but few Hellenistic elements; but when
it spread to the diaspora, it was transformed by the
notions of its Greek-speaking and Greek-thinking
adherents.   The doctrine of Jesus in the Gospels is
Hebraic; the doctrine about Jesus in the Epistles is
Hellenistic.   Judaism contributed to the new creed
the social and moral ideal, Hellenism the ideal of
individual redemption.[81]   The Hellenistic writers
of the New Testament, such as the authors of the
Epistle to the Hebrews, or the Gospel according to
St. John—both, it is surmised, Alexandrians—
prove how far, in the second century, foreign ideas
had undermined the pure Jewish standpoint.   Their
use of allegorical interpretation is illuminating in
this connection.   The manna and the brazen serpent represent for the Palestinian symbolists the
Law and faith; by Philo they are associated with
the Logos; by the writer of the fourth Gospel they
are identified with Jesus incarnate.[82]   Again, the

writer of the Epistle to the Hebrews, giving a new turn to Philo's personification of the Logos as high priest and as Melchizedek, speaks of Jesus as " a high priest who passed into heaven, who was in all points tempted as we are, yet was without sin "; and later he writes: " After the similitude of Melchizedek there ariseth another priest . . . . and this man, because he continueth ever, has an unchangeable priesthood. Wherefore he is able to save them to the uttermost that come unto God by him, seeing he ever liveth to make intercession for them." [83] The ideas of the incarnation of God in human form and of human redemption by a divine individual, both in antipathy to the Jewish conception of God, and derived from the Hellenistic mysteries, are emphatically marked. When the fundamental bonds of unity were loosened, the beliefs which Jewish separateness was designed to preserve were likewise impaired. The doctrines of the Logos and the Powers were in the first and second centuries of the common era so developed, that the unity of the Jewish God and His divine communion with man was lost in the speculations about intermediaries and trinities and in " a phantasmagoria of angels and demons." The movement which began with the Septuagint translation

of the Bible ended with the Epistles of the New
Testament and the Creeds of the Christian Church.
Theological Christianity, with its rejection of the
Law and the national hope, its background in the
ideas of the Greek mysteries, and its dogmas of the
incarnation and redemption by the Savior, was
the last outcome of Alexandrian allegory. It was
the final stage in the syncretism of Judaism with
foreign cultures, which, up to a point, had nourished and fructified Jewish thought, but when it
passed that point, produced a new religious species.
Alexander's hope for the marriage of Europe and
Asia was consummated in the field of religion, and
the New Testament is the offspring of the union."

The Jewish communities of Alexandria and
other Hellenistic centres did not disappear with the
spread of Christianity. The Alexandrian colony
persisted till the beginning of the fifth century,
when it was violently expelled by the Christian
bishop. But the congregations of the diaspora
were no longer clearly distinguished from the
catholic body of Judaism. From the end of the
first century no extant literature marks a division
between the Greek-speaking and the other Jews.
But from the same period date numerous writings

of Christians and Gnostics, whose doctrines were, in large measure, a development of Hellenistic Judaism. Those who remained Jews accepted the rabbinic authority. They adopted the Palestinian Canon of the Bible, and rejected the additions to the biblical books and the apocryphal works which were contained in the Septuagint translation. The Christian Origen (flourished about 220 C. E.) refers to the books of Tobit and Judith and the additions to Daniel and Esther as being no longer in the Jewish Canon.³⁵ A large part of Hellenistic Jewry must have been absorbed in the new religious bodies, and Hellenistic Judaism perished as a distinct branch of the religion. The Palestinian teachers sought to defend Judaism against Hellenism, the Alexandrian teachers to defend it with Hellenism. The alliance, however, was dangerous, and in the early centuries of the Christian era, when the crisis came, Hellenistic Judaism was saturated with so many strange doctrines that it lost its centre of gravity and was unable to stand the shock, and its traditions and ideals were transformed through the intermingling of Oriental ideas into various heresies. The sublime faith of Hebraism and the clear reason of Hellenism were lost in the blended product. Neither Jewish nor Hellenistic religion prevailed in the fusion of cultures, but they were absorbed in a cosmopolitan creed which combined elements from many sources in an impure syncretism.

CHAPTER V

THE HELLENISTIC-JEWISH
LITERATURE

The history of the Hellenistic movement in Judaism is mainly to be sought in literature; and we have already dealt with several monuments which mark its progressive stages: the Septuagint translation, the books of the Maccabees, the Wisdom of Ben Sira, the Wisdom of Solomon, and the culminating achievement in the works of Philo-Judæus. Much of the product of the blending of the two cultures has disappeared, and is known to us either by name only, or in fragments; but in addition to the books mentioned several others have survived which illustrate the progress of Hellenization both in Palestine and the diaspora, and mark different aspects of its influence and its effect. The Rabbis, indeed, when the dangerous consequences of religious syncretism were apparent, contrived to exclude the whole of the literature from the works used for public reading or public teaching in the schools, so that it played scarcely any direct part in later Jewish thought. It was preserved, however, by the early Christians, and it lived on under the protection of the Church fathers and Christian monks who regarded it with great veneration, for the same reason that the Rabbis discountenanced it—that it contained the germs of Christian teaching.

That some Jews, as early as the latter part of the fourth century B. C. E., were well acquainted with Greek, is proved by the comments upon Judaism of certain pagan authors, which must have been derived, if not from translations of portions of the Scriptures, at any rate from verbal information. But it is the Septuagint translation which marks the entrance of Judaism into the stream of the world's culture. Round it is grouped the whole of the Jewish literary output in Greek during the third and second centuries: the books of the Apocrypha and the Apocalypses, the poetical and literary paraphrases of the Bible, the apologetic and propagandist writings. The two aims that run through the writings of the period are: first, to strengthen the hold of Judaism upon the Jewish people by developing and expanding its religious ideas, and showing their harmony with the intellectual civilization of the environment; secondly, to make Judaism known to the Gentiles and honored in their eyes, and to rebut calumnies about its sacred books and beliefs. When Greek was spoken by all cultured people, each nation was anxious to write its history in that language, so that it should be available for all. Literature like society was cosmopolitan. The Septuagint translation of Scripture, however, if we have regard only to its linguistic character, was fitted for the study rather of the Jewish community than of their Gentile neighbors. As Schürer says, it was written in a new language, swarming with such strange Hebraisms that the Greeks could hardly understand it.

Short and concise histories of Jewish antiquities were composed in more intelligible Greek for the general public. The earliest Jewish historian of the kind, of whom we have fragments, is Demetrius, who lived about the end of the third century. The remains of his work, with those of most of the early Hellenistic Jewish writers, are preserved in the collection of Alexander Polyhistor, a voluminous author of the first century, which again has come down to us through excerpts in the Ecclesiastical History of Eusebius.[1] Demetrius, it seems, was a jejune chronicler, who set out in chronological order the leading events of the history of Israel and Judah from

the time of Abraham. Eupolemus, who wrote
a book on the kings of Judah, has more pretence
to literary skill. He freely handles the scriptural
history, and he makes Moses the inventor of the
art of alphabetical writing which was handed on
by the Jews to the Phœnicians, and by them to
the Hellenes. Freudenthal ingeniously identifies
him with the Eupolemus whom Judas Maccabeus
sent on one of his embassies to Rome; and his awkward Greek style makes it probable that he was a
Palestinian Jew, while his use of the Hebrew, instead of the Septuagint text of the Bible, and his
freedom from any allegorical embellishment of the
Scripture narrative suggest that he was a loyal
Judean unaffected by Greek influence. These
early historians are Greek only in language, not in
thought; and even their language is a foreign medium in which they are by no means at home.

On the other hand, traces of a crude religious
syncretism are found in the slender fragments of
two Samaritan historians which are preserved in
the same source. Malchos Cleodemos associates
Abraham's offspring by Keturah with Heracles, the
Greek and Phœnician hero-god; while pseudo-
Eupolemus [2] identifies Abraham with Nimrod and
Belos, and speaks of Argerizim (i. e., Mount Geri-

zim) as the mount of the highest deity. And Theodotus, a poet who wrote an epic on Shechem, the
holy city of the Samaritans, ascribes the city's foundation to one Sicimos, a son of the Greek god
Hermes. Among the half-Jewish Samaritans,
then, in the second century a distinct movement
existed toward the adoption of the cosmopolitan
Hellenistic religion which was in vogue throughout
the East. The presence of a Greek colony both
in Samaria and Shechem doubtless fostered the
movement. A different kind of syncretism is contained in the writings of pseudo-Artapanus, of
which our remnants are more considerable. He
wrote a history of the Jews, and is especially concerned with the story of Israel in Egypt. He certainly was an Egyptian Jew, and his knowledge of
Greek literature is greater than that of the writers
hitherto mentioned, extending to the composition of
lines in different Greek metres. He is master, too,
of the more obvious devices of rhetoric, and he has
something of the skill of the writer of fiction. The
general principle of his writing may be defined as
confounding the chronology and perverting the
Scriptures, in order to associate the Hebrew heroes
with the heroes of the nations. According to his
improved Exodus, the leader of Israel was the

same person as Musæus, the legendary teacher of
Orpheus; he was the inventor of philosophy and of
hieroglyphics, and a great warrior and builder to
boot; he built the city of Hermopolis, and he even
established the Egyptian religion. The Egyptians
called him Hermes because of his skill in herme-
neutics. The patriarchs likewise founded Egyptian
cults, and Abraham instructed the Pharaoh of his
time in astrology. The author was writing not for
the Jewish but for the pagan community, and he
was writing not history but apology, which is history with a purpose and without a conscience.

From the beginning of the second century a feud
raged between the Hellenized Egyptians and the
Jews, which was largely fought with the weapons
of literary falsehood. The Jews thought fit to
defend themselves against the calumnies of their
detractors, who spread scurrilous accounts of their
origin and their beliefs, by spreading equally false
accounts of the glorious part their ancestors had
played in Egyptian civilization. The syncretism
of a pseudo-Artapanus then is not a sincere expression of opinion, but a conscious pose, designed
to impress the ruder section of the population
among whom the Jews lived. It betrays the not
very happy influence of Hellenistic models upon the

Jewish littérateurs of Alexandria. They imbibed a disregard of truth, together with the capacity to write ornate periods, and acquaintance with poetical mythology led them to turn their own sacred records into fiction.

Freudenthal, on the strength of certain correspondences between the fragments of Artapanus and the Letter of Aristeas, ascribes the famous letter to the same author. Further he attributes to him a large part of the Jewish pseudepigraphic literature which was composed in Greek verse. His thesis savors of the method of the Bacon-Shakespeare controversialists; but whether he is right or only ingenious, whether one bold man was responsible for the fictitious version of Exodus, for the imaginative record of the origin of the Septuagint translation, for the monotheistic tags that are appended to Sophocles and Orpheus, and for the exhortations to Judaism which the Sibyl utters in hexameters full of false quantities and sound doctrines, or whether a school of literary forgers divided the work between them, undoubtedly a common trend runs through all the apologetic literature, and a single spirit prompted its composition. The purpose was to glorify Judaism and the Jewish people in the eyes of the Hellenistic population by the

adoption of Hellenistic standards and the use of
Hellenistic forms. To effect this object, accuracy
and truth might be sacrificed, and the intrinsic
excellence of the teaching might be tricked out
with fictitious testimonials of Greek thinkers. The
apologetic literature has a curious blend of the missionary and advertising spirit. But it is absurd
to attribute its fiction to the inherent vice of the
Jew. Scaliger, the seventeenth century scholar,
spoke of falseness as " Judæorum natura insita,"
but in truth the Jewish writers were only copying
what others had done for Chaldean, Egyptian, and
Hellenistic antiquities.'

The Letter of Aristeas, which has survived in
its integrity, professes to be a contemporary account of the translation of the Pentateuch into
Greek in the time of Ptolemy Philadelphus (285-
277). It purports to be sent to Philocrates by his
brother Aristeas, who was an official at the court,
and went on an embassy to Jerusalem to induce the
high priest to send sages who should make the version of the Hebrew Scriptures for the royal library.
Possibly the writer assumes the name of Aristeas in
order to identify himself with a Jewish historian
of that name, of whom a short fragment dealing
with the story of Job is preserved. But scholars '

agree that letter cannot be contemporary with the events described. The writer naively betrays his later date in several particulars, as when he says that the arrangement for the reception of foreign guests at the Alexandrian court may *still* be seen in operation, and that " all histories *used to be* translated by these kings," *i. e.,* the Ptolemies. Scholars agree also that he must have been an Alexandrian Jew. The balance of evidence as to his approximate date is in favor of the end of the second century B. C. E. The story of the embassy to Jerusalem, of the choosing of sages for the translation, " who had not only acquired proficiency in Jewish learning but had also given profound study to that of the Greeks," of their reception at Alexandria, and of the miraculous outcome of their labors, has already been touched upon. The narrative contains also several romantic letters which passed between Ptolemy and Eleazar, the high priest, a detailed description of the royal presents to the temple, and a gorgeous but shadowy description of Jerusalem, bespeaking the literary craftsman rather than the eye-witness. But what is more notable for the study of Hellenistic thought is the apologetic account of the Law which is put into the mouth of Eleazar. It is, perhaps, the first example of the propagation of the Mosaic legislation in the light of Greek ethical ideas. " I believe," says the writer by way of introduction to this section of his work, " that most men have some curiosity about the regulations of the Law concerning meats and drinks and the animals which are considered unclean." ° Eleazar, having first expounded the monotheistic principle of Judaism and contrasted it with the lower ideas of God held by other peoples, explains that these laws are designed to secure the purposive separateness of the Jews. " To the intent then that we should not become perverted through joining in the pollution of any people . . . . he fenced us round on all sides with laws of purification of meat and drink and hearing and seeing. For, speaking generally, all these, if viewed in the light of their inward meaning, are directed by a single power; and in every detail there is a profound reason for the things which we abstain from using, and those of which we make use." °

The method of Aristeas is like that of the *Dorshe Hamurot* of Palestine; but he extends to the Halakah the symbolical interpretation which they, for the most part, confined to narrative passages. He points out a symbolical value in the various dietary laws. " The winged creatures of which we partake, such as doves, geese, and the like, are tame and distinguished by cleanly habits, using wheat and pulse for their sustenance. On the other hand, those that are forbidden are wild and carnivorous, and use their powers to oppress the remainder of their kind. Hence the lawgiver signified that those for whom the laws are ordained must be outwardly righteous and oppress none through confidence in their strength, but must direct their lives by righteous motives." Symbolism is closely akin to allegory, and the apologist offers other interpretations of the Mosaic law which are more distinctly allegorical. The parting of the hoof and the dividing of the claws " symbolize discrimination in directing every action to a good end; for the strength of the whole body, in order to display itself in action, is dependent on the arms and legs. Again, the chewing of the cud to thoughtful minds clearly indicates memory; for it is nothing else but a calling to mind of one's life and existence." '

In the last part of the letter the writer describes a symposium between the king and the translators, extending over seven days, which gives him an opportunity of bringing out the supreme wisdom of

the Jewish sages. This section of the work recalls
the stories in the Talmud about Alexander's discourse with the wise men of Judea; but its distinctive feature is the combination of the Hebraic idea
of righteousness with Hellenic ethics. All wisdom
is derived from God, and the prince of Aristeas is
counselled to secure the prosperity of his realm by
godliness. Again, when the king asks what is the
greatest glory, he receives the reply: " To honour
God, and that not with gifts and sacrifices, but with
purity in the soul, and in the devout conviction that
all things are fashioned and directed by God in accordance with His will." ⁸ When he asks: " Can
wisdom be taught? " (a famous Greek question),
he replied: " The soul is through God's power so
adapted as to accept all that is good, and reject what
is contrary thereto." Throughout, insistence is laid
on faith; and trust in God is emphasized as the
foundation of wisdom and virtue. There is clearly
a tacit controversy with the position of the Greek
schools, and more especially of the Stoics who,
making man the measure of all things, placed supreme reliance on reason. The Jewish sages " far
excelled the philosophers, in that they took God
for their starting-point."

The Letter of Aristeas is a specimen of the didactic novel; and another monument of Hellenistic Judaism, the so-called Fourth Book of the Maccabees, is a specimen of the artistic homily. The title given to the latter by its author was " On the Supremacy of Pure Reason "; it is on the face of it not a historical narrative, but a moral exhortation or series of sermons supported by historical argument and embellished by rhetorical ornament, designed to point out the excellence of the life under the Torah, and drawing its examples from the Seleucid persecution. In default of a known author, it was long ascribed without good reason to Josephus. Freudenthal [9] suggests with more plausibility that it is based on the history written by Jason of Cyrene, of which our Second Book of the Maccabees is an epitome. But whoever its author and whatever its date, it constitutes in a way one of the most perfect blendings of Hellenism and Hebraism which have come down from the period. The purpose of the homily, like that of the Letter of Aristeas, is to glorify the Jewish Law and the Jewish way of life; but it is carried out with greater loyalty to the spirit of Judaism. Doubtless the difference in standpoint is partly due to the fact that the preacher is addressing Jews or proselytes in a synagogue, while the Letter was addressed to the Gentiles outside the synagogue. Though he wrote with full mastery of the arts of Greek rhetoric, he is in his ideas a loyal Pharisaic Jew, full of national pride and of love for his religion. Nor does he allow his knowledge of Greek philosophy to weaken in any way his faithfulness to legal observance: rather it confirms and deepens it. Judaism remains for him the best system of life. " For our philosophy " (*i. e.,* the Law), he says, " teaches us temperance, so that we master our pleasures and desires, and it exercised us in fortitude so that we willingly undergo every toil. And it instructs us in justice, so that in all our behaviour we give them what is due; and it teaches us to be pious, so that we worship the only living God in a manner becoming His greatness."

He makes an ethical defence of the dietary laws which, then as now, were the target for a type of shallow rationalism. " When we long," he says, " for fishes and fowls and four-footed animals, and every kind of food which is forbidden to us by the Law, it is through the mastery of pious reason that we abstain from them. For the affections and appetites are restrained and turned into another direction by the sobriety of the mind, and all the movements of the body are kept in check by pious reason." In this fashion he sets up the Mosaic code as the embodiment of a loftier reason than the pleasure-seeking, self-indulgent materialism which was based upon a superficial acquaintance with Greek philosophy. Yet it is a sign of Greek influence that he feels compelled to find an ethical justification for the prescriptions of the Law. He invokes the Greek idea of reason as the foundation of virtue; but he avoids the allurements of symbolism and allegory. The Mosaic code as a whole is the rule of reason; and wisdom, which is the knowledge of affairs both human and divine and of their causes, is attained by the discipline and instruction of the law. Aristotle had taught in his *Ethics* how moral virtue based on good habit must precede intellectual excellence, which was the goal of human endeavor. The author of our homily, applying this teaching, acclaims Judaism as a positive system of the best life. The commandments not to reap the corners of the field, and not to cut down the trees of the enemy in war, bear witness to its humanitarian character. And for the practical influence of the Law he points to the story of Hannah and her sons, which is embellished with all the artifice of the accomplished rhetorician.

His reflections manifest the influence of Stoic thought, which is also apparent in the Wisdom of Solomon and the works of Philo. Many of his philosophical concepts are directly taken from Stoic writings, but he adopts only those elements of Stoicism which are in harmony with the Jewish outlook. The impersonal Providence of the Greek school becomes with him the Providence which protected the patriarchs; and he asserts the union between the body and the soul in the creation of God. He holds fast to Jewish moderation, and shows no favor to asceticism and other-wordliness. Piety consists in strong self-control, not in flight from the world. Jewish faith is deepened by contrast with pagan godlessness; and the heroic deeds of the Maccabean martyrs are illuminated by the light of Hellenistic ethics.

A third apology for the Jewish law, of which we know not the real author, is preserved in fragments under the name of Aristobulus.[10] The passages profess to come from a treatise on " The Interpretation of the Holy Laws," written by that Aristobulus [11] who appears at the beginning of the Second Book of Maccabees as a leading man among the Egyptian Jews and the teacher of Ptolemy. If the work were properly ascribed to

him, it would date from the beginning of the second
century B. C. E.; but though it is possible that the
historical Aristobulus was an early exponent of an
eclectic Græco-Jewish philosophy, the internal evidence points to an origin some three centuries later.
The fragments reveal a more advanced stage of
Hellenization than is shown by the Letter of Aristeas, and the Fourth Book of the Maccabees. The
book is first referred to by Clement of Alexandria
who flourished about 200 C. E., and modern scholars have concluded that it is later than the works of
Philo whom the writer copies, though often not
understanding him aright.¹² The position assumed
is that Greek philosophy is derived from the Hebrew wisdom; and the thesis is supported by spurious quotations from popular Greek poetry of pre-
historic times. These ideas and methods were
commonly accepted in the second century, the golden
age of literary forgery, by early Christian scholars,
and through them passed into the thought of the
Middle Ages. Several of the fragments contain
justifications of the Mosaic law, based on allegorical interpretations or the attachment of Greek conceptions. Thus a passage on the meaning of the
Sabbath contains a Pythagorean dilation on the
power of the number seven, which may be com-

pared with the treatment of the Book of Jubilees.[13]
The apologists whom we have hitherto considered
were essentially concerned with the defence of the
Mosaic laws by their interpretation according to
Greek notions. Aristobulus is partly engaged on
the same object, but he is also anxious to associate the Hebraic idea of God with the theology
of the Greek philosophers, and at the same time
to explain away the anthropomorphisms of the
biblical narrative. These were the motives also of
the Philonic allegory; and though not nearly as
elaborate as the doctrine of the Logos in Philo, the
conception of God's activity which appears in Aristobulus is the same in kind. Commenting on the
narrative of the creation, he said: " It may all be
ascribed to the Wisdom; for all light cometh from
her; and some of the Peripatetics have said that she
is the torch-bearer." He warns Ptolemy against
taking literally the passages of Scripture which as-
cribe to the purely spiritual God hands and arms
and face and feet; and calls on him to attend to the
philosophical interpretation; for Moses often hid
his meaning beneath allegories. The physical
miracles which attended the decalogue are ecstatic
illusions of the assembled Israelites; and when the
Bible speaks of the hand of God being heavy on the

Egyptians, it signifies the divine power, because all power and energy are conceived to lie in the hand.

We must now turn back to the more popular Jewish propaganda which was spread by pseudepigraphical works, partly in prose and partly in the guise of archaic Greek poetry. There is little to guide us to the authors or the age of its various components. As to the most famous part, the Sibylline oracles, it is clear that their composition was spread over a long period, and represents several religious standpoints. They cover, indeed, the whole progress of the Jewish advance against paganism, from its original outburst after the Maccabean triumph to its final transformation into Christianity. Among the pseudo-historical glorifications of Judaism the most remarkable are two books on the Jews and on Abraham which were composed in the name of Hecatæus of Abdera. The genuine Hecatæus was a court historian of Ptolemy Soter (about 280 B. C. E.) who wrote a history of Egypt, dealing not only with outward events but with the beliefs and laws of the peoples who were brought under the Ptolemaic sway. A Greek historian, Diodorus, has preserved fragments of his description of the Jews in which he recognizes their lofty idea of divinity and their staunchness to their ancestral faith, though in characteristic Greek fashion he represents that the heavens were their sole God. But the spurious Hecatæus, who is first quoted in the Letter of Aristeas and may be the creation of the writer of the letter, far outdoes his model in praise of the Jews. " They undergo," he says, " with exemplary courage all manner of tortures and the most cruel deaths rather than break the institutions of their ancestors." The motive for their settlement in Alexandria was that Alexander wished to honor their courage and their loyalty. He explains the absence of any mention of the people of Israel in the ancient writers on the ground that the teaching of the holy books of the Jews was too pure and too sacred to be understood. Lastly he quotes a number of apocryphal verses of the Greek tragedian Sophocles in favor of the divine unity, and others purporting to be from the comic poet Philemon about the punishment of hidden sins by the all-knowing and just God. In brief, pseudo-Hecatæus says just the things which the Jewish apologists wanted the Greeks to believe of their creed, and provides just that evidence which the Jewish apologists required to impress the Hellenistic world.

The Judaizing poem ascribed to Phocylides, a famous Greek moralist of early times, is similar in purport. Already in the seventeenth century Scaliger, the scholar who took a harsh view of the morality of this literature, pointed out that the poems revealed either a Hellenistic-Jewish or a Christian author; and the later researches of Bernays [14] have proved that the former is the true alternative. Occasionally, as the text stands, notions appear which are derogatory to pure monotheism; but Bernays has shown ingeniously that these passages contain glosses or mistakes, and can be emended so as at once to get rid of the offending words and improve the sense. The moralist emphasizes those aspects of the Mosaic law which obviously breathe a broad humanitarian spirit, and he forbears from denouncing pagan degradation. He says nothing of the sabbath or of sacrifices, but expatiates on the commandment against the taking of a mother-bird with her young from the same nest,[15] or the eating of anything torn from wild animals. Writing perhaps at a period when the Jewish mission was not yet self-confident, he does not directly attack the worship of idols, but, on the other hand, he speaks of God as a unity. Tentatively and covertly he propagates the Jewish teaching as " the mysteries of righteousness," conveying his medicine, so to say, in a tasteless pill, and investing it with the attraction of a secret cult.

The Jewish sages of the Middle Ages distinguished between the statutes and ordinances which have a validity for mankind and those which are the special heritage of Israel and concern ritual. The pseudo-Phocylides, in the same spirit, selects only the former for recommendation to the Gentiles whom he wished to affect. It probably is not that Hellenistic influence led him to disregard the national observances of Judaism; but in preaching broadcast a moral mission, it was expedient to keep them in the background and to emphasize the ethical precepts.

A bolder standpoint marks the earliest of the Sibylline Oracles, which is generally admitted to be the third of our numbering. The present collection comes from a Christian monk of the sixth century, and is in hopeless disorder. It contains fourteen books all in hexameter verse, and dating from the second century before the Christian era to the time of Constantine (about 300 C. E.). The Judaizing purpose and doctrine of some of the oracles are so thinly veiled that even the critics of antiquity recognized a Jewish Sibyl. Pausanias, the famous archæologist of the third century, in discussing the various Sibyls, says: " One of them was an oracle-giving seeress on behalf of Palestine, named Sabbe; some called her, too, the Babylonian, others the Egyptian Sibyl." ¹⁰ The greater part of the third oracle and the prologue of the first, which appear to be the work of one author, have demonstrably an Egyptian origin, because there is a deliberate and sustained attack on the Egyptian worship. Animated with greater daring than the writer who used the mask of Phocylides, the poet at once bursts into an invective against idolatry: " Are ye not ashamed, ye mortals, to make gods of cats and brutes, fools to adore snakes, dogs, weasels, and birds of air, and creeping things of earth and images of stone, statues made by hand, and cairns by the roadside? " He passes on to praise the Jewish people, not by name, but by clear indications: " There is a race of pious men, who live about the temple of Solomon and have their origin from Ur of the Chaldees. They do not worship the sun or the moon, nor pay heed to miracles or sorcerers or astrologers. They practise justice and virtue, and have no greed for money; they have just weights and measures; they do not rob each other, nor remove the landmarks of their neighbours. The rich man does not oppress the poor or afflict the widow, but gives them part of his harvest according to the sacred law of God." [17] The Sibyl claims to be the true prophetess sprung from Babylon, and she attacks Homer for the false doctrines which he *will* utter in times to come to the Greeks, suggesting, forsooth, that Homer was the plagiarist, and she the original writer of hexameter verse. " A false-writing seer will appear among them . . . who will master my words and my verses." Without a doubt the Jewish writer had his fair share of *hutz-pah*. He passes judgment upon the other nations, Babylon, Egypt, Gog and Magog, Rome and Libya, and foretells their downfall in the spirit of a Hebrew prophet. He is equal to making a play on words in Greek,

> Samos shall be sand, and Delos deleted, and Rome a ruin,[18]

where he adroitly imitates the assonance in Zephaniah (2. 4):

> For Gaza shall be forsaken
> And Ashkelon a desolation.

If, as can hardly be doubted, the writer had the Hebrew model before him, it shows how fully Jewish he was in mind and training. The promise of the Messianic kingdom and the description of the

Messianic age likewise follow the traditional Hebrew ideas: " From the East God will send a king
who will put an end to all war on earth, killing
some, and fulfilling the prophecies for others. And
he will act not according to his own counsels, but in
obedience to the righteous commands of God.
Peace shall prevail among the kings of the earth,
and God shall set up an eternal kingdom over all
men." [19] Throughout the poem he offers little indication of Hellenistic thought, save that he betrays a special affection for Hellas, and associates
the Greek myth of the giants with the Bible story
of the flood. But in his conclusion, where he foretells the ultimate triumph of the Jewish return,
and the Paradise that awaits the righteous, his
voice is the voice of a Jeremiah or a Malachi,
though his meter is the meter of Homer. " The
glorious restoration of Jerusalem, and the ac-
knowledgment by the whole world of the religious
doctrines of the Jews, are to him not matters of
faith but certainty." [20]

The fourth oracle is likewise, in all probability,
the work of an Alexandrian Jew. It praises the
Jewish people by allusion, in the manner of the
earlier poem: " Happy shall be those who love the
great God, praising Him before meat and drink.

Nought have they to do with sanctuaries and altars, the seat of dumb stones soiled with the blood of animals. Other peoples imitate not their piety and their ways, but in their folly sneer and mock, imputing to them their own evil doings." The fifth oracle, though in its present form it contains considerable Christian interpolations, has been ascribed to a Palestinian Jew. Written after the destruction of the temple, it is full of lamentations for the national disaster, but it breathes a hope in the coming reappearance of a savior, who is described in the allusive manner of the apocalypses of the time. " An excellent man will come from Heaven, the best of the Hebrews, whose hands approached the fruitful rod; who once stayed the sun (comp. Joshua, 10. 12), and spoke with beautiful speech and holy life."

Possibly the expected savior is Joshua, whom the Samaritans especially revered, and in that case the author would be a Samaritan Jew. Many of the succeeding oracles are by Christians who early adopted this form of propaganda, and were dubbed by Celsus in reproach " Sibyllistae," so fond were they of using it for missionary purposes." But as late as the fourth century of the Christian era there are prophecies of the restoration of Jerusalem

222

which must be the work of the Jews. Sibylline
verses were co-terminous with the Jewish missionary activity, and formed one of its most notable
expressions.

The Sibylline Oracles and the apocalypses, it
has been said, are twins; but they are twins easily
distinguished in character and appearance. The
Sibyllines were addressed to the pagan masses
by way of exhortation and warning, the various
apocalypses to the Jewish people by way of encouragement; the Sibyllines are uniformly composed in Greek hexameter verse, the apocalypses
are written either in prose or in the prose-poetry
of the prophetic books of the Bible. In times of
trouble and stress, such as were frequent from the
time that the Jews came under Roman sway, part
of the Jewish people, more particularly the less
educated and the less staunch, desired the Messianic
visions and glorious promises of Israel's future in
the books of the prophets to be expanded for them.
In their longing for a knowledge of the working
of God, they required accounts of the creation more
detailed than the opening of Genesis; and affected
by the astrology and mystical lore of the time, they
loved to hear accounts of the celestial wonders
which were stored up in the heavens above. Lastly,

in the gloom of Roman oppression and the conviction of the immortality of the soul, they hungered for pictures of the rewards and punishments in the future world which they could not find in the Hebrew Scriptures. These yearnings prompted the apocalypses, which date from the Persian period of Jewish history. Apocalypse therefore in one way continues the message of the prophets in the light of the Persian and Hellenistic culture, but it differs markedly in its form. The prophets conveyed their teaching by direct spoken utterance; the apocalyptic writers by symbols and parables, as a kind of secret wisdom to be understood only by the initiated. Their work bears the same relation to the classic Hebrew prophecy as the far-fetched conceits of the Jacobean poets to the full and outspoken utterance of the Elizabethans. The prophets spoke in their own name, the apocalyptics ascribed their revelations to the hoary figures of the past or to the heroes of by-gone generations.

The biblical books which stand midway between classical prophecy and apocalypse are Zechariah and Ezekiel, which in their form are of the same class as Isaiah and Jeremiah, but in much of their content are parallel with the celestial visions of a later age. The book of Daniel is a more purely apocalyptic book which found its way into the Hebrew Canon of Scripture. It purports to be written during the Babylonian captivity; but its detailed account of the Seleucid dynasty under the guise of prophecy shows that it was composed in the Hellenistic period and under Hellenistic influence. The other works of this class, though originally composed in Hebrew, have survived only in Greek or Aramaic, or some other version.

As the Jewish missionaries to the heathens used the name of a mythical seeress or a popular poet to convey their sermons, so the apocalyptics regularly used one of the progenitors of the race, or some famous teacher of historical times, to cloak their speculations. The visions and prophecies bear the names of Adam and Eve, Noah, Enoch, and the patriarchs, or of Baruch and Ezra and Jeremiah. An exception to the rule is the book known to us as the Book of Jubilees or as " the little Genesis." [22] Its general design is an amplification of the Book of Genesis, with various fantasies about angels and dreams, and the nature and ordering of the celestial bodies. The whole purports to be a revelation to Moses on mount Sinai by an angel of the Presence. It is the earliest example of haggadic Midrash, and it contains many

legends which appear in later Midrashim. But
what gives the book its title, and what is peculiar
to it, is the holiness which is predicted of certain
numbers, notably of seven and fifty, and the elaborate attempt to formulate a chronology by them.
The mystical veneration of numbers was a commonplace of Hellenistic culture and typical of its
looseness of thinking. Derived from Chaldea, and
fostered by the Pythagorean brotherhoods, it
seized on the civilized world as a cardinal principle
of thought. Philo and Aristobulus as well as the
author of Jubilees are affected by it in their treatment of the Sabbath, but with the difference that
they point out the virtue of numbers in relation to
universal things, while he does so in relation to
Jewish observance and beliefs. There are seven
days of Passover and Tabernacles, and seven days
of Holy Convocation. The Fast of Atonement is
observed in the seventh month; there are seven
pieces of holy furniture in the Tabernacle, and seven
branches of the Holy Candelabra. Seven is the
number of forgiveness, of the covenant, of holiness,
perfection, and rest. Of other Hellenistic influences in the book there is little indication, and, on
the other hand, the writer emphasizes the separateness of the Jewish people. Israel may not asso-

ciate or intermarry with the Gentiles because they sacrifice to the dead and worship evil spirits; because their ways are unclean, and they will be destroyed from the earth. The original language was probably Hebrew or Aramaic. With the rest of the apocalyptic literature it dropped out of general Jewish tradition in the second or third century; but it was known to the writers of Midrash and of the gaonic period, and also to the Karaites, and it remained a holy book to the remote branch of the people in Abyssinia which has survived in the Falashas.

Another apocalypse preserved through the veneration of the Abyssinian sect is the Book of Enoch, of which an Ethiopic version came to light in 1773. Enoch was a favorite figure with the authors of revelations, because of the mysterious saying of the Bible about him: " And Enoch walked with God, and he was not; for God took him." [23] Besides the Ethiopic book, which itself is a compilation of five sources, a " Book of the Secrets of Enoch " is preserved in the Slavonic. The older Book of Enoch, it is conjectured, is derived from a pre-Christian Hebrew original. It is the most comprehensive of the apocryphal books; it reveals the secret of the creation of the world, of the kingdom of the angels, of the last judgment, of the Messianic age, and of the cataclysms in nature which are to precede it. The secrets are conveyed in visions which Enoch receives in his passage through heaven; the vision of Wisdom, where he imparts in the form of parables the revelation of the spiritual world, and also an explanation of the great natural phenomena based on a confused medley of the physics of the day; the vision of the revolution of the lights of heaven, which is likewise a rambling recital, in poetic language, of the popular astronomy; and the vision of the historical world-process, which is in the normal manner of prophetic teaching. The vision of the Messiah manifests a blending of Hebraic and Hellenistic conceptions. The Anointed of the pure Jewish conception, who appears first in Isaiah's prophecies, was to be a national hero of the house of David, ushering in the era of righteousness and peace:

> And there shall come forth a shoot out of the stock of Jesse,
> And a twig shall grow forth out of his roots.[24]

Now the development of the conception under the stimulus of foreign persecution during the Maccabean period is clearly shown in the Psalms of Solomon, a liturgical composition of the first century before the common era. " God will raise up a prince of the house of David to rule over Israel, to crush their enemies, and to purify Jerusalem from the heathen . . . . The heathen nations will serve him, and come to Jerusalem to see the glory of the Lord. He is a righteous king, taught of God, and there shall be no unrighteousness in his days." [25] This form of the Messianic hope found permanent expression in one of the earliest prayers of the liturgy, the Eighteen Benedictions, and was adopted in Pharisaic Judaism as an integral part of Jewish belief. But Hellenistic speculation fostered the notion of a more etherealized and, so to say, theological Messiah. The Primal or Divine Man, who plays a large part in the work of creation, was one of the fixed ideas of the current theology. He is the central figure in Orphic eschatologies; and perhaps through this source, perhaps by a less direct fusion of thought, he found his way into the circle of Jewish apocalyptics, and changed the notion of the Messiah from a terrestrial king to the celestial being. So Enoch, who in one verse tells of the coming of the national redeemer, in another passage sees dwelling in heaven the Righteous One, " the Elect who is chosen and hidden before God before the creation of the world, and will be before Him for evermore." [26] He is spoken of variously as " the Son of

Woman " or " the Son of Man," [27] and many of
the attributes of the Wisdom and the Logos are
transferred to him: " His name was called by God
before the sun and the signs of the zodiac were
created . . . . He sits on the throne of God; the
source of Wisdom pours forth from the thoughts
of his mouth." [28] The Heavenly Man in the Greek
myth is the intermediary of creation; in the Jewish apocalypse he is the divine agent at the end of
the world-process. " At the end of time the Lord
will reveal him to the world, in order that he may
judge all creatures in accordance with the end to
which God has chosen him from the beginning." [29]

Side by side with the idealized conception of
the Messiah, the Book of Enoch and the Ascen-
sions contain materialistic pictures of the after-
world, from which the finer instinct of the old
Hebrew prophecy held back. Sensuous earthly
hopes find expression in the description of Paradise; foreign elements taken from Egyptian and
Chaldean sources are combined with prophetic
images, and jumbled together in a confused pic-
ture we have " green meadows and sulphurous
abysses; white horses and frightful beasts."
Strange again to the simple Hebraic idea of God's
working is the introduction of evil angels, Azazel,

who has the functions of a Power of Darkness, and Peniel, who tempts men with dangerous gifts,[20] including the gift of writing. We may find parallels for these features in the contemporary religious literature; and in general it may be said that the apocalyptic literature is impregnated with elements borrowed from the ethical-religious philosophy and the realistic theosophy of the environment, and imperfectly fused with the Jewish teaching which formed the basis of the vision. The Alexandrian sages syncretized Greek philosophy with the Torah; the authors of the Palestinian apocalypse syncretized Hellenistic mysticism with Jewish prophecy.

A section of theosophists and gnostics went beyond the standpoint of the author of our apocalypse, as is shown by his denunciation of "those who altered the words of truth, and treated the words of the holy and great One as lies." They perpetrated lying works, and wrote books about their speech; and they abandoned the inheritance of their fathers which endureth for ever. They were akin, it seems, to those excessive followers of the allegorists of Alexandria, attacked by Philo, who made their spiritual interpretation a ground for rejecting the observance of the Law. These extrava-

231

gant searchers into the secret doctrines were so intent on the affairs of heaven and the orbits of angels,
that they ceased to regard the law of conduct in this
world. They established a dualism between
heaven and earth, and sought to fill the gulf they
had created by intermediary powers. In this they
wandered from the spirit of Judaism, and opened
the way to dangerous heresy. The pseudepigraphic Enoch enlarges quaintly upon the dangers of writing, by which these disloyal teachers are
able to perpetuate their doctrines.[31]

The Slavonic Book of Enoch, which is derived
from a Greek original (though parts of the work
may have been founded on Hebrew writings), bears
unmistakable traces of Greek influence not only in
doctrine but in certain suggestive details. Thus
Adam's name is derived from the initial Greek letters of the four quarters of the world:[32] "And I
gave him a name from the four substances, the
east, the west, the north, and the south."[33] As
the root *Adam* has only three letters in the Hebrew, the fancy here must be Greek. Moreover
the writer several times follows the Septuagint in
preference to the Hebrew Bible, and he reproduces
the words of Ecclesiasticus, apparently from the
Greek version: "God made man in His own image

after His own likeness, and placed in him eyes to
see, and ears to hear, and a head to undrestand." "
His doctrine is occasionally reminiscent of the speculations of Philo and the Wisdom of Solomon, as
when he says that the existent was created from the
non-existent, and the visible from the invisible; and
that every soul was created eternally before the
creation of the world.   Is it strange that these
books, with their mingling of Greek and Jewish
cosmology and with their strange doctrines of
angels, incurred the disfavor of the Rabbis?   Like
the sensational fiction of our day, they filled their
readers with wild ideas, and nourished dangerous
expectations.

Another work of this class, but recently discovered in the Syriac, is the Apocalypse of Baruch,
which seems to be a translation of a lost Greek
version.   It may have sprung from a Palestinian
original, for it contains few traces of Hellenistic
philosophy; and parallel passages are found in the
Midrash on Lamentations.   The writer, indeed, emphatically declares for the creation of the earthly
before the heavenly sanctuary: " Dost thou think
that this is the city of which I said ' by the palms of
my hands have I graven thee '?   It is not this building which is now built in your midst.   It is that which

will be revealed with all that was prepared beforehand, from the time when I took counsel to make Paradise, and showed it to Adam himself before he sinned." But the notion of an ideal creation preceding the material world, if indeed it did not spring from native Hebraic fancy, was known early to Palestinian theology.

The Testaments of the Twelve Patriarchs [35] was probably in origin a Hebrew product. But we have it only in its Greek version, filled with Christological interpolations. Greek influence shows itself in the feature that each patriarch typifies a particular virtue. Joseph stands for moderation; Naphtali for natural goodness; Gad for hatred. The habit of associating a biblical character with a special attribute is distinctively, if not exclusively, Hellenistic; and the influence of Greek models is shown in the form of the addresses of each patriarch, which are exhortations after the style of the moral tract known as the " diatribe."

Another Hellenistic composition which has been handed down full of Christological interpolations, but probably was Jewish in its original form, is the book of the Odes of Solomon. The Odes have not as marked a national character as the Psalms of Solomon, which are undoubtedly the work of a

Palestinian Jew; but on the strength of references to the temple at Jerusalem, scholars tend to the opinion that they were written before the destruction of the sanctuary.[36] The writer has carried to a further point than any contemporary Jew the tendency to symbolism and the use of Hellenistic imagery. His odes resemble the Græco-Egyptian hymns such as we find in the Hermetic literature, and parallels with many of his specific images may be found in Philo.

Philonic doctrine is recalled in another book of revelation, the Assumption of Moses, which is preserved only in a Latin version. As Philo identifies Moses with the divine Logos, so in the Assumption Moses declares of himself: " From the beginning of the world I have been stored up with God to be the mediator of His Law." Notions of mediating powers and their incarnation in human form were subsequently to play a large part in Christianity. The raw material of Christian theology, indeed, is to be found in either the apocalyptic literature of Palestine or the allegorical exegesis of Alexandria, which were fused together in the second century.

The most attractive and the most sublime creation of the whole apocalyptic class is the Book of

Ezra, generally designated as the Fourth." It was written in Hebrew, though now surviving only in versions, and it is true almost throughout to the Pharisaic standpoint of Judaism. Composed shortly after the destruction of the temple by Titus, it offers an admirable contrast to the outlook of the prophets of the Restoration, and indicates the new elements which Judaism had absorbed into its creed from its contact with the world since the Babylonian captivity. The soul of the prophet, after much struggle and questioning, receives through a series of celestial visions assurance of God's grace and justice, and of the coming of the blessed age of the Messiah. The messages are conveyed sometimes directly by God, but for the most part by angels, in allegories and parables. The book is full of profound national sentiment. The question which Job in his agony had asked in relation to the individual righteous man, Ezra, after the fall of the second temple, asks in relation to the righteous nation: Why has God afflicted His chosen people? "Are they of Babylon better than they of Zion? Or is there any other people that knoweth Thee beside Israel? Or what generation hath so believed Thy covenants as Jacob? And yet their reward appeareth

not, and their labour hath no fruit." [38]   The angel
Uriel makes answer: "Thy heart hath gone too
far in the world, and thinkest thou to comprehend
the way of the Most High?"   In a second vision
Ezra asks: "Why hast Thou given this one
people unto many, and upon the one root hast
Thou prepared others?   And why hast Thou scattered Thy only people among many?   If Thou
didst so much hate Thy people, yet shouldest Thou
punish them with Thine own hand."   And the
angel asks in answer: "Lovest thou that people
better than He that made them?"   He calls on
the prophet to show him "the image of a voice
.   .   .   . then I will declare to thee the thing that
thou labourest to know."   The last judgment and
the solution of all these problems shall be the work
of God Himself.

After seven days' fasting Ezra has a third vision.
Having declared the wonder of creation, and
his faith that this was performed for the sake
of God's people, he asks: "Why do not we possess an inheritance with the world?" [39]   To this the
angel answers that the people now tread a straight
and difficult road, but at the end of it good things
are laid up for them.   A Christological passage,
which is an interpolation, follows in our text, stat-

ing that the coming age will be ushered in by God's
own anointed son.[40]   Then Ezra offers up beautiful prayers for mercy, in the style of a *Selihah*;[41]
and the angel consoles him by the assurance that a
remnant shall be saved.   " For as the husbandman
soweth much seed upon the ground and planteth
many trees, and yet the thing that is sown good in
his season cometh not up . . . . even so, of them
that are sown in the world, they shall not all be
saved." [42]   This theme is repeated in the next
vision: " The earth giveth much mould, whereof
earthen vessels are made, but little dust that gold
cometh of." [43]   Very striking, too, is the simile
about the immortality of the Law of Israel, which
survives the nation.   " For though it is a custom
when the ground hath received seed or the sea a
ship . . . . that that being perished wherein it
was sown or cast into, that thing also which was
sown or cast therein doth perish . . . . Yet with
us it hath not happened so.   For we that have received the Law perish by sin, and our heart also
which received it.   Notwithstanding the Law per-
isheth not, but remaineth in its force." [44]   The consolation in the national calamity is found in the conviction of a second life, wherein the good and evil
shall receive their due reward.   The ways of the

future world are broad and safe, and yield the fruit
of immortality.[45]   Those that contemned the Law
" shall not obtain entrance into the mansions of
the Highest; but shall stray without in bitter an-
guish, sorrowing with a sevenfold sorrow."   And
those that followed God's will in this life " shall
behold with joy unspeakable the transcendent
might of Him Who hath caught them up to be with
Himself, where their joy shall be sevenfold increased." [46]

The search for secret wisdom did not serve to
weaken in the writer the love of his people and the
veneration for the Law.   In the following chap-
ters he turns away from the national tragedy, and
bursts into prophecies about the Last Judgment;
and in the seventh and last vision, where he describes the revelation of the Sacred Writings to
himself, he throws a flood of light upon the motive
and the origin of the apocryphal and apocalyptic
literature.   Ezra is chosen by God to make known
to His people the whole of the divine wisdom, of
which part was given to Moses that he should reveal and part that he should keep secret.   Together with the acceptance of an oral law, which
supplemented the written law and was afterwards
embodied in Mishnah and Talmud, the people held

a belief in a secret doctrine of God and His works
which supplemented the Torah and the Prophets.
Ezra, who, according to tradition, was the first to
write down the Bible, is appointed also to write the
whole of the secret lore; but he is to publish only
a part, and part he is to show secretly to the wise.
With the aid of five chosen men he writes ninety-
four books," and is ordered to publish the first
twenty-four books (*i. e.,* the Bible) " that the worthy and unworthy may read it "; but to keep the
seventy last " that thou mayest deliver them on
to such as be wise among the people . . . . For
in them is the spring of understanding, the fountain
of wisdom, and the stream of knowledge." Philo,
in the same spirit, constantly speaks of his allegories of the Law as divulged only to the wise and
those initiated by piety and study into the inner
mysteries. Revelations in Palestine and theosophy
in Alexandria were in theory reserved for the
chosen few; but in fact they were vulgarized by
being committed to writing.

Apart from the apocalyptic literature and a number of the Sibylline Oracles, Palestinian Jewry produced during the Hellenistic period several works
which manifest more distinctly the influence of
Greek thought and Greek models. The one

Palestinian Hellenist of lasting repute was Josephus, the historian and apologist. But he was not the sole writer of Jewish history in Greek who sprang from Palestine. Nicholas of Damascus, in the generation before him, was the chronicler laureate of Herod and one of the chief sources which Josephus used for his work. It is well-nigh certain, however, that Nicholas was not a Jew, but one of the Greeklings whom Herod liked to gather around him. But Josephus had a hated rival in Justus of Tiberias, who, having opposed him as soldier, afterwards as historian competed for the favor of the Græco-Roman world. Justus wrote an account of the Roman wars and a chronicle of the Jewish people from the time of Moses to the death of Herod. We can form no independent judgment of its value, since not even fragments have been preserved. Photius, the bibliographer of the ninth century, praises its conciseness of style. Josephus, not an impartial critic, attacks its perversion of the truth. It speaks somewhat at least for its usefulness that it survived by the side of the *Antiquities* and the *Wars,* which were so much favored of the Church, till the time of Photius.

Josephus himself has gained renown less from his intrinsic excellence as a writer, or his reliability as a historian, than from the fact that he was the sole authority for a period of Jewish history in which the Christian Church was especially interested. He is a striking example of a conscious and artificial Hellenist who acquired a foreign culture with the fixed purpose of "Hellenizing his compatriots" and of spreading a truer knowledge and a more favorable idea of his countrymen among their conquerors. Reared with a Jewish education, and never master of Greek speech, he set himself in middle life to represent Jewish history and Jewish life "sub specie Græcitatis." He lived in Alexandria for some time after his surrender to the Romans,[48] and while resident there was brought in touch with Hellenistic-Jewish literature. But he did not gain more than a varnish of Greek culture; Greek philosophy seems to have remained a sealed book to him, and his works show little knowledge of the profounder Jewish Hellenism. Apologetics are the limit of his constructive powers. At the end of the *Antiquities* he proclaims his intention to write three books concerning Jewish opinions "about God and His essence, and about our laws; why according to them certain things are permitted, while others are prohibited"; but he did not carry

242

THE HELLENISTIC-JEWISH LITERATURE

out his intention, and probably we are not much
the poorer.

There is little that is original in the apologetics
of the *Antiquities,* which are a Hellenized version
of the Bible and post-biblical history. The most
remarkable of his writings from this point of
view are the two books commonly entitled
" Against Apion," but known to some of the
Church fathers as " To the Hellenes." In one of
these he establishes the antiquity of the Jewish
people; in the other he refutes with force and
knowledge the calumnies of Apion the anti-Jewish
writer of Alexandria, and expounds the profound
religious foundation, the broad humanity, and lofty
morals of the Jewish legislation. He explains in
an illuminating passage the superiority of the Mosaic law over other systems." The Greek philosophers, he says, only disclosed their lofty ideas to a
few, " but our legislator who made conduct agree
with the laws, not only prevailed upon the people
of his own time to accept his ideas, but imprinted
the faith in God so firmly on all their posterity that
it never could be removed. The reason why this
legislation was better directed to the common weal
than any other was, that Moses did not make religion a part of virtue, but ordained other virtues

to be part of religion. I mean, justice, fortitude, temperance, and a general concord of the members of the community with one another. For all our actions and studies and words have a reference to piety towards God. He has left nothing indefinite or undetermined. There are two ways of arriving at any sort of doctrine and a moral conduct of life: the one is by instruction in words, the other by practical exercise. Now other lawgivers have separated these ways in their systems: choosing one, they neglected the other. But our legislator skilfully combined the two methods of discipline, neither leaving the practical exercises to go on without theory, nor the hearing of the law without exercise; but from the earliest infancy and from the ordering of the daily diet, he left nothing of the smallest consequence to be done at the pleasure and whim of the individual." Josephus gives here a clear exposition of the fundamental feature of Judaism as a religion of daily conduct as well as ethical teaching, which seeks to sanctify the common actions of life. And no other Jewish apologist of antiquity put it so well. For the most part, however, his writings leave the impression rather of an industrious and learned literary worker than of an original personality like Ben Sira or Philo, or the author of the Fourth Ezra or the Wisdom of Solomon. He may be taken, in fact, as the type of the assimilating Jew who has lost the Jewish intensity without gaining the deeper spirit of Hellenism. Doubtless there were many of his kind, if not of equally remarkable talents, and like the assimilating Jews of other epochs, who have not seldom sought fame in writing the history of their people or rebutting the attacks of anti-Semites, he is in no way representative of Jewish thought. He dropped out of the knowledge of the community till the Middle Ages, and his influence was mainly external. The Alexandrian Hellenists were expressing their own culture, which, if confused, was sincerely and passionately felt. Josephus, on the other hand, merely imitated the ideas of a foreign culture, and wrote to please in a medium which was so strange to him that he had to get friends to assist him in making his composition correct.[50]

After the loss of the national independence and the consequent intensification of Jewish life in Palestine, a Palestinian Jewish Hellenist becomes almost inconceivable; and literary monuments in Greek cease from the country which still remains the centre of Jewish culture and Jewish learning. More remarkably, however, we have few subsequent records of Hellenistic Judaism, hitherto so prolific in literary work. For about one hundred years the Jews in different parts of the diaspora were engaged in a desperate struggle for life against heresies within and enemies without. They required all their energy for that struggle; the polemic that was called for was of a sterner sort than an Artapanus or a Josephus had provided. Apologetics at such a crisis would have been ridiculous : the times did not invite to philosophy and poetry. The cultured Jew often figures in the Christian dialogues, and controversies between Jews and Christians must have been frequent in the Hellenistic world, but no literary record of them from the Jewish point of view has survived. Probably the monks took care of that. As the Hellenistic-Jewish literature began with the Septuagint version, so it virtually ceased with two translations of the Scriptures. The first Greek version came to be regarded as the holy text by the Christian sect and the other heresies which sprang up in the second century. For this reason alone it would have been suspect to the Rabbis; but it was, moreover, not a faithful reproduction of the Hebrew. More particularly in the version of the later books, the translators had allowed themselves a wide license both of addition

and modification. Their work was rather " Targum " than exact translation of the Hebrew, em-
bracing much of the floating Haggadah which
gathered around the Bible characters. When the
mischief caused by the Hellenistic movement became apparent, the Rabbis traced its origin to the
Septuagint translation; and since it was requisite
still to have a Greek version of the Bible for the
large numbers of Greek-speaking Jews—there were
some in Palestine itself—they had the work done
afresh under their guidance.

The Revised Version was made by Aquila, a
proselyte from Pontus and a pupil of Rabbi Akiba,
who together with Rabbi Eleazar and Rabbi
Joshua supervised its preparation.[51] So pleased
were the sages with the work, that they applied to it
the verse: " Thou art fairer than the children
of men; grace is poured upon thy lips ";[52] but a
more impartial literary judgment has stated of
its language that " it is such awkward Greek
that it is almost good Hebrew." [53] Aquila's object
was not to provide a translation which should find
favor with the Greeks, but to give an accurate rendering from one language into the other, word for
word, which was accommodated to the halakic
tradition. So strict was his standard that, regard-

247

less of Greek syntax, he inserted the word συν
(*with*) where the Hebrew particle את occurred in
the text. Here he was very clearly following the
Rabbis, who, emphasizing the importance of every
letter in the Hebrew text, in the first verse of
Genesis laid particular stress on the particle as the
refutation of heretical teaching.[54] The other translator of Scripture, Theodotion, who, according to
the Church fathers, was a Jew of Ephesus, pursued the same aim. But he was not so concerned to
differ from the Septuagint. He left, however,
many Hebrew words untranslated. His version
had little influence on the Jewish people; and so
far as a Greek Bible was required, Aquila, who had
rendered only the books of the Hebrew Canon, took
the place of the Septuagint among the loyal body
of Jews.[55] His translation is frequently referred
to in the Talmud in a favorable manner.[56] It is due
to the abiding influence of his work that the Amoraim down to the third century expound not a few
biblical passages by the Greek equivalent of the
Hebrew word.

The two translators of the Hebrew Bible in the
second century came from the Asiatic diaspora.
Whether the Rabbis distrusted the Jewish culture
of Alexandria, or whether Hebrew there was so

utterly neglected that nobody was able to make a new version, it seems that from the second century the Alexandrian hegemony over Hellenistic-Jewish thought passed away. The catechetical school at the Egyptian capital was the nursery of Christian theology; but the Jewish school of philosophy comes to an end. Professor Krauss has unearthed from the buried ruins of neo-Platonic philosophy a Jewish neo-Platonist, Domninus, who hailed from Egypt in the fourth century; [57] and possibly one Atticus, another minor philosopher of the same period, who wrote to show that the doctrines of Plato agreed, and the doctrines of Aristotle disagreed, with the teachings of Moses, was also an Alexandrian Jew. [58] But these single instances only serve to show the general literary barrenness of Alexandrian Judaism after the fall of the nation. The product of Hellenistic culture on Hebraic soil during the second and third and fourth centuries must be looked for in the New Testament, the patristic philosophy, and the gnostic outpourings. The Epistles, the Homilies, the Cosmogonies and the Pleroma were the aftermath of the Septuagint, the apocalypses, the Wisdom of Solomon, and Philo.

CHAPTER VI

THE RABBIS AND HELLENISM

It is a bitter irony of history that the Jewish hero
who fought to deliver his people from the Seleucid
yoke was the first to bring them into relation with a
power which in the end placed a heavier yoke upon
them.   Rome was a dangerous friend, for she had
a way of making alliance a prelude to conquest.
She was, too, a harsh conqueror, intolerant of national life in her subjects, and an adept at breaking
down the spirit of a people.   The maxim that her
greatest poet gave her was: " To spare the conquered and war down the proud "; it was her imperial policy throughout to crush any spirit of independence.   The Jews who were first her allies were
soon to feel her iron heel.   In 63 B. C. E., Pompeius, called into Judea through the civil strife of
two claimants for the throne, outraged their feelings upon entering Jerusalem by forcing his way
into the Holy of Holies.   From that time forward
they maintained a passive resistance, which burst
out at intervals into open conflict, until the final
hundred years' struggle for national independence

began. The Roman statecraft at the outset sought to break up the cohesion of the Jewish nation by supporting the Hellenized Syrians against them. Pompeius restored the Greek cities of Philistia and the Decapolis; and Herod, the perfect Romanizer, found favor with his patrons by encouraging Greek culture and introducing Greek fashions into his kingdom. Julius Cæsar, indeed, who had a larger vision than the typical Roman ruler, was not only tolerant, but actually careful, of Jewish individuality. He saw to it that the Jewish communities throughout the empire enjoyed their full privileges and their separateness; but the harsher antinational imperialism reasserted itself among his successors. From the beginning of the common era the Palestinian Jews were faced with a new struggle, fiercer than any they had yet encountered. They had to fight at once against the external forces of Rome and against internal enemies; at once for national existence, and for the preservation of their religion and their culture. Rome did not come like Hellas with the bait of a brilliant civilization, but with an administrative tyranny which she tried to force on her subject peoples. And Judea was the single country within her far-flung empire which so stubbornly resisted her " peace."

251

It is in the light of this renewed struggle for existence that we must regard the rabbinic attitude towards Hellenistic culture in the civil era. We have not any full record of the opinions of the Palestinian schools before the first century; and by that time the Jews were already putting on their armor, so to say, against the intellectual aggression as well as the military force of Hellenized Rome. They were suspicious of anything which seemed to facilitate disintegration. Yet indications are not wanting that at an earlier period the Rabbis looked with favor on the Hellenistic development of Judaism. They applied the verse in Genesis, " God enlarge Japhet, and He shall dwell in the tents of Shem," [1] to the translation of the Scriptures into Greek; and in the same spirit it was said that the Torah cannot be adequately translated except into Greek. [2] The Gemara relates that an Aramaic Targum was made from the Greek, and it is with reference to Aramaic rather than Greek versions that some of the Tannaim expressed their disapproval. [3] Some have even thought that the Targum Onkelos—the Aramaic paraphrase of the Bible—was so-called because based on the Greek translation of Aquila. The scrolls of the law [4] and the bill of divorce [5]

might be written in Greek. So, too, with the
lituigy, the Rabbis allowed the Shema', the grace
after meals, and the Eighteen Blessings to be
recited in Greek, and indeed in any language.
According to Rabbi Simon ben Gamaliel, the Scriptures may be written in Greek only (besides
Hebrew).⁶

The only early attack upon Greek is the curse
which, it is related, was uttered against the teaching
of " Greek Wisdom " during the civil war between
the Maccabean princes, which led to Pompeius' invasion of Palestine.⁷ The Rabbis were seldom
particular about chronology, and as the same story
is told of a period two hundred years later, there
is probably an anachronistic reference, designed to
point the lesson that the Hellenistic leanings of a
section of the people led to the national catastrophe. If the prohibition were made at the time
stated, it would have been a " war-emergency "
measure, directed to the special need of the moment. The record of the life and thought of the
oldest Tannaim, or masters of the tradition, bears
witness to the early tolerance of Pharisaic Judaism to the Greek language. Sparse as is our knowledge of these sages, it indicates that they were in
regular communication with the Jews of the dias-

pora. At the beginning of the first century before
the common era, whence we date the oldest parts
of Mishnah and Midrash, the heads of the Sanhedrin were Simon ben Shetah and Judah ben
Tabbai. The former, during the persecution of the
Pharisees by Alexander Jannæus, fled for refuge
to Alexandria, where he answered a number of
problems which were put to him by the community.
Simeon and Judah were succeeded in the headship
of the schools by Shemaiah and Abtalion, both,
according to tradition, proselytes,⁸ and therefore in
all probability in touch with Greek thought. We
may infer their teachings from the records of their
most famous successors, Hillel and Shammai.⁹ If
any man can be said to represent that which is best
in rabbinical and Pharisaic tradition, it is Hillel. It
is therefore the more striking that he is excelled by
no teacher of his age, or perhaps of any age, in his
recognition of the universal value of Jewish law
and its ethical aspects. His maxims are sufficient
answer to those commentators who assert that the
preaching of a universal Judaism was the special
characteristic of Hellenistic Jewry, and due to
Hellenistic influence, and that the benighted Pharisees of Palestine merely added precept to precept.

The sayings which have been preserved in
the name of Hillel suggest that he was directly
or indirectly acquainted with Greek doctrines. It
is related of him that he paid special care to the
health of the body, saying that the body was the
image of the divine.[10] The maxim represents the
standpoint of Greek ethics, though it has biblical
support in the text that " God created man in His
own image." Noteworthy, also, are the questions
of religious philosophy which were disputed between him and Shammai. So long did they argue
whether heaven was created before the earth, that
the Shekinah came down and inspired them to accept the belief in a simultaneous creation of heaven
and earth.[11] The Talmud relates elsewhere that
Alexander the Great asked the same question of the
wise men of the South;[12] and in Plato's Timæus—
the Gospel of the neo-Platonists and the Gnostics—
it is written: " The earth is the oldest of all deities which have been created within the heaven." [13]
Beneath the surface of the dispute lay the question
whether an ideal creation preceded the physical,
which is one of the central doctrines of the philosophy of Philo. This was the point upon which
Hillel and Shammai must have been at variance;
and while Hillel said earth was created before all

(*i. e.,* there was no intermediate step between God's will and the bringing into existence of the world), Shammai maintained that heaven was created first (*i. e.,* an ideal plan preceded). A similar difference of opinion between Hillel and Shammai is expressed in relation to another controversy upon the period of day at which God accomplished the creation. According to Shammai, the plan of creation was made by night and the creation itself took place by day; Hillel, on the other hand, said that both took place together in the day.

It is further related that for three years the two schools discussed " whether it is better for a man to be born, or not to be born." " Again the subject of their dispute was the subject of a famous Greek controversy. One of the oldest Hellenic poets had declared: " Best of all is it not to be born." The question, it may be, arises among all peoples in their reflective stage, and it is raised in the apocryphal book of Esdras; but these broad philosophical problems were, not less than questions of religious law, matters of the deepest interest to the Pharisaic school at the beginning of the Christian era. Lastly, a rival piece of allegorical exegesis, ascribed to Hillel and Shammai, shows that they were in the habit of deriving symbolical lessons even from the ritual-

istic points of the Torah. Shammai traced an allegorical value in the two lambs of the daily sacrifice: that they pressed down the sins of Israel, the
word for lamb being identical with the root for
to press. Hillel, however, objecting that what is
pressed down rises up, and reading כבס for כבש,
derived from the word the value that the sacrifices
washed clean the sins of Israel.[15]

The extant Midrash, which may be regarded as
a condensed edition of the oral tradition, preserves numerous speculations about an ideal creation. Instead then of a rigid separation between
Alexandrian and Palestinian Jewry, or between the
philosophical and the legalistic exegesis, which is
postulated by some critics anxious to decry the
Pharisaic narrowness and to exalt Hellenistic universalism, the fact seems to be that a regular communication of thought existed between the two
branches of Jewry, and that speculation about cosmology and the ultimate nature of things was a
favorite study among the Pharisees as well as
among the Hellenists, albeit more thoroughly
Judaized by the former body.

The philosophical doctrines of the Palestinian
school were embodied particularly under two
heads: the *Ma'aseh Bereshit* and the *Ma'aseh Mer-*

kabah; the first representing ideas about the creation or cosmology, the second ideas about the
heavenly kingdom and theology and angelology.
A modern writer [16] has endeavored to trace in
them, respectively, " a doctrine of ideas " and
" a doctrine of emanations." We have not the
material from which to derive such a theory, and
it is hardly consonant with the general nature of the
Jewish Haggadah to attribute definite philosophical divisions to the Palestinian Tannaim.
The Jewish mind was essentially imaginative and
intuitive and averse to exact metaphysics or close
reasoning; the fragments of philosophical thought
from the early Midrash contain not a few indications of the influence of Hellenistic speculation,
which, however, is converted from metaphysical
doctrine into poetical fancy, from dogma to literature. While the imaginative ideas of the Hebrew
prophet or poet were transformed at Alexandria
under Greek influence into a theology more or less
systematic, that theology, when it passed through
the mind of the Palestinian Tanna and Amora,
was again resolved into a number of striking but
unsystematic fancies. The Jewish genius, that is,
when not moulded by foreign culture, instinctively
avoided casting its thought about God and creation

into a formal and definite doctrine, because it realized the danger of dogma for a pure religious monotheism. Theology remained a matter for individual study and pursuit, but not a part of the discipline of the school or of the national tradition.

Mystical and gnostic speculations, however, were popular among the sages. The Talmud and the Midrash record many fancies about the pre-existence of certain holy things created before the rest of the world, a conception which was probably induced by acquaintance with the idealistic philosophy of the Hellenists. According to some, six things existed before the creation, according to others, seven, *viz.:* the Torah, the name of the Messiah, Gehenna, the Garden of Eden, The Throne of Glory, the Sanctuary, and Repentance.[17] Again, the Midrash knows the doctrine of the pre-natal life of the soul,[18] that " our birth is but a sleeping and forgetting," which came perhaps through the Alexandrian Wisdom of Solomon from the Platonic and neo-Pythagorean tradition. An angel, it is said, causes the soul to forget before birth the whole Torah in which it had been educated. So, too, the Book of Enoch[19] says that every soul was created before the foundation of the world. Again, the Talmud contains references to the doctrine of the creation of an upper and a lower world, and of a celestial and earthly Adam, which give a new coloring to the Alexandrian speculation about the kingdom of Ideas and the Primal Man. These doctrines were possibly derived from Babylon, and had thence entered the thought both of the Jewish and Hellenistic peoples. The influence of these doctrines can already be traced in an early prayer which is recorded in the Talmud: " May it be Thy will, O Lord, to make peace in the family above and the family below." [20]

Several fancies are derived from the variation in the second chapter of Genesis in the spelling of the Hebrew *Wayyizer* (" and He formed "); where the creation of man is spoken of, it is spelt with two Yods, and where the reference is to the creation of the brute, it is spelt with one. [21] The two Yods, it is said, point to the duality of human life, in this world and the next world, or to the original dual formation of man from the lower and the upper beings (*i. e.,* the angels). Here we have a parallel with Philo's teaching that the races of men are twofold: one is the heavenly man and the other the earthly man. The first man, said the Rabbis, was co-extensive with the universe: his dust was gathered from the whole world, and he stretched from the earth to the firmament."

The doctrine of creation by Wisdom also finds a place in Palestinian tradition. The Targum Yerushalmi gives as a translation, or rather as an interpretation, of the first verse of Genesis: " With wisdom God created the world," and it frequently ascribes God's action to the *Memra* or Word. The Midrash enumerates as the seven *Middot,* or attributes of God, which carry out His will and, as it were, form divine powers: Wisdom, Righteousness, Justice, Kindness, Pity, Truth, Peace; and Rab, a famous Babylonian teacher, spoke of ten *Middot* by which God achieved the creation. When Philo interprets the seven cities of refuge as the seven various stages in the knowledge of God, the upward progress of man to the complete communion with the deity through apprehension of His attributes, it would seem that he is developing to a new value a poetical tradition of his people. But the central figure of Palestinian idealism is not the Primal Man or the Wisdom, or the *Memra,* or the attributes, but the Torah itself, which is already the subject of a psalm in the book of Proverbs. Many are the fancies in which its divine nature is expressed—as many as Philo's images of the Logos. The Torah is God's counsellor and agent, His plan in the creation, His desirable instrument by which the world was created. " God looked on the Torah and then created the world." [23] Another interpretation of the first words of Genesis makes the Torah declare: " By me, the beginning (בי ראשית), God created Heaven and Earth." [24] The verse in Proverbs (8. 30), " Then I was by Him, as a master-workman (אמון) ; and I was daily all delight, playing always before Him," was applied to the Torah's part in the creation. The sages explained the word אמון variously: some held it equivalent to פדגוג, schoolmaster (Greek παιδα-γωγός); others to a workman; and others understood it as hidden away or covered. The latter interpretation may reflect Egyptian influence, for the name of the great Egyptian deity Amon meant "hidden." Like the Wisdom or the Logos in Alexandrian literature, or the Messiah in the apocalypses, the Torah is conceived as a divine power stored with God before the creation. Ben Sira [25] already has this fancy when, identifying the Law with Wisdom, he says God created her and saw her, and poured her out on all His works. The doctrines of Greek idealism were thus adapted in Palestine by the sages to glorify the divine Law.

There can be no doubt that the sages were influenced by Hellenistic literature, which is shown by the mere fact that in many of the cosmological and even legal passages of the Midrash Greek words are found in abundance; but it is incorrect to give the name of philosophy to their fancies, and the Greek thoughts, when moulded afresh in the Hebrew mind, were expressed in terms of religious poetry.

The secret teachings embodied in the *Ma'aseh Merkabah* had, as their special feature, a theosophical gnosis such as appears in a cruder form in the apocalypses and testaments, and in its finer development in the esoteric writings of Philo.[26] These ideas were part of the common thought of the time, and were especially popular at Alexandria. They reached the height of their favor in Palestine during the first century, when the trials and miseries of the nation induced men to seek hope and consolation in the inner religion and secret teachings. Rabbi Johanan ben Zaccai, who, after the destruction of the temple, held the Jewish people together at the crisis by means of his school—the famous vineyard of Yabneh—was, according to the Midrash, a devotee of such speculations. Many stories illustrate his fondness for them; and most of his disciples, who were the Tannaim of the next generation and played a great part in the organization of Jewry in exile, imbibed it from him. That he acquired the love of gnostic speculation from a knowledge of Hellenistic literature is made the more probable by another characteristic reported of his teaching. He was a master of the form of exegesis known as חמר or מין חמר, which was cultivated by a special school.[27] The word means, according to some scholars, "a string of pearls," and according to others, "the essential"; but, be this as it may, the school of interpreters were those who, like the *Dorshe Reshumot,* "the searchers of symbols," [28] looked for a deeper meaning underlying the letter of the law, and allegorized the commandments. Few of their interpretations have been preserved, but it is striking that those we have correspond with suggestions which occur in Philo.[29] Thus the command "And his master shall bore his ear, " [30] referring to the treatment of the slave who would not accept his proffered freedom in the year of release, was interpreted by R. Johanan according to the method of *Homer* as follows: [31] "Why has the ear been distinguished from all other organs of the body to be bored? The Holy One said: The ear that heard my voice on Sinai crying:

For unto Me the children of Israel are servants—[32] and not servants to other servants—shall be bored through, when this man takes a master for himself." The true significance of the law, which tallies with Philo's interpretation, is to impress on the slave the lesson of freedom.[33] The talmudic passage goes on to say that Rabbi Simon the son of Rabbi Judah the Prince interpreted the following words: "His master shall bring him to the doorpost," in similar fashion. The door and the doorpost were chosen because they were the witnesses of the divine redemption of Israel in Egypt, when God passed over the lintel and the two side-posts.

The Tosefta [34] quotes five other sayings of Rabbi Johanan ben Zaccai in the same method, of which the most striking is the homily on the law: "An altar of stones shalt thou build; thou shalt lift up no iron tool upon them." [35] The law forbids the use of iron because the sword is made of iron, and the sword is the symbol of punishment and revenge, while the altar is a symbol of forgiveness and reconciliation. Stones cannot hear, nor see, nor speak; yet because they bring about conciliation between the people of Israel and their Father in Heaven, the law forbids us to lift an iron tool upon them. These passages bespeak the preacher's homily;

and the allegorizers of Palestine equally with the allegorizers of Alexandria may have developed their ideas in sermons for the synagogue. The correspondence with the Hellenistic school is striking not only in their method, but in their detailed interpretation of the few biblical verses of which the Midrash has preserved the record. The *Dorshe Reshumot* looked for symbols in the narrative but not in the legal parts of the Torah; but the *Dorshe Hamurot,* following the Alexandrian habit, applied allegory equally to the Law.

At the crisis of the struggle, in the second century, between Judaism and the Hellenistic syncretism, the leaders of the Palestinian schools detected the danger of this allegorical development, as well as of other importations from Hellenized Judaism. The Mishnah prohibits the moralizing method in reference to the command against taking the mother with its young from a nest.[36] By laying stress on the moral idea which the law was alleged to symbolize, as against the positive prescript, the allegorizer tended to whittle away the observance, or to provide an excuse for its neglect.

The New Testament proves that the method could be, and was in fact, applied, on the one hand, to abolish the fundamental practices of Jewish life, circumcision, the Sabbath, the dietary laws, and, on the other, to undermine the binding force of the Torah altogether. Several passages in the Pauline Epistles mark this extreme but logical development of the antinomian tendency. Thus Paul, allegorizing the story of Abraham and Hagar, says: " For it is written that Abraham had two sons, the one by a bondmaid, the other by a free-woman. But he who was of the bondwoman was born after the flesh, but he of the free-woman was by promise. Which things are an allegory; for there are the two covenants, the one from the mount Sinai which gendereth to bondage which is Hagar. For this Hagar is mount Sinai in Arabia, and answereth to Jerusalem which now is, and is in bondage with her children. But Jerusalem which is above is free, which is the mother of us all." [37] In the same spirit again he declared: " For he is not a Jew that is one outwardly, neither is that circumcision which is outward in the flesh. But he is a Jew which is one inwardly; and circumcision is of the heart, in the spirit and not in the letter, whose praise is not of men but of God." [38] The observance of the law was not so much an inferior way for the extreme antinomian as a stumbling-block in the right way. " For as many as are of the works of the Law are under the curse "; and again: " Christ hath redeemed us from the curse of the Law." [39] It remained only for Barnabas and Marcion, the Gnostics, to take the further step, and deduce from allegorical interpretation that the Jewish God was the power of evil against which Christ, the good power, had to struggle, and that the observance of the Law is the seduction of the devil; [40] or that the Jewish worship, exacted by the ceremonial Law, exhibited the peculiar depravity and iniquity of the people. [41] The rejection of the Law naturally appealed to the Greeks to whom the Christians preached, and within a century became the basis of a cleavage in the Christian sect, so that Clement could write: " If the Gentile carries out the Law, he is a Jew; if he neglects it, he is a Greek (Christian)." [42]

A radical discrepancy existed between the allegorizing habit, when applied to the Torah, and the spirit of Judaism. For Judaism essentially holds its members together by law and observance. It allows freedom of speculation in the region of ideas and large freedom of doctrine; its firm anchorage is in a fixed way of life, and to that anchorage it must hold if it is not to be shattered. Warned by the spread of heresies in the second

century, the Rabbis detected in the outlook of
the allegorical interpreters a destructive and disintegrating force. Blasphemous interpretations [43]
called into question the sacredness of Scripture.
Just as in art symbolism is a good servant but a
bad master, so in religion: for, in either case,
the symbolical habit tends to run to excess and
sweep away sane thought. The Palestinian Rabbis therefore cut out of the tradition these interpretations of the Torah. The works of the
prophets and " the Writings," such as the Song
of Songs, which were part of the traditional lore
of the nation, might be treated as allegories; but
the Torah itself, the divine revelation in a special
sense and the national way of life, must not be
made the text for humanitarian homilies and mystical reflections, lest it should be degraded to the
mere pretext for them, and cease to be a law. According to the thirty-two canons of exegesis drawn
up by R. Eliezer ben R. José of Galilee, they allowed allegorical exegesis to be applied to the
Torah in the case of three verses only, where the
literal meaning had been definitely supplanted in
practice. The menace was felt the more in Palestine, because there heresy made greater strides than
in Babylon, and the Jewish teachers were engaged

in frequent polemics with Hebrew and Gentile Christians and Gnostics, who regularly appealed to allegorical interpretations in arguing the superiority of their beliefs. Clement of Alexandria and Origen, the two founders of Church philosophy, not only summon the method in general to the support of Christian theology, but use the particular interpretations of Philo as weapons against the religion which he was endeavoring by these means to propagate among the Gentiles. An extraordinary national-religious instinct prompted the Rabbis to discard part of the heritage of even the most revered teachers of a former generation, because it threatened the centre of gravity of Judaism. Johanan ben Zaccai was dear to them, but dearer still was the preservation of Judaism in its integrity.

The speculation into the secrets of the Torah, which contained many foreign elements, was also discouraged. Johanan ben Zaccai, though he was famous as a master of mystical doctrine and spoke of it as " the great subject," uttered the warning against undue reflection upon the mysteries of the universe. When questioned on such things by his pupil R. Eliezer ben Hyrcanus, who had mystical leanings, he replied: " " What answer gave the

Bat-Kol (the heavenly voice) to that wicked one who said: ' I will ascend above the heights of the clouds; I will be like the Most High.' "? [45] And R. Eliezer in turn repeated the warning against speculation, saying: " Keep it far from thy house." Other followers of Rabbi Johanan, nevertheless, did not succeed in observing the mean he laid down. The Gnostic crisis, if we may so call the struggle between Pharisaic or Catholic Judaism and the mystical ideas professed by some of the foremost teachers, reached its turning-point about the middle of the second century. Judaism was beset by dangers within and without. The desperate attempt to recover national independence in the reign of Trajan was put down with ruthless severity; the Christian heresy was rapidly spreading among the communities of the diaspora; it was marking itself off more and more clearly from the Jewish people, and taking up a hostile attitude to the Torah and the national hope. Syrian and Persian religious cults with their fantastic theosophies were seizing hold of the Græco-Roman empire. The devotees of Gnosticism, who hitherto had indulged their ideas in esoteric circles, were openly abandoning the law, spreading their heresy, and exhibiting separatist tendencies. Lastly, some of the most

271

distinguished Rabbis of the schools were so carried away by the attraction of the secret wisdom, that they introduced strange notions into Jewish monotheism, and modified the Jewish idea of creation on the lines of Hellenistic cosmogony.

The Mishnah describes the dangerous trend of the time in the form of a characteristic allegory: " Ben Zoma, Akiba, Ben Azzai, and Elisha ben Abuyah entered Paradise together. Ben Zoma looked and became demented; to him they applied the verse: ' Hast thou found honey? eat so much as is sufficient for thee, lest thou be filled therewith, and vomit it.' [46] Ben Azzai looked and perished; to him they applied the verse: ' Precious in the sight of the Lord is the death of His saints.' [47] Ben Abuyah plucked up the plants; of him they said: ' Suffer not thy mouth to bring thy flesh into guilt.' [48] Akiba alone passed through scatheless; of him they said: [49] ' Draw me, we will run after thee.' " [50] Paradise (פרדס) is a name given by the sages to theosophical speculation and secret wisdom; and the story has reference to the mystical movement of the period. Three of the four sages who indulged in it fell a victim to its blandishments. Ben Zoma, though celebrated for his erudition in the Halakah, was devoted to cosmological speculation.

He reported to R. Joshua the result of his meditation upon the creation in these words: " I looked between the upper and the lower waters, and I saw that between both there is only three fingers' breadth." [51] From this it may be inferred, perhaps, that he held that the world was not created *ex nihilo,* but that water was the primitive element; which had been the starting-point of Greek philosophy. R. Judah ben Pazzi, in the next generation, declared likewise that the world was originally water in water: the water became snow, and the snow became earth.[52] Akiba, on the other hand, is recorded to have uttered the warning on entering Paradise not to say: " Water, water," [53] *i. e.,* not to accept the Greek theory of a primeval stuff.

R. Joshua said of Ben Zoma, in relation to his mystic speculation: " He is still ' outside.' " [54] The spoken as well as the written word which fostered gnostic leanings was external to the tradition. He was termed the last of the *Darshanim* (the preachers) ; and Ben Azzai, famous for his piety as Ben Zoma for his scholarship, was termed similarly the last of the *Shakdanim* (*i. e.,* diligent expounders). A mystical interpretation concerning the revelation, that God's voice took the form of the angel Metatron, is ascribed both to him and

273

Ben Zoma. He was also an ascetic, holding that the flesh was an impure vessel with which the divine element in man could not be associated. Possibly the statement of the Midrash that he died prematurely from his excessive devotion to mystical speculation has reference to his extreme asceticism.

The tragedy of Ben Abuyah was graver. He was the Jewish Faust, the type of the scholar lost by his eagerness for knowledge. A maxim, prophetic of his fate, is ascribed to him: " Knowledge without observance is like a horse without a bit, which throws its rider." [55] He became a definite apostate, and his name was not even uttered by the Rabbis, who referred to him as *Aher* (" the other "), to mark his exclusion from the congregation of Israel. The exact form of his heresy is not recorded, but it seems to have extended over doctrine and practice. It is related that Greek songs were continually in his mouth, and heretical books dropped from his lap in the schools; and that when he entered Paradise, he saw Metatron by the throne of God and exclaimed: " There are two divine powers." [56] Metatron is the supreme angel who occurs frequently in the talmudic and later apocalyptic literature; some explain the word as the Hebraized form of μετὰ θρόνον (*by the throne*); others as the He-

braized form of the Latin " Metator " (*divider*),
and suggest a connection with the dividing Logos
of Philo, or the Horus of Egyptian theurgy. Any-
how, under the influence of Hellenistic and Mani-
chean culture, Ben Abuyah seems to have adopted a
form of dualistic theology in place of the pure
Hebrew monotheism. Of his apostasy in regard to
Jewish practice, the Talmud relates that he rode on
the Sabbath, and plucked fruit on the Day of Atonement.[57]

It is clear from passages in the Talmud, and
is confirmed by others in the Midrash, that Akiba
himself had theosophical leanings. He declared
that a throne is set for the Messiah by God—a doctrine which is popular in the apocalytic literature—;
and José of Galilee, hearing this, cried out against
him : " How long wilt thou profane the Shekinah ! "
(*i. e.,* the Glory of God).[58] The great systema-
tizer of the law of conduct had a philosophical
mind. The saying in Pirke Abot attributed to him
deals with the metaphysical problem of the freedom of the will. " All is foreseen, yet freedom
of the will is given." [59] He regarded the Song of
Songs as a complete allegory, and the profoundest
book of Scripture;[60] and according to the Christian scholar Origen, his mystical exegesis was sub-

sequently forbidden in the schools to those who were not of mature years.[61] In virtue of his fame as a master of the mysteries of the Law, several of the earlier kabbalistic works which date from the eighth and ninth centuries, the *Sefer Yezirah* and a cosmogonical *Alphabet,* were ascribed to him.

Pre-eminence at once in secret wisdom and in halakic teaching marked a contemporary of Akiba, R. Ishmael. He it was who drew up the famous thirteen rules of halakic interpretation of Scripture; and from him are derived a large part of the halakic Midrash to Leviticus and to Deuteronomy, the Mekilta and Sifre. But at the same time he was renowned as a master of the Kabbalah. Later tradition ascribed to him the theosophical *Hekalot* ("Halls of Heaven"). R. Hai Gaon (died 1038) quotes both a greater and a smaller *Hekalot;* and the books that have been preserved deal with the ordering of the heavens and the heavenly hosts, the Messiah, the description of the throne and the celestial temple, and theories of the cosmogony. The attribution of these particular doctrines to Ishmael may be spurious, but it is suggestive that tradition pointed to the two most distinguished jurists among the Tannaim as masters of the secret lore. In the golden age of rabbinic wisdom the mystic and the legalist were combined.

Nevertheless, the outstanding greatness of Akiba was not his mystical speculation but his purification of Judaism. Tradition says that he was sprung from non-Jewish parents, but he inherited from his master Joshua ben Hananiah a profound conception of Judaism and an instinct for what was false to its teaching, which made him at the crisis of its fate the great bulwark of its integrity. Joshua ben Hananiah, who flourished in the preceding generation, appears in midrashic legend as the brilliant champion of Jewish wisdom against Hellenism; and he began that spiritual fight against Hellenistic contamination of Judaism in which Akiba was the protagonist. The latter is described paradoxically as *Scholasticos,* the Greek word for *scholar* being used in the sense of champion of the Law.⁶² The Midrash Ekah contains a collection of tales illustrating how Jewish *Hokmah* prevailed over the Greek dialectics. Elsewhere Joshua's dialogues with Hadrian about the nature of God and of his victory over the philosophers of Athens are reported.⁶³ The Jews of Alexandria put to him twelve questions which he brilliantly answered: three on practical observances, three on Haggadah, three on

Derek Erez (or worldly wisdom), and three problems.[64] These stories typify the conscious antagonism and struggle which were renewed between
Hellenism and Hebraism after the loss of national
independence.

The circumstances of Akiba's life and times were
such as to reinforce the spirit which he inherited
from his master, and to deepen the recognition of
that antagonism. He took, as is well known, a
leading part in the rising under Bar Cochba against
Hadrian, when the Jews made a desperate attempt
to recover their independence; and he was one of
the martyrs in the campaign of slaughter which
followed it. The agony of Israel in this conflict
may be gathered not only from the Talmud and
the Midrash Ekah (which are full of harrowing
tales of the war), but from the reports of the
Church chronicler Eusebius, and the pagan historian Dio Cassius.[65] At first the Jews prevailed
over the Greeks, both in the diaspora and in Palestine, and, if the accounts are true, killed tens of
thousands of their foes. But the whole strength
of the Roman empire was brought against them.
Severus was summoned from Britain, and after
three years of heroic resistance the revolt collapsed.
Hundreds of thousands of Jews were massacred

in Cyrene, Egypt, Palestine, and Mesopotamia:
600,000 are said to have perished at Palestine
alone; some provinces lost the whole of their Jewish population, and the attempt was made to ex-
terminate a people who could not be subjugated.

The plague within was as terrible as the sword
without. The decay of national life, the atrophy
of human reason, and the incursion into the Græco-
Roman world of " Orientalism " produced such a
welter of superstitions and heresies as has never
been before or since. All creeds were in the melting-pot; the one national-religious system that survived was endangered for a time by the centrifugal
tendency. Israel did not go into exile, it was said,
till twenty-four orders of heretics were formed.[6]
The Judeo-Christians scoffed in the synagogue,
Gnostics sought to warn the people against the observance of the Law, syncretistic creeds with their
troops of angels and mediating powers offered to
a world that was fast losing its reason and its hope
a seductive consolation in misery. The peril was,
in truth, graver than that which threatened Judaism three centuries before in the time of the Maccabees. Against compulsion to idolatry it was easy
to rally the forces of the Jewish nation, but the
sages of the second century had to fight with spirit-

ual weapons against the invitation to a universal spiritualism which was leading some of the best minds away from the Jewish teaching of God.

Akiba was the leader of the Puritan movement. Paul had travelled through the diaspora to carry his mission to the Gentiles, and Akiba travelled through the scattered communities of Israel to strengthen them in their loyalty to the Law. He was at Rome, in Mesopotamia, in Egypt, and Arabia. It was necessary, in the first place, to get rid of the peril of Gnosticism, and the basis of his teaching was "Back to the Torah," the pure source from which Judaism had sprung. An apologue told of him is characteristic.[67] When the Jews were prohibited by the Roman emperor from studying their Law. Akiba refused to abandon his studies. In reply to Pappos ben Judah, who warned him of the danger, Akiba told him the fable of the fishes who, being perturbed in the water, were invited by a fox to come to land. The Torah was Israel's element,[68] and if they left it because of outer disturbance, they would stand in peril of their salvation. Similarly, when asked by his nephew whether, having learnt all the Torah, he might now study the Greek wisdom, R. Ishmael quoted to him the verse: "And thou shalt meditate therein

280

day and night." * " If," he added, " thou canst
find an hour which is neither day nor night, then
thou mayest study Greek." [70]

For a time, indeed, Greek books and Hebrew
books written under Greek influence, were altogether eschewed. The literature which the Jews
had composed in the Hellenistic period was none
of it holy, and much of it in the eyes of the sages
dangerous in tendency, in that it opened the way
for foreign non-Jewish influences to affect the Jewish belief and the Jewish way of life, and was
freely used by the heretics for their purposes. The
extreme consequences of Hellenistic allegory and
mystical speculation had been drawn, and were
proved to amount to the repudiation of Judaism.
Hence, to preserve their heritage, the Rabbis determined to cut out the impurity root and branch.
The external books, that is, the books not admitted
by the Synagague to be holy or to be included in
the Canon, were prohibited in the schools. The
sage might read them for himself, but they were
not for the study of the scholars. It was said, in
the hyperbolical fashion of the Mishnah, that those
who read external books are excluded from the
future life. [71] And again: " He who brings to his
house any other than the twenty-four books of the

Bible, such as the book of Ben Sira or Ben La'anah, brings confusion into it."[72] Speculation has been unable to settle what is meant by the book of Ben La'anah, or by the books of Ben Togla and Homeros, which are elsewhere classed in the same category of forbidden literature. Homeros may be a general term for Greek poetry; but it has been suggested that it is a transliteration of the Greek Himeros, and refers to Greek books of light literature.[73] Elsewhere the books of the Sadducees are placed together with Ben Sira among those which may not be read.[74]

Though the books now included in the Protestant Apocrypha never formed part of the Hebrew Canon, the wisdom of Ben Sira was often quoted by the early sages.[75] Some desired to withdraw from public reading (גנז) other books which were commonly recognized as holy. Thus it is said that the scribes intended to withdraw from public use Ecclesiastes and Proverbs and the Song of Songs,[76] until the Great Synagogue arose and interpreted them;[77] and that Hananiah ben Hezekiah prevented Ezekiel from being withdrawn.[78] These suspected books were to form a class reserved for the study of scholars; and the name Apocrypha (i. e., things hidden away) is perhaps derived from the *Sefarim Genuzim* of the Jewish sages. The rabbinical term, however, is applied to works which, with one exception, were included in the Canon.[79] The twenty-four books which were finally admitted as holy are the books of the Hebrew Bible as we have it now, and are commonly called the Hebrew Canon. They correspond to the twenty-four writings which pseudo-Ezra is told to reveal to all the people, and to the twenty-two books which Josephus—either joining Ruth and Judges, and Jeremiah and Lamentations, or dividing the historical books differently—declares to comprise the Hebrew Scriptures.[80]

The Jewish people recognized no definite list of holy writings before the second century. In the Hellenistic age the Alexandrian Bible mixed up indiscriminately with the books of the Hebrew Canon writings now regarded as apocryphal, the Maccabees and the Wisdom of Solomon; and on the other hand, discussion still raged in the Palestinian schools as to the final admission of certain books. There was a fresh trial and judgment at the crisis of the struggle with Gnosticism. The Books of Ecclesiastes and the Song of Songs were those longest in suspense, perhaps because they were suspected of having their origin in the Hellenistic period, but in the main because of their peculiar doctrines.[81] Of the apocalyptic literature Daniel alone was included in the Canon, and that, because the first part of the book was regarded as historical. The other books of the kind, even those composed in Hebrew, the Testaments of the Patriarchs, the Assumptions of the Prophets, the Enoch writings, were rejected, and dropped out of the tradition, but did not altogether disappear from private study. Their infusion of gnostic ideas and their somewhat crude eschatology compromised pure monotheism; and the fact that they were regarded with special favor by the various Minim or sectarians, especially by the Christians, and were interpolated by them in their polemics, caused the Rabbis to look on them with suspicion. They became a source of false doctrine, and their new service emphasized their dangerous tendency.

A section of the Mishnah of Hagigah indicates the collective rabbinical attitude toward cosmological and theological speculation. " It is forbidden," runs the law, " to study the mystery of creation, except alone, and the mystery of the Merkabah, not even alone, unless the individual is able himself to form a judgment. He who busies

284

himself with four things, what is above and what below (the earth), what before and what after (life), better were it for him that he had not been born; and better were it that he who has no thought for the glory of his Maker had not been born." [82] The doctrines of the Pleroma and Hell, of the pre-natal state and the last judgment, were the peculiar interests of gnostic wisdom, and the passage is really a warning against the gnostic leanings in the schools. The Jewish position was that the limits of human knowledge were fixed; and it was dangerous for the ordinary scholar to try to transcend them.

Judged from this standpoint, the apocalypses were antagonistic to true humility. During the first century of the Christian era the power of reason universally decayed, so that philosophy meant not rational but mystical speculation. Yet man will always want to peep through the partition between the two worlds, and, despite the rule of the Mishnah, Jewish sages continued to enquire what is above and below, before and after. Bar Kappara, a contemporary of R. Judah, the compiler of the Mishnah, is said to have expounded the *Ma'aseh Bereshit;* and the secret doctrine remained popular in the schools both of Babylon and Palestine. [83] The

writers of apocalypses, however, were concerned
overmuch with such things, and, therefore, their
influence upon the people tended to heresy. It was
said in the name of R. Eleazar, that after the fall
of the temple, the standard of thought of the whole
nation was lowered: " The sages became as
scribes, the scribes as attendants in the synagogue
(Hazzanim) ; the Hazzanim as students, and the
students as the 'Am ha-Arez, and the 'Am ha-Arez
became feeble, no one questioning, and no one investigating. Our help is in God in heaven." [84]
Hence the common people were the more easily
attracted by the apocalyptic appeals, and swelled
the ranks of the heretics. According to the Christian Jerome, the Ebionites—the Christian sect of
Jewish origin which held that the Mosaic law was
binding on them—were so called because they were
poor in understanding (אביונים). Another early
Christian writer, Tatian, claimed that learning was
a bar to true faith.

The resolution to purify Judaism of foreign admixture and to preserve it from the heretical fever,
which sprang from foreign influences and from the
confused theosophy of the time, prompted the
prohibition against teaching Greek culture. The
study of the Greek language also was prohibited,[85]

but only during the crisis of the struggle against the Græco-Roman armies. It was a measure ordained during the war of Quietus (in the time of Trajan) to prevent informing. At that period the Gentiles aimed at nothing less than the extirpation of the Jewish people, and the Jews were compelled to the most desperate measures to preserve a remnant. But when the pressure was reduced, knowledge of the Greek language became regular again among the Palestinian Rabbis; it is expressly recorded that even during the crisis the Rabbis allowed the school of Gamaliel II, the head of the Sanhedrin, to study Greek.[86] Gamaliel's son, Rabbi Simon, relates that in his father's house five hundred pupils were instructed in the Torah and five hundred in Greek. A half-century later R. Judah recommended that in Palestine the people should speak either Hebrew or Greek; and Aquila's Greek translation of the Bible was made under the auspices of the great Tannaim.[87] Greek as a language was not long under the ban, and a rabbinical saying has come down: " The language is honored the literature is rejected (לשון יונית לחוד וחכמת יונית לחוד)."[88]

During the three centuries which had elapsed since the Maccabean rising, the degradation of that

culture in the East had steadily continued, till now
it was a travesty of the civilization of Athens and
Ionia. No Hellene could have recognized in the
fantastic trinities, theosophies, and cosmogonies of
the Gnostics and neo-Platonists a development of
the philosophy of Plato and Aristotle. Baffling
mysticism displaced clear reason; moderation of
thought gave place to limitless extravagance, the
desire for scientific truth to utter distrust of the
intellect and self-abandonment. The force of
Hellenism spent itself by the second century, and
was then overpowered by the Oriental reaction.
The gulf between God and man, which Hellenic
philosophy had tried to bridge, was now widened
by the sublimation of the Godhead into an abstract
negation, and by the depreciation of this world and
the life of the flesh. Instead of relying on reason
and contemplation, man yearned for redemption
and expiation by means of angels and demons.
The Rabbis instinctively recognized a canker in this
medley. Their legal sense, moulded by a study of
the Halakah, gave them an aversion to its confusion of ideas; their religious sense made them
rise above its clouded conception of God. It was
not Pharisaic narrowness on their part, but a clear
intuition of the essence of Judaism and of the

overpowering necessity of preserving its outlook uncontaminated, which led them to set up fences against foreign incursion. They were opposed not to freedom of thought, but to free play for demoralizing influences; and if their attitude was one-sided, at the moment one-sidedness was necessary to sanity.

In this spirit of distrust of the Hellenistic movement they said figuratively that the making of the Septuagint translation—which marked the introduction of Hellenism into Jewish life—was comparable with the making of the golden calf; and they appointed a fast-day (the eighth day of Tebeth) to mark the calamity.[89] They expressed their feeling of bitterness at the contamination of the Scriptures in the saying that God would not let Moses write the oral law for fear that it should be translated and appropriated by the Gentiles, as it is said: " I have written to him the great things of My Law, but they were counted as a strange thing." [90] The Mishnah was God's mystery which He revealed only to His saints.[91] Greek culture, in the sense of philosophy and theology, was banished from the schools from the end of the second century. Exceptionally we find a teacher who must have studied it for himself and used it polemically

289

against Minim and pagans; and the knowledge of the Greek language was to continue in Palestine for more than two centuries. Yet the study of secular science, and more especially of astronomy and medicine which was derived from Greek science, continued both in Palestine and Babylon; according to the doctrine of R. Eleazar Hisma, recorded in the Ethics of the Fathers, it was to be regarded as an after-course of Wisdom," *i. e.,* to be pursued only after a complete mastery of the Torah was attained.

The exclusion of Greek thought from education corresponded with the exclusion of idolaters and heretics from Jewish society. In either case the motive was to preserve Judaism in its integrity. The rabbinical laws against association with pagans are set out in the tractate Abodah Zarah. The regulations about what things may not be sold to or bought from Gentiles seem excessive in our day, but when it is remembered that they are directed solely against pagans to prevent the introduction of idolatrous practices, the reason for the stringency is clear. As for the desirability of separating the Jews from the pagan society of the time, the description of Græco-Roman life by the pagan

290

satirists Juvenal and Persius provides ample support.

The struggle of the Jewish teachers against the Minim was more assiduous than that against the pagans. They were fighting in the one case against an open and visible foe; in the other they had to deal with heretics in their own midst. Both the meaning and the derivation of the word Min are disputed. Some have held it to be a form of מנאי, and to stand for Manichee or a follower of Oriental dualism; others say that it is connected with מאמין, and was applied to those who believed in gnostic creeds. But, whatever its original meaning, it was certainly applied in the Talmud to various orders of heretics in general, and to Judeo-Christians in particular. Some kinds of *Minut* were known before the spread of Christianity. The embryo of the later sects, as has been seen, existed in Philo's time.[93] The Cainites chose as their hero the biblical character who was bound by no law, and their doctrine seems to have been an organized religious anarchy—a teaching which finds its devotees even to-day. The Sethites, who made Seth their ideal figure, the Ophites, who regarded the serpent as the divine power, and the Hypsistanae, who recognized a supreme god ruling over a number of powers, each

professed certain peculiarities of theology and cosmogony, but were allied with the Cainites in rejecting or neglecting the Law. When they appear as
organized and distinct heresies, they are treated as
Christian-gnostic sects; but it is likely that they
derived their tenets from Jewish Gnostics who
sprang from the heretical hotbed of Alexandria.

The Minim began to be prominent in rabbinic
literature from the time of the destruction of the
temple, and the Midrash contains endless stories
of polemical controversy with them. The rise of
Christianity, coming at the same time as the shock
to the national life inflicted by the destruction of
the temple, emphasized the peril of *Minut*. The
Gentile Christians under the influence of Paul had
early adopted an extreme antinomian outlook, and
the fourth Gospel and, still more, the apocryphal
Christian writings are full of gnostic theories.
Many of the Judeo-Christians at the same time
professed to remain members of the Jewish community, and faithfully practised its observances.
The danger of the infection was thereby increased,
and to meet the crisis, the Rabbis took measures to
excommunicate the heretics. The supplication
against slanderers (ולמלשינים) directed against
Minim was added to the Eighteen Benedic-

tions.[94] Warning was given not to admit into the schools those whose inner ideas were not in harmony with their outer practice. Their scrolls and books were to be burnt, and though they contained God's names, they were not to be rescued from the fire. " Let them burn with their incantations (אזכרות)," it was said in the name of R. Tarphon and Ishmael; " heretics only sow hatred, jealousy, and dissension between God and Israel." [95]

The Christians, indeed, once the cleavage between them and the Catholic body of Judaism had asserted itself, rapidly widened the breach. They welcomed Hellenistic influence and syncretistic conceptions as much as the Rabbis discountenanced them. All those elements of Alexandrian mysticism, which had been fluid in Philo, became crystallized in the early patristic teaching, passing from literature to dogma : and the antinomianism which Philo had impugned as involving Chaos in religion was presented as a step towards salvation. As Judaism became more thoroughly Judaized, Christianity was more and more Hellenized. As the one strengthened the national-religious hold, the other expanded its cosmopolitan appeal. The contrast between the two movements is shown in the favor which the Church showed to the store of

apocryphal and apocalyptic literature, on the one
hand, and the exclusion of it from the Synagogue
and Bet ha-Midrash, on the other; in the Greek
rendering of the whole of the New Testament, on
the one side, and the abandonment of the Greek
development of Judaism, on the other; in the use
of the Septuagint by the Church, and its replace-
ment by the translation of Aquila in the Synagogue.

The dialogue between Trypho and the Jew,
which is ascribed to Justin, though probably a
spurious work, is an early record of the Christian
polemic, and illustrates the development by the
Church of the Alexandrian-Jewish theology as an
engine of attack upon monotheism. Wisdom is
presented as an independent power existing before
the creation of the world, and the writer attacks
those who do not regard it as separate from God.
The Gospel ascribed to St. John shows a similar
application of Alexandrian theology counter to
Jewish monotheism; and its opening decisively
marks the introduction of the idea of the incarnation that was to become the foundation of dogmatic
Christianity: " In the beginning was the word,
and the word was with God, and the word was God.
The same was in the beginning with God . . . .
And the word was made flesh, and dwelt among us,

and we beheld his glory, the glory as of the only
begotten of the Father, full of grace and truth."
The writer of the book, almost certainly an Alexandrian, represents the transition of Jewish-Hellenistic speculation about God into Trinitarian mysticism. Hellenism had produced a double offspring, Christianity and Gnosticism: both repudi-
ated the Law, both compromised Hebraic monotheism. The Church itself was soon like to be
engulfed in the witches' cauldron of gnostic fancies,
and engaged in a life-struggle with hydra-headed
heresies. All the aberrations from the Judaism of
the diaspora which were produced by the mingling
with the degenerate syncretism of the time found
their way into one or other of the opposing camps;
but Palestinian and Babylonian Judaism, preserved
in its integrity by the Word of the Law and by the
devotion of the Rabbis, confirming the solidarity
of the people, continued to hold aloft, though in
isolation, the Hebraic ideal.

Deprived of their temple, of their national centre in Judea, and to some extent of their independent organization and their autonomy, and
reduced to the level of a subject population, the Jewish people were compelled to draw tight the cords
of their tent, and to give over for a time their hopes

of universal expansion. But the loss of the external bonds and the outward forms of nationality led them to increase the strength of the inner ties and the moral and religious unity. Their more complete dispersion among the Hellenistic peoples induced a firmer hold on their national culture and resistance to foreign influences. The downfall of the sanctuary increased the power of the synagogue; the intensity of the national crisis aroused the spiritual forces of the people; the combined invasion of Hellenism and Orientalism was met by the intensification of the Hebraic spirit.

CHAPTER VII

THE AFTERMATH

By the end of the second century, the severity of the struggle against Rome and against Hellenism had passed. The Jews settled down to their life in exile, hoping indeed that a Messiah would soon arise to deliver them from the foreign yoke, but no longer bursting out in desperate rebellion. They had won from their conqueror by their heroic resistance the privilege of being a *religio licita,* a recognized denomination possessing a large measure of self-government; and partly through the central Sanhedrin which was still established in Palestine, and partly through the organization of the Synagogue in all parts of the Roman empire and beyond, they strengthened their internal cohesion. The Jewish communities, if no longer colonies of an independent nation, were branches of a distinct and separate nationality; and the loss of a territorial centre was compensated by the more complete ordering of conduct upon a national basis. Amid contempt and persecution they cherished their language and law, their history and poetry, with all their old pride and devotion.

Largely as a safeguard against heretical interpretations of the Torah, R. Judah (about 200 C. E.) compiled the Mishnah, which formed the authoritative text of the oral law, binding on all sections of the people and supplementing the Torah. The consolidation of the Halakah (the way of life) strengthened the hold of the national tradition. At the same time the fear of disintegration and denationalization led to the gradual withdrawal of the Jewish people into itself, and to the diminution of the proselytizing which had been in the main the work of Hellenistic Jewry. The Jews were to attract the Gentiles by their example, not to proselytize.[1] The progress of Christianity and the triumph within the Church of the antinomian and anti-national tendency, pointed the dangerous side of the missionary activity to the Rabbis. But it must not be thought that the activity ceased; the Haggadah of the Tannaim and Amoraim is full of beautiful thoughts about proselytes, among which the saying of Simon ben Yohai is typical: "Of the pious it is said they love God; but of the proselytes: God loves them. Hence we learn that the proselytes are more excellent than the pious."[2]

Another teacher declared that the whole world was
made for the sake of " those that fear God," ' and
Rabbi Eleazar thought that God dispersed the
Jews to aid the work of conversion. Nevertheless,
the influence on the Jewish congregations of the
Greek-speaking fearers of God gradually dimin-
ished.

Palestine remained, for more than two centuries
after the destruction of the temple, the chief centre of the Jewish people, and the seat of Jewish
learning. The Sanhedrin and the great rabbinical
schools were established there, and it is mainly of
the Palestinian Tannaim and Amoraim that we have
record in the older parts of Talmud and Midrash.
Even more completely than while they enjoyed
national independence, the Jews were living amid
a Greek-speaking and a Hellenized population.
Driven from Jerusalem and Judea, they had concentrated in Galilee, which was largely settled by
non-Jews. Moreover, as the Christian teaching
spread, large numbers of Christians made Palestine their home. Greek-speaking and Hellenized
like the pagans, they were prone to engage in polemics with the Jews, and formed an intellectual
leaven in Jewish life. Especially at places like
Cæsarea and Lydda, which were Christian bish-

oprics and prominent centres of Christian scholarship, Jews were thrown together with them, and
engaged in frequent controversy. The campaign
of Akiba and his followers against Hellenism and
the prohibition of the study of Greek wisdom did
not involve the cessation of intercourse between the
Aramaic-speaking Jew and the Greek-speaking
Gentile. Rather the reverse was the case: the
warnings and prohibitions were called for by the
temptation to mingle. Discussion between Rabbis
and Greek philosophers in Palestine is frequently
recorded in the Talmud and Midrash, and most of
the supposed traces of the influence of Greek philosophy on rabbinical thought occur in the Haggadah of the Rabbis who flourished later than the
second century. It may be that these doctrines
had already entered into the current thought of the
schools, and were not derived from direct contact
with Greek writings; but it is also possible, and in
some cases probable, that the Palestinian teachers
themselves studied the Greek wisdom. Although,
too, the Hellenistic and apocryphal literature had
been placed under the ban, considerable traces of
the ideas contained in it appear in the Midrash, and
preserved an abiding impression of the Hellenistic-
Jewish movement.

300

The most striking result of the national struggle was not the elimination of Hellenic ideas in Palestinian Jewry, but the dwindling of the importance of Hellenistic Jewry. The communities of Alexandria, Cyrene, and Libya never recovered from the decimation which followed the risings against Trajan and Hadrian. Estranged from the main body of Jews by their neglect of Hebrew, and rent by heresy and faction, their reduced numbers were little by little won over to gnostic and Christian ideas. Marcus Aurelius, the philosopher-emperor, spoke contemptuously of the Jewish rabble at Alexandria; and what had once been the most productive centre of Hellenistic-Jewish literature gave not a single Jewish record to the world after the second century. Christian scholarship, on the other hand, soon took up its chief abode in Alexandria; and when the city again became celebrated as a seat of philosophy and learning, it was through the patristic school of Christian writers. The destruction of the temple and the consequent disappearance of the deputations, which had used to come up to Jerusalem at the great festivals, would have tended to cut off the stream of influence that had passed from the diaspora to Palestine; and the disintegration of the Alexandrian community itself widened the breach.

The Haggadah attributed to the generation which succeeded R. Akiba reveals but little trace of foreign thought. The antipathy toward the Greek people and everything Greek was still too strong, the need for emphasizing what was Jewish still overpowering. Thus R. Meir, the most distinguished disciple of R. Akiba, who had also learnt from the apostate Ben Abuyah, emphasizes the self-sufficiency of God's chosen people. Israel is the metropolis in which everything is gathered; from his midst come priests, prophets, and writers, as it is said: " Out of him came forth the corner-stone, out of him the stake." [4] That is to say, the Jews needed not to learn anything from other peoples: their culture was complete in itself. A similar separatist tendency is shown in his prohibition to visit the Greek theatres. They were the seats of the scoffers, and R. Meir [5] applied to them the verse of the Psalmist: " I hate the gathering of evil-doers, and will not sit with the wicked." [6] The antipathy to the theatre and circus and amphitheatre is a commonplace of rabbinical literature. Nehunyah ben ha-Kanah, who belonged to an earlier generation, thanked God that his lot was among those who sit in the synagogue and not among those who sit in the theatre.' The places of amusement of the degenerate and demoralized populace of the empire, in which human beings were made to kill each other, or were devoured by wild beasts in order to provide a thrill for spectators, typified all that was low and base in the pagan civilization, and aroused the disgust of the Puritan conscience of the Jews. To frequent them was in public life what *Minut* was in thought—a denial of God.

R. Meir, however, albeit a stern upholder of the Jewish spirit, was celebrated for his mystical speculation, and engaged in intercourse with a noted Greek philosopher, Oenomaus of Gadata,* who knew the Jewish Scriptures, no longer a rare thing for a pagan philosopher. A Syrian neo-Platonist of the same period, Numenius of Apamea, is the reputed author of the striking saying: " What is Philo but Moses speaking in Attic Greek? " and he referred to the opening chapter of Genesis in support of his cosmological doctrines. Truth, he said, must be obtained by a comparison of the holy records of the Jews and Persians with the teachings of the Greek philosophers. So, too, the unknown author of the famous treatise " On the Sublime," which is the most striking piece of literary criticism that has come down from the period, quotes from the beginning of Genesis, and classes Moses with Homer as a master of style. " In the same way (*i. e.,* like Homer at his best)," he writes, " the legislator of the Jews, no mean man, wrote at the very beginning of the Laws: ' God said.' What? ' Let there be light, and there was light; let the earth be, and the earth was.' " [9] While Jewish teachers were rejecting the current syncretism, Gentile philosophers were endeavoring to fuse Judaism with their systems. Tolerance had become a fetish, and on all sides there was an outcry against Jewish particularism. Celsus, the famous pagan impugner of Christianity, complains: " If the Jews were content to observe their laws, nobody would reproach them; but since they pride themselves upon perfect knowledge and refuse to mix with other men, they are in the wrong. For their religious ideas are not peculiar to them, nor is there any indication that they enjoy the esteem and love of God to a higher degree than others, or that they alone have the privilege of receiving messages from heaven." [10] The taunt at the Jews on account of their lowly position is a commonplace among the Christian apologists, and represents the current opinion of the enlightened world. But the Jew held to his aloofness, conscious that he stood for something truer than the dominant easy-going conciliation of everything.

The one teacher of R. Meir's age who shows in his mystical teaching a correspondence with Hellenistic ideas is R. Judah ben Ilai. To him the saying is ascribed: " God looked at the Torah when he created the world." [11] Another piece of poetical mysticism, which reflects Hellenistic speculation, is his conceit that this world and the future world were created by the two letters of God's name. A remarkably large number of Greek words occur in the Haggadah which has come down in his name; and it is probable that he sojourned for some time in Alexandria. He uses the Nile as the image of a moral lesson, and the description of the beauty and size of the great Alexandrian synagogue is ascribed to him. [12]

While social intercourse with their Hellenistic neighbours was forbidden to the Jews, and the study of Hellenistic literature was discouraged, yet, even during the period of stress, no attempt was made in Palestine to prohibit the use of the Greek tongue. The praise which R. Judah bestowed on the Greek language has already been mentioned. When the danger of the Hellenization of Judaism was passed, the Rabbis found it possible to admire the excellence of the Greek tongue, as the earliest teachers had done before the danger was apparent. It was spoken of as " that which had no fault." [13] Compared with Latin, the language of the cruel Christian and Roman persecutors, Greek gained a new charm. Rab Huna (about 250 C. E.) said: " The Greek kingdom was superior to the Roman in three things: in law, science, and language." [14] Latin was essentially the language of brute materialism and of idolatry; whereas Greek fitted philosophical and spiritual ideas. Another late Amora, R. Jonathan of Eleutheropolis, said in the same spirit that the Greek language was excellent for poetry, Latin for war.

The vocabulary of the rabbinical writings likewise bears witness to Greek influence. It has been calculated that there are three thousand borrowed words, mostly Greek, in the Talmud; Greek transcriptions are used not only for official and legal terms, but for names of animals and plants, for abstract and scientific ideas, and even for synonyms of the most cherished Jewish institutes, as Νόμος for the Torah. Some scholars have maintained that there existed in Palestine and in the western Jewish communities a Judeo-Greek dialect, comparable with the Judeo-Arabic of later centuries, or with the Jüdisch-Deutsch of more modern times.[15]

We have further proof that many of the Tannaim and Amoraim (though they spoke and wrote in Aramaic), knew the foreign language, in that they frequently resort to an interpretation of biblical words based on a Greek transliteration of the Hebrew, in order to draw some improving homily or some striking meaning. Joël has ingeniously shown how the Rabbis detected a peculiar value in the Greek translation when they came to attach the traditional lore to the text. Holy Writ had a meaning in other languages as well as Hebrew; and to the Torah-intoxicated mind of the commentator the assonance of the Greek equivalent with some other Hebrew word could not be an accident.[16] One Rabbi explains the name Jeremiah as derived from the Greek *Eremia*—desolation; and another associated the Torah with *Theoria,* the Greek word for contemplation. Doubless the use of Aquila's translation suggested some of the interpretations, which are due not to indifferent philology of the Rabbis, though the Rabbis were neither exact philologists nor exact theologians, but to their zeal in the search for homilies. Other indications of knowledge of Greek occur where a Greek

image is used; as when R. Hanina compares the
soul leaving the body to a cable threaded through
a mast—a translation of a Greek proverb—," or
when R. Eleazar ben Pedat quotes a Greek maxim,
" unwritten law is before the king," in support
of God's excellence, which is shown in that God,
unlike a king, obeys His own laws.¹⁸ Possibly
the maxim was written up above the Basilica, i. e.,
the law-court of the city in which the Rabbi lived.
Again, R. Simon ben Lakish quotes the words of
a prayer in Greek: " Thou hast sent abundant
rain, O Lord." ¹⁹

The sudden appearance of Greek phrases in the
Talmud is not rare, and single Greek words are as
common as Latin tags in eighteenth century English. A few of the Rabbis of the later period not
only patronized the Greek language, but also
showed favor to Greek culture. R. Johanan bar
Nappaha, one of the Amoraim of the generation
following R. Judah, in commenting on the story of
Noah and his sons, placed Shem, the ancestor of
the Jews, and Japheth, the ancestor of the Greeks,
on an equality. Shem has obtained the Tallith,
the emblem of religious zeal, Japheth the pallium,
the philosopher's mantle. The Jewish Haggadist
thus anticipated the English essayist in distinguish-

ing the functions of the two great civilizing peoples. His contemporary Bar Kappara, a famous mystical teacher, whose knowledge of Greek is vouched for in the record of his tradition, interpreted the same verse in a way still more favorable to the Greek tongue. Playing on the Hebrew יפת he said: "The words of the Torah shall be recited in the speech of Japheth (*i. e.*, Greek) in the schools and synagogues." [20]

In the generation of the Patriarch Judah's disciples (*i. e.*, the first part of the third century), several facts suggest a partial breaking-down of the wall of seclusion between Jews and Gentiles, and a closer acquaintance among the Jewish sages with Hellenistic ideas. The bitterness of the era of conflict was mitigated, and the Jew, confirmed in his religious faith, could afford to mingle with the Christian apologist or the pagan philosopher. R. Johanan is said, on the authority of R. Abbahu, to have taught his sons and daughters Greek. He explained, in justification to those who expressed surprise, that a knowledge of Greek protected a man from slander and was an ornament for an educated woman, and that the prohibition against learning it was a temporary measure designed to prevent informing during the struggle against the Roman

commanders.[21] Another Rabbi of the third century, R. Levi bar Haitah, reports that he heard the
Shema' recited in Greek at Cæsarea, and a ruling
was given that the Shema' might be recited thus, so
that the commandment of understanding its meaning might be fulfilled.[22]

Cæsarea, the foundation of Herod and the
chief port of Palestine during the early centuries
of the common era, was the principal city in which
Jewish teachers were in contact with Hellenistic
civilization, and intercourse between Jews and
Gentiles was particularly fostered. After the destruction of Jerusalem it became the capital of
Palestine, and it rivalled Alexandria as a meeting-
place of cultures. The Rabbis called it the metropolis of kings,[23] but it was rather a metropolis of
scholars. Origen, the most distinguished of the
earlier Christian apologists, and the compiler of
the Hexapla Bible, recounts that he conversed there
with Jews. He must have derived from them his
not over-abundant Hebrew knowledge, as centuries
later Luther derived from the Rabbis of Germany
acquaintance with the Hebrew Bible. It is a happy
conjecture of Graetz that among the Jewish sages
whom Origen consulted was R. Hosha'ya, a disciple of Bar Kappara (whose favor toward Greek

has been quoted). The Midrash records dialogues which R. Hosha'ya held with a philosopher.
They discussed, among other things, the reasons
for the necessity for circumcision [24]—one of the
subjects on which the Church was ever ready to
contend with the Synagogue. It may well be that
the philosopher was none other than Origen.[25] To
R. Hosha'ya tradition ascribed the passage at the
opening of the Midrash on Genesis, which says
that God created the world by the aid of the Torah,
in the same way as a king employs an architect to
draw plans of his palace. The image of the architect and plan corresponds strikingly with a pic-
ture which Philo gives of the creation; and as
Origen was a faithful follower of Philo's allegorical method, and possessed at Cæsarea manuscripts
of all his works, it is possible that the Midrash is
an indirect adaptation of the Alexandrian allegory, induced by ideas which passed from Origen
to R. Hosha'ya.

R. Joshua ben Levi is another Amora who introduced pieces of religious idealism, which may
perhaps be adapted from a Hellenistic source. He
declares that all things were originally created by
God in their perfection [26]—a poetical variation of
the theory of creation through ideal archetypes.

R. Joshua, as well as R. Hosha'ya, lived and taught at Cæsarea; and thus may have come to know Alexandrian teaching, either directly or indirectly through Christian disputants. The Christian teachers in Palestine, who loved to find—or foist—Christological passages in the Hellenistic literature, were not slow in confronting the Jews with the allegorical interpretations in the religious philosophy of Philo and Aristobulus and the other writers of the Alexandrian school whom they had adapted to their own ends. The works of Origen and Clement are full of passages from these books which pointed, as they held, to the truth of Christianity. And that Christian scholars argued on these things with loyal Jews is clear enough, on the one hand, from the dialogues, which have come down to us, between Justin and Trypho and Jason and Pasiphaos, and, on the other, from the frequent reports in the Midrash of disputes between the Rabbis and philosophers or *Minim* or Roman emperors." If only for the purpose of controversy, it was necessary for the Jewish sages to have a knowledge of the literature on which their opponents relied; and hence some influence of Hellenistic Judaism crept surreptitiously into rabbinic

Judaism, and colored the religious cosmology and the theology of the Midrash.

References to Greek renderings of biblical passages appear in the Haggadah of the fourth century teachers, such as R. Joshua, R. Reuben, and R. Judah. Thus the contact with Greek was never entirely suspended in the rabbinical schools till the Christianizing of the Roman empire and the consequent persecution and isolation of the Jews. The infiltration of Greek knowledge was not restricted to the Palestinian colleges. Babylon began to vie with Palestine as the home of Jewish learning from the beginning of the third century, and many of the most famous heads of the schools in Palestine came originally from the East. Greek culture cannot have been as firmly established in Mesopotamia as in Galilee, and little by little it was supplanted, as the Roman power weakened and the Persian prevailed. Yet the Babylonian Amoraim not only used Greek words frequently, but adapted Hellenistic conceptions to their Hebraic outlook.

Perhaps because the danger of contamination by foreign influence was less strong than in Palestine, the mystical and allegorical teachings of the Hellenistic epoch were not as severely repressed in the Babylonian schools. Rabbah, a great Babylonian

Halakist of the earlier part of the third century, was the author of the idea that God accomplished the creation by means of ten ideas or attributes: Wisdom, Understanding, Justice, Love, etc. To him also is ascribed a certain Midrash about Bezalel—the artificer of the tabernacle—which shows a remarkable correspondence with the idealistic allegories of Philo. Interpreting Bezalel's name according to its Hebrew etymology as " the shadow of God," Philo says: " The shade of God is really His wisdom with which He made the world "; [28] while Rabbah explains that Bezalel knew how to combine letters by which the heavens and the earth were created.[29] The notion of creation by letters occurs in another midrashic fancy that this world is the work of the ה, and the world hereafter the work of the ' in the divine name.[30] Such fancies concerning creation by means of letters appear to be the prototype of those kabbalistic notions which took strong hold of a section of the Jewish people in the early part of the Middle Ages. The mystic doctrine of cosmology and the myths about angels, which had been produced, or at least stimulated, by the combination of Hebrew religious feeling and Greek speculation, were current in Palestine before the Christian era. The lore was partly preserved in the esoteric teachings of the rabbinical schools which were not committed to writing, and partly turned into the rank growth of heresies which sprang out of the soil of Hellenized Judaism. Struck out of the public teaching of the schools, it was never entirely eliminated, either in Palestine or Babylon, from Jewish tradition, and was nourished from time to time by the outside influence of syncretistic culture. Those Rabbis who were reputed masters of the secret wisdom, such as R. Judah ben Ilai and Bar Kappara, and manifest also a knowledge of Greek, formed a kind of liberal school in the colleges, and no attempt was made to prohibit their speculation.

The mystical teaching was established as part of the thought of the people; and when the struggle with Hellenism had ended, there was not the same necessity for excluding the record of it from the Midrash. Yet, as late as the fourth century, the warning is uttered by R. Ami not to disclose the secrets of the Torah save to him who is a leader and pre-eminent in wisdom and understanding.[31] It was only after the hold of the Law had been strengthened by centuries of discipline that the speculation into the before and after became an interest of the general body; and then it could no

longer work the mischief which it had threatened
at the crisis of the Jewish Puritan Reformation.
It plays a large part in the later Midrashim and the
so-called neo-Hebraic apocalypse, which date from
the seventh century; a much larger part, indeed,
than is allotted to it in the earlier Haggadah. But
there is no reason to doubt that, though the last
section of the tradition to be written down, these
Midrashim had their origin in early speculation.
The permanent influence of Hellenistic ideas on
Jewish tradition lies in the mystical notions, which
are not prominent in the older collections of rabbinical wisdom, just because they were treated as a
secret and higher wisdom which was not to be
divulged. They find expression occasionally in the
Midrash of the Tannaim and Amoraim through
some fancy about the Torah, or the creation, or
the wisdom of God; and occasionally the less mystical idealism of Hellenistic Judaism is reproduced
in the rabbinic theology. Dr. Neumark has attempted [32] to trace a definite and systematic philosophy running through the Haggadah, divided in
proper form into a doctrine of Ideas and a doctrine
of Emanations (the *Ma'aseh Bereshit* and *Ma'aseh
Merkabah,* respectively), and derived in regular
succession from Hillel and Johanan ben Zaccai, like

the teachings of the Greek schools; but this attempt is more heroic than convincing.

Jewish tradition preserved from the Hellenistic era rather a mystical than a philosophical doctrine. Mysticism is the outcome of the fusion of the religious with the inquiring sense; the attempt to transcend by vision what cannot be attained by reason; and thus it represents the natural consequence of the combination of Hebraism and Hellenism. How it developed in Palestine and Babylon between the time of Philo and eight hundred years later when we begin to get a full record, we cannot tell; but that it was sustained through all that period is shown first by the constant references to mystical and gnostic teaching in the age of the Tannaim, by the considerable fragments of mystic doctrine which occur in the Haggadah of many of the Amoraim, and finally by the Hellenistic and mystical coloring of the later Midrashim. The war which R. Akiba declared upon Greek wisdom and external books was an episode rendered necessary by the storm and stress of the time and the machinations of heretics, and it saved Judaism from disintegration. But if he and his successors effectively checked the excess of gnosticism, and succeeded in establishing the Law and

the Halakah as the solid basis of Jewish life in
the dispersion, they did not succeed—and they
could hardly have desired to succeed—in cutting
out the mystical yearnings of the people for a
closer communion with God, and a fuller understanding of His workings. At any rate those yearnings persisted; they lay hidden for a time under the
great growth of the legal literature; but when Judaism again came out into the light, and new influences from without were introduced to fertilize
its teaching, they received fuller play. They outlived the time when Hellenistic development of
Judaism was already forgotten in the schools, and
when Greek had become an unknown language not
only to the masses but to the sages of the people.

In the course of time the knowledge of Greek
disappeared in the East, though it was maintained in the schools and communities of the West.
The centre of Jewish learning, however, was now
fixed in Mesopotamia, where the Persian kings
gave the Jews a large measure of autonomy; and a
new Erez Israel was formed to give a glamor to
the exile. Knowledge of the foreign language
gradually dwindled in these schools, far removed
from Greek influence. But Greek culture, like the
phœnix, was immortal; and from its ashes in the

Orient a few centuries later another creation arose, which fructified Jewish thought, and led it to produce a new philosophical literature.

In the West it was not so much the barbarians as barbarity which cut off Jews from contact with the Greek-speaking world. The emperors had maintained a consistent attitude of tolerance until Christianity was established as the creed of the empire. Severus, indeed, was dubbed " archisynagogus "—president of the synagogue; and he placed in his bed-chamber texts from the book of Genesis. Even Constantine, who by imperial rescript made the revolutionary change in the State religion, declared that it was impossible to force belief on anybody. But that idea was not restored in Europe till the day of Voltaire. As Christianity prevailed, the position of the Jews became worse; the bitterest of wars raged between Church and Synagogue, though war it can hardly be called, since the Christians had at their back the whole force of the empire, and the Jews had only their Torah. The tradition of tolerance, which was inherited from the pagan times, mitigated the oppression for a time; and the short-lived advent of the pagan emperor Julian brought relief to the Jewish people. He it was who summed up his opinion of Christianity in the words ἀνέγνων, ἔγνων, κατέγνων, " I read, I knew, I condemned," and in hatred of the Church he proposed to restore the Jewish temple at Jerusalem. But the favor of the pagan emperors was the measure of the hatred of the Christian patriarchs and bishops, who, from the beginning of the fifth century, were for the most part supreme in the counsels of the empire. Ambrosius, the celebrated father, demanded insistently that the Jews should be completely isolated, and should not be allowed to hold converse with Christians. The mission which was still preached from the synagogue in Greek, was a hated competitor of the Church; the very existence of the synagogue was an eyesore and a menace. The Jews must be allowed to survive as " a witness " to the truth of the Church's teaching; but their life must be made miserable for the same end. Cyril, the "most Christian" bishop of Alexandria, expelled all Jews from the city of Alexandria, and persecuted them bitterly when any were found in the land of Egypt. Thus the greatest Jewish community of the Hellenistic diaspora was finally broken up. Augustine at Rome, who was under the influence of Ambrosius, and who stamped his ideas upon European civilization during the Dark and Middle Ages, taught that the Jews had no place in the Christian state: their law was a " most baneful schoolmaster " (*molestissimus paedagogus*), their synagogues must be put down. The campaign of the teachers of the Church produced the bitter anti-Jewish legislation of Theodosius and Justinian in the fifth and sixth centuries. No new synagogue might be built, and an attempt was made to close those which existed. It was declared a capital offence for a Jew to proselytize, and for a Gentile to be converted to Judaism. Jews were forbidden to hold slaves of any other nationality, and marriage between Jew and Christian was stringently prohibited. Thus the isolation of the Jews was gradually accomplished, not, as is often supposed even by Jews, by the meticulous regulations of rabbinical law, but by the calculated hostility of the Church which claimed to be universal and to bring with it an Evangel of Peace for all mankind.

Down to the time of Justinian many Jews of the Byzantine empire must have been in the habit of reading the Bible in Greek as well as in Hebrew. The emperor in the year 553 issued a famous *Novel* concerned with Jewish ritual, which is the first legislative attempt by an external power to fix Jewish belief and practice, and is a document of the first importance upon the attitude of the Jews of the later empire both to the Greek language and the rabbinical tradition. The *Novel* recites that, according to reports, some of the Jews hold exclusively to the Hebrew speech and desire to use it for the reading of Scripture, while others claim to use the Greek language as well for the liturgy. The champions of the tradition were opposed to this usage, but the emperor ordains complete liberty to either party to follow their desire and to use any language for the reading of Scripture in the synagogue, so that all may understand. He threatens capital punishment and confiscation of their property against any dignitaries of the Jewish clergy who excommunicate or punish those who read the Bible in any language but the Hebrew. Further, he restricts the Greek texts which may be used to two: the Septuagint and Aquila's version; and strongly recommends the former " which is far more exact, and is remarkable for the fact that, though the translators were separated and gave their interpretation in different places, they nevertheless all reached one result. And though the Seventy lived long before Jesus, they yet presaged his coming, and inserted the tradition of it by a kind of prophetic grace . . . . But in order not to exclude alto-

322

gether the other renderings, we give them liberty to use that of Aquila, though he was a proselyte, and does not accord well with the Seventy in regard to certain meanings." The imperial preference for the Septuagint contrasts with the rabbinical favor toward Aquila.

The Christian legislator was in more direct opposition to Jewish tradition and feeling in prohibiting absolutely the use in the synagogue of the oral law, which, he declared, had blinded them to the Christian teaching. " By abandoning themselves to their insensate interpretations, they have wandered away from the true light. We ordain, therefore, that they have liberty to come together in their synagogues and read the sacred books in the Greek tongue, but that no liberty is to be given to the interpreters among them, who hand down only a Hebrew tradition, to pervert that according to their own sweet will, and to cover their false doctrine under the ignorance of the mass. That second edition, as they call it, we prohibit altogether, because it has no connection with the Scriptures. It has not been transmitted to us by the prophets, but it is an invention of men who spoke only of earthly things, and had not the divine spark." [33] Some have inferred from the *Novel* the existence of

a Greek translation of the Mishnah; but the prohibited " second edition " is more probably to be
identified with the Haggadah; nor is it at all clear
that this " edition " referred to existed in a Greek
form.²⁴ What may be deduced, however, is that the
struggle between Hebrew and Greek was still maintained in the Synagogue to the sixth century, and
that in some countries, despite the rabbinical ban,
a section desired the Scriptures to be read solely
in the version of the Septuagint or of Aquila,
unaccompanied by the recital of the rabbinical commentary. The imperial legislator saw that in the
Hebrew Bible and its Hebrew or Aramaic interpretation lay the strength of Judaism, while the Septuagint version of the Old Testament was a step
toward Christianity. Justinian went on to menace
with exile and the extreme penalties of the law all
Jews who dare to maintain that there is neither
resurrection nor last judgment, or that the angels
are not divine beings. It would seem that a party
in the Jewish communities persisted in maintaining
the standpoint of the ancient Sadducees, and formed
a link between them and the Karaites. And the
emperor was an enemy of heretical teaching among
the despised Jews; for heresy was infectious.

324

The Jews were more completely thrown back
on their rabbinical tradition as the Church began to
press them in more narrowly by the construction of
ghettos. In remote corners of the civilized world,
in the far west of the North-African coast, in Abyssinia, and in the vicinity of the great African desert,
a few Hellenistic colonies remained out of the
reach of Christian oppression; preserving not indeed the Greek tongue, but some of the syncretistic
ideas and beliefs which had sprung up during the
Hellenistic period. Greek, indeed, was still spoken
by Jewish congregations in the Provence in the Middle Ages. But otherwise the knowledge of Greek
seems to have completely disappeared among the
Jews.

Intercourse with Hellenistic thought was again
brought about in the Jewish schools in the eighth
century. The first half of the gaonic period, when
the law was arranged and codified and the Talmud was written down, manifested little or no
movement toward the production of philosophical
and mystical literature. But the conquest of the
Persian dominions by the Arabs and the development of Arabic culture in the Jewish environment
brought anew, though indirectly, into Jewish literature a vigorous Hellenistic influence. Under the

wise rule of the Abbasid Caliphs, the Arabs developed a remarkable philosophical culture, and assimilated a great part of the literature of the classical and Hellenistic age, which had been translated into Syriac. The Jews, quick to take part in the intellectual revival, again became acquainted through Arabic writings with outside culture, and, at second hand, with the thoughts of their people which, before the Dark Ages had fallen, had sprung from the mixture of Hellenism and Hebraism. The apocalypses and the mystical wisdom had not entirely passed out of knowledge; and under the fresh impulse, their study revived. A new Hebrew apocalyptic literature was composed, claiming indeed to be ancient, and imitating and reproducing the ideas of the Old Testatment visions. A Hebrew book of Enoch, a Hebrew Assumption of Moses, the Mystery of R. Joshua ben Levi, containing revelations supposed to have been received from Elijah, and apocalypses of Elijah and Zerubbabel, have survived from the period. The divine Power plays a large part in most of these books, and the idea of a heavenly hierarchy and of a series of heavens is common to them all. Enoch, who had been the favorite figure of the older apocalypse, appears with a new prerogative as a divine agent in creation. He is identified with Metatron—the archangel and divine potency—and the *Sefer Heka-lot*, in which Metatron plays the chief rôle, is also called the Book of Enoch.

From the eighth and ninth centuries also date the pseudepigraphic books of the Secret Tradition, or Kabbalah, as it was simply called, which claimed the authorship of the great Tannaim, but manifestly was not composed before the gaonic period. The secret doctrines about the Creation and the Chariot, which had hitherto been handed down orally, were now committed to writing and embellished with current images of divine beings and demons, and fancies about angels, and cosmogony by letters. This mediæval speculation shows the influence of neo-Platonic philosophy, which was itself the outcome of the mixture of Oriental with Greek thought. The most celebrated of the Kabbalist books is the *Sefer Yezirah*, described as the first philosophical book written in Hebrew; and others of the same genus are the Greater and Smaller *Hekalot*, the Book of Raziel, and the *Sefer ha-Yashar*. It is said at the beginning of the *Sefer Yezirah*: " By thirty-two wonderful paths the Eternal has created the world in three forms: number, letter, and speech; ten numbers self-

contained and twenty-two letters." The mystical
cosmogony was characteristic of the thinking of the
age, and led on to the more philosophical doctrine
of *Sefirot* or emanations, which appears later in the
more developed kabbalistic literature.

The latest of the Midrashim, the *Midrash Tadshe* and the *Midrash Konen,* were compiled during
the same period. The first purports to be the work
of the saintly Tanna R. Phineas ben Jair, and has
remarkable correspondence with the Book of Jubilees and also with some writings of Philo.[35] The
inference is that it was composed of floating allegorical and mystical teachings which were derived
from a time when the Hellenistic influence was
strong on Judaism. The second book, which derives its title from the verse in Proverbs (3. 19),
" The Lord by wisdom founded the earth; by
understanding He established (כונן) the heavens,"
portrays the pre-existence of the Messiah, and its
descriptions of Hell and Paradise betray Arab-
Greek influence. The later kabbalistic literature
derives largely from these sources, but includes in
addition a large amount of neo-Platonic theology.

Of higher intellectual value than this mystic
literature was the new development of Jewish philosophy. Fostered likewise by Arabic writers, it

starts with Saadya in Egypt in the tenth century, reaches its zenith with Ibn Gebirol and Judah ha-Levi in Spain in the eleventh, and culminates with Maimonides in Egypt in the twelfth, and Crescas in Spain in the fourteenth century. The Judeo-Arabic school borrowed their system, in large measure, from the Muhammedan philosophers who had adapted and combined the Aristotelian and neo-Platonic systems to be an intellectual support of Islam. They knew no Greek themselves, but they acquired their knowledge through the Arabic translators and adapters. And while a great part of the Hellenistic-Jewish literature was unknown to them, and the very name of Philo never occurs in their writings, yet indirectly the influence of Hellenistic-Jewish thought affected them through its absorption in the later Greek and early Christian schools, from which their own masters started. Hellenistic-Jewish theology had, in fact, by the Middle Ages become part of the world's intellectual possession. Saadya knows of the book of the Maccabees, the Wisdom of Ben Sira (which he refers to as the Book of Instruction), and the Book of Jubilees.[36] Perhaps the Hebrew text or an Aramaic translation of the apocryphal works had been preserved in Egypt, where Jewish learning was never altogether extinguished.

A new epoch of Jewish thought began when the mediaeval masters of Jewish learning sought—as the Alexandrians had done—to defend Judaism with the aid of Hellenism, to recast the substance of the one in the form of the other. The conflict between Hebrew and Greek culture seemed for a time to have ended with the victory of the Jewish religion; for Greek wisdom in the Middle Ages was its humble servant. Hellenic speculation was used to bolster Hebraic belief, and Greek ethics to justify the Jewish Torah.

CHAPTER VIII

CONCLUSION

At the end of the fourth century of the Christian era the wheel of civilization, which seven hundred years previously had been turned in the direction of a cosmopolitan culture, seemed to have achieved a full circle. The Jews were more isolated and more exclusively national than at the end of the fourth century before the Christian era, when they were first brought into relation with Hellenism and began their expansion. They had indeed given to the civilized world a large part of their heritage, and spread their moral teaching far and wide; they had inspired the neo-Platonic philosophy, and provided the basis for a world-religion, but they seemed to have received little in return save hatred. An outside observer surveying the position might judge the Hellenistic movement to have left no trace on the religion of Israel, and to have been an aberration rather than a development; but if we look over the field more closely, we shall find that that view is not altogether correct.

331

The Jews and the Hellenes stand out from the other peoples, at the beginning of the period, by their strongly marked national character and their contrasted ideals, which were the outcome of generations of national life disciplined in a particular way. Hebraism was devoted to conduct, or, as a Jew would say, to the Torah; Hellenism to the full development of all human faculties. The acceptance by the people of a lofty moral law constituted the greatness of the one; the harmonious ordering of life by the individual devoted to the state, the greatness of the other. Virtue to the Jew meant righteous life; to the Hellene, physical and intellectual and moral excellence. Both nations were eager for knowledge; but the Jew sought for knowledge of God, the Hellene for knowledge of nature. Both again were conscious of a high purpose which raised them above other peoples; but the Greeks were filled with the idea of intellectual superiority, the Jews with the conviction of a moral and religious mission. To the Greek philosophical speculation about the causes of things was of supreme interest; to the Jew, the study of his history, in which he traced the working of a personal God executing the law of righteousness on the nations. By the conquests of Alexander the Great, Hellenism

332

expanded beyond the national society which had
produced it. It was deliberately spread, as a
Church militant, over the eastern world, through
the foundation of Hellenistic cities and colonies on
the pattern of the city-states of Hellas; but the conditions of its expansion caused its rapid deteriora-
tion. The culture of the Hellenic people was the
immediate and direct expression of a political national life, and the spirit that had thrilled it died
when that life ceased. Pure Hellenism—the Greek
spirit—was never brought to Palestine, and was
never imbibed by the Jews; what did come, and
what was imbibed by some classes, was a mixed
product of Hellenic wisdom and Oriental civilization, which presented much of the outward show of
Greek life, but did not offer what was most precious
in it.

Had the Jews met Hellenism on its own soil and
in its prime, a true harmony between the two might
possibly have resulted and produced a civilization
more splendid and more complete than the world
has yet known. But Providence did not work in
that way, and in fact the Jews encountered a Hellenism debased by transplantation to a strange soil.
The Greek culture with which they came in contact
in Palestine was contaminated by Hellenized

Syrians with their crude materialism and mysticism.
Judaism, on the other hand, was in the stage of
vigorous development, and strongly entrenched in
its national life, which gave it a mould of resistance
to foreign ideas. But it was not yet fully self-
conscious, and had not reflected on the basis of its
religious intuitions.

The superiority of the external products of the
Greek people, of their art, their pleasures and their
literature, and the glamor of their political and
military prowess were strong enough to exercise
a large influence in Judea. The Greeks had conquered the East, and the tendency is always for the
subject to imitate the manners of the ruler. Hence,
there was much outward imitation of Greek fashions, and among some circles an inward assimilation of the Greek point of view. But when the
attempt was made to hasten the process, and to ex-
tend it from manners to morals and from morals to
religion, the deep-seated feelings of the people were
roused, and the struggle between the two cultures
began. The core of the nation was sound; they
resisted with heroism the endeavor of Greeks and
Graecizing Jews to coerce them, and prevailed.
The struggle ended in the utter rejection of the

foreign culture in Judea, and its discomfiture in the whole of Palestine.

Tested in the trial of moral strength, Judaism had become self-conscious, and the Jew had gained a fresh pride in his religion, a fresh consciousness of his mission. The conception of the unity of God and the hold of the Law were strengthened by contrast with the paganism which the Hellenizers had tried to substitute for it. The Jews passed from passive resistance to aggressive iconoclasm, and in turn spread their ideas beyond the limits of their country. But traces of the Syrian Hellenism, which had been implanted among the less educated masses, endured; and the victorious Judean people harbored a growing semi-Hellenized crowd who had neither grasped the pure Hebraic faith, nor received the pure Hellenic spirit. This populace fostered the apocalyptic literature with its fantastic and yet somewhat materialistic spirituality, which, while it was largely an expression of the Hebraic mind and a development of the prophetic vision, shows the marked impress of foreign doctrine. A more distinct relic of foreign ideas in their spiritual form remained in the sect of the Essenes, who represented the ascetic attitude, which had sprung up in the Greek society out of the decay of national life and intellectual contemplation. But the bulk of the people were confirmed in their ancestral faith, and the renewal of the independence of national life, together with the teaching of the Pharisees, strengthened the hold and deepened the conception of Judaism.

In the diaspora, where the Jews formed a considerable and well-knit element in the midst of a Greek-speaking population, their relation with Hellenism proceeded otherwise. They pursued their own learning in the synagogues, but at the same time they became eager to know the ideas of their neighbors. More particularly at Alexandria, which from its foundation was at once the principal seat of cosmopolitan culture and a great Jewish centre, they had about them a purer and more genuine Hellenism than had been imported into Palestine. By their munificent patronage of art and the organization of their museum and library with its fifty thousand books, representing the literatures of all peoples, the Ptolemies contrived to bring to their capital the best of the Hellenic genius of the Silver Age. On the other side, the hold of his national culture could not be as strong on the Jew in dispersion as on the Jew in his own land. Hence, though the Jewish mind had not acquired that imitative skill and assimilative capacity which are characteristic of it to-day, the Alexandrian community felt the attraction of Hellenism more rapidly and more deeply than the Palestinian. They adopted the language of their environment, and endeavoured to adjust their religious ideas and observances to the intellectual standpoint of the dominant culture. The translation of the Scriptures into Greek was a vital step in the adjustment. A further step is marked by the abundant apologetic literature, in which the Jewish Law is interpreted as a code of rational ethics, and a deliberate attempt is made to adopt Greek theology to the support of Judaism.

Knowledge of Greek philosophy stimulated the Jews to fresh development of their religious ideas. At the same time the Maccabean triumph and acquaintance with the weak side of Hellenistic culture aroused an aggressive missionary spirit. They preached and propagated Judaism to the Gentiles about them, and denounced the surrounding paganism and immorality with a zest which did not scruple to use fictitious authorities for the purpose of moving the populace. Not only at Alexandria, but in Mesopotamia, in Syria, in Asia, and in the islands and cities of Hellas itself, the Jewish communities gathered around their synagogues a number of proselytes or " fearers of the Lord," and inculcated the moral teachings of the Mosaic law in those who were not willing to become full converts to the national religion. But as the semi-Judaized and semi-Hellenized populace of Palestine was a source of weakness to Jewry, because of the impure notions to which it clung, so the crowd of converts and semi-converts who were gathered around the synagogues of the diaspora were a danger to the integrity of the Jewish faith. They retained, to a large extent, their earlier habit of mind, and they brought into the Jewish congregation doctrines which were not in harmony with pure monotheism. The literature which was designed to win them shows frequent trace of the impurities and of the compromizing spirit to which Pharisaic Judaism was a stranger. A large part of Hellenistic Jewry remained true to the Torah and the ancestral way of life, but a part, under the influence of foreign ideas, tended to whittle away the national-religious heritage in a vague universalism.

The finer aspect of the heightened Jewish self-consciousness showed itself not in the popular missionary movement, but in the development of Jewish philosophy, in which the religious Jewish idea dominates intellectual conceptions derived from the Greek thinkers. The Alexandrian teachers adhered to the study of the Torah as their proper and sufficient wisdom, but looked to the interpretation of Scripture not simply for new didactic lessons, but for the indication of philosophical ideas. One splendid figure, who sums up the deepest aspirations of Hellenistic Judaism, achieves something approaching a harmony between Jewish religion and Greek wisdom. Philo does not harmonize the spirits of Hebraism and Hellenism—that was impossible in his day—but he does fuse the spiritual teachings of the two, and that not in an artificial and conscious way, but sincerely and spontaneously. He created something new in literature and thought. His philosophical mysticism, expressed in a poetical prose, was the most striking combination of the religious and the intellectual ideals which the ancient world produced, and represented the resultant of the union of the Greek searching for knowledge of causes and the Jewish yearning for God.

The Jew created no original philosophical system, but he used the intellectual forms of others for the expression of his distinctive outlook. Under the dominance of the religious spirit, the transformation of Greek philosophy was bound to end in mysticism, the Jewish adoption of Greek intellectual contemplation ($\theta\epsilon\omega\rho\iota\alpha$) in a longing for ecstasy.

Mystical thought is, however, always exposed to the danger that it tends to leave the firm anchorage of reason and the law of conduct. Philo points out the existence of such an excess in his day. He himself held fast to the Law while he indulged his philosophical ardor, and contrived to find a true balance between national religion and universal mysticism. But the influence of Hellenistic philosophy was to lead away a large class of his contemporaries from the national manner of life into that maze of mystical ideas which is called gnosticism. The observance of the national-religious law was endangered by the inordinate desire of the individual to penetrate into the secrets of the universe; men sought to transcend reason in wild visions and imaginations. Moreover, the Hellenistic thought which the Alexandrian sage endeavored to fuse with Judaism was mixed with a number of speculations and notions which were fundamentally opposed to the genuine Jewish outlook. Egypt, the cradle of mythology, has always been antipathetic to Judaism in its religious conceptions, and the intermediary powers and divine hypostases, which were the product of the syncretism of Graeco-Egyptian and Hebraic theology, were brought into the Hellenistic-Jewish philosophy with dangerous consequences. They were held by Philo in a loose solution, and in such a way as not to impair the worship of the one God of the Hebrew conscience; but they were crystallized and defined by his successors and became the basis of hybrid sects and heresies. Graeco-Roman society in the first and second centuries was lapsing into an extreme of irrationalism, and its thought was in process of degradation. The Jewry of the diaspora, weakened by its proselyte following, was not proof against the influence. By the abandonment of Hebrew as the language of its literature and its ritual, it gradually lost touch with the Catholic Jewish feeling; and when the temple service was brought to an end, the centrifugal tendency became more pronounced. Hellenistic Jewry became a medley of struggling heresies and sects. Animated by the desire to convert the Gentiles, it had sacrificed its particularism and weakened its defences; and by the reception of a large number of converts with a foreign outlook, and by the infusion of non-

Jewish notions in its theology and philosophy, it lacked the cohesion which preserved the strength and individuality of the Palestinian community.

When the Christian teaching of the Messiah come to redeem humanity—which was itself derived from the Hellenized literature of apocalypse —was disseminated among the Jewish communities, it was Greek-speaking Jews who were prominent in developing it, and Greek-speaking converts and " fearers of the Lord " to whom it mainly appealed. It accorded with their opposition to the Law, with their desire for a universal creed for all people, with their notions of an intercessor between man and God. Hellenistic Jews, on the other hand, introduced into the simple doctrine of the redeeming Messiah, which was the starting-point of the Christian doctrine, many of their theological ideas, and thus started the radical modification of Jewish monotheism which was to culminate in the Trinity of the Church. The history of Christianity ceases to be a part of Jewish history from the time when the mythical and metaphysical element, derived from Alexandrian decadence, obtained the ascendancy.[1]

Hellenism in the diaspora, then, nurtured a creed which was true neither to the cardinal points

of the Hebraic or the Hellenistic genius, nor
to the intuitive apprehension of the one God of
history, nor to the eager search for truth and knowledge. The strange doctrines had been less forcibly
resisted there than in Palestine, and obtained a
firmer lodgment; but no stable and lasting synthesis
with Judaism had been accomplished. At the time
of the first preaching of Christianity mystical ideas
were prevalent also in Palestine. They were
brought possibly by the Greek-speaking Jews who
were constantly coming to and from the Holy
Land; possibly they were the outcome of the Oriental Hellenism which still survived in the Jewish
environment. Whatever their origin, they threatened the growth of heresy similar in kind to the
heretical efflorescence in Egypt and Syria. The
inner disintegration coincided with the last desperate struggle to preserve the national independence; and the failure of that struggle emphasized
and deepened the crisis in the spiritual life. While
a national centre with a standard of Judaism endured, esoteric speculation could be allowed so long
as it did not undermine the loyalty and faith of the
main body. But it became an element of disso-
lution when the outward bond of cohesion was

343

rent asunder, and had to be repressed in order to preserve a Catholic Judaism.

The greatest crisis in the struggle between Hellenism and Judaism was reached when Hellenistic syncretism threatened, as three centuries before Hellenistic paganism had threatened, Jewish monotheism and the observance of the law. In face of the peril the Jewish spirit made a supreme effort. A Puritan revival, parallel with that which had been experienced in Babylon, marked the beginning of the Roman exile. The heads of the schools perceived that the heretical teachings had their origin in the introduction of Greek theology and Greek forms of thought into the Jewish mind. The Greek culture of the time was fatal to Hebraic religion, and therefore they blamed it rather than compromise their Judaism in any way. Mystical teaching, which bore the stamp of foreign influence, and the allegorical interpretation, which sought to combine it with the Bible, were discouraged. The Hellenistic-Jewish literature, which harbored non-Jewish elements, though preserved by the Gentiles to play a part in the intellectual development of Europe for over a thousand years, was cut out of the Pharisaic tradition. Jewish culture was pruned of its luxuriant growth, in order that it might retain its strength and withstand the storm which beat about it.

In the thorough purgation of Judaism, the Rabbis showed a true appreciation of the conflict which existed between Hellenistic theology and Jewish monotheism. That theology was in fact but a reincarnation of the old pagan mythology; and when Christianity ceased to be a Jewish heresy, it proceeded to incorporate with its Jewish element a large part of the myths of the Aryan and Semitic peoples. The abiding paradox of metaphysics has been pointed out by Anatole France. " Any expression," he says, " of an abstract idea can only be an allegory. By an odd fate the very metaphysicians who think to escape the world of appearance are constrained to live perpetually in allegory. A sorry sort of poets, they attack the colors of the ancient fables, and are themselves but collectors of fables. Their output is mythology, an anæmic mythology without body or blood." The early Greek philosophers had endeavored to destroy the myths of the popular religion, but their successors weaved around their philosophical reflections about God the same mythology in another form. And the Jewish Hellenists had been beguiled by them into compromises of monotheism.

They had sought greater exactitude by allegorical interpretation, contained in a vague metaphysic, which, as it became stereotyped, was made the basis of a non-Jewish mythology. The image and symbol were taken for reality, and obscured in the coarser thinking of the later age the ideas they were designed to explain. The Rabbis, interpreting more truly the genius of Judaism, eschewed the dialectic of the metaphysician and the reasoning of the theologian. When they desired to describe the divine attributes or the transcendental nature, they turned frankly to fable and allegory.

Nevertheless, though the Hellenistic branch was lopped off from the trunk of Judaism, though the Hellenistic theology was rejected, and the Hellenistic wisdom placed under the ban, the mystic doctrine, which had been fructified by Hellenistic influence, lived on in the background, or rather underground, of Jewish thought. The written record of Hellenistic Judaism was discarded, but an oral tradition of esoteric speculation endured in Palestine as well as the diaspora. Greek ideas were transfixed in this wisdom, and thus entered into the thought of the people, coloring the Jewish intuition of the one transcendental God with something of the Greek Gnosis or search for

346

knowledge. The undercurrent of mystical thought, of which we know little but hear much in the early Haggadah of the Talmud, outlived the Alexandrian influence which had nourished it. But it did not find a permanent literary expression till a fresh stream of Hellenistic influence was brought into the Jewish world in the early part of the Middle Ages.

Cut off from the outer intellectual world for some five hundred years, and engaged in a constant struggle to preserve their individuality, the Jews had no leisure for philosophical speculation. But they were again brought, in the tenth century, into relation with it through the Arabic culture which flourished about them in Egypt and in Spain. The Renaissance in the East preceded that in the West. While Europe was sunk in the obscurantism of the Dark Ages, the systems of Aristotle and the neo-Platonists were stimulating the Arabs to philosophy, and, through the Arabic medium, came again to affect Jewish ideas. Indeed, Saadya Gaon, the first Jewish philosopher who deserves the title, recognized the logical hegemony of Aristotle, but contrived to distinguish between the Jewish and the philosophical outlook. His successors embraced the Greek metaphysics more whole-heartedly. The revived Hellenism, however, which entered into Jewish mediæval thought, was not a dangerous dissolvent. In the first place, it was, so to say, in a strait waistcoat, subjected already to the service of religion by the Muslim philosophers from whom the Jews derived it. Moreover, it no longer stood for a theory of life, nor was it associated with a competing religious outlook, but it was simply a body of knowledge and reflection about physics and metaphysics. Jewish life and thought, on the other hand, were even more thoroughly consolidated and organized than they had been in the period of the great struggle. A thousand years of life under the Law, together with the constant study of the ever-growing mass of tradition in Mishnah, Talmud, Midrash, and later commentaries, had made the mind of the people proof against the seduction of foreign doctrine. In the Golden Age of Spain the influx of Hellenism aroused the emulation of the Jewish spirit, and served to deepen it, without producing any aftermath in the form of heresy and sectarianism. The expansion of the mystical teaching led, indeed, to a cleavage between two sections of Jewry; and the introduction of Greek philosophical ideas into the interpretation of the Bible was strenuously opposed by some of the greatest

348

thinkers of the time. But the religious philoso-
phies of Ibn Gebirol, Maimonides, and Gersonides,
though they evoked opposition, were accepted into
Jewish literature, and brought permanent influence
of Hellenistic metaphysics into the Jewish schools
which endured through the Middle Ages to modern
times.

The new Hellenism was a stimulating force, and
it was harnessed to the service of the Jewish religion; but it had, from one aspect, an untoward
effect on Jewish thought. The Greek master, to
whom most of the Arab-Jewish school looked up,
was Aristotle, who was the greatest logician and
rationalist of the ancient world. So deep was their
respect that they endeavored to attach him to
Judaism. According to one account,² he was a
pupil of Simon the Just, the high priest at the time
of Alexander the Great; according to another,
which more boldly disregarded chronology and lo-
cality, he was associated with Gamaliel when the
latter visited Rome in 96 C. E. A third account,
still bolder, declared him a Jew of the tribe of Ben-
jamin, who took away the secret books of wisdom
from Solomon's palace when Jerusalem was captured. Similar stories had been told by the
Christian scholars, Clement of Alexandria, and

Eusebius; but it was in the revival of Jewish
thought in Spain that they first found acceptance
among the Jews.

Certain correspondences could be detected between the Aristotelian theology and the Jewish
creed. Aristotle, at the end of his *Metaphysics,*
declared for monotheism; and he believed in a tele-
ological ordering of Nature which harmonized
with the demand of the religious consciousness. He
could be made then to give rational support to the
intuitional Jewish conception of God. But the conciliation was more apparent than real. Judah
ha-Levi, who vigorously opposed the new Hellenism and asserted the right of Judaism to " autonomous intellectual existence," pointed out the
contrast between the Jewish personal God of history and the Greek impersonal principle of being,
the Prime Mover. " By no means is the God of
Aristotle the God of Abraham; the way to the latter lies through emotion and the inner living feeling, and for Him the soul aspires. The way to the
former is through abstract thought, and the heart
beats not for Him." Aristotle, in truth, with his
intense rationalism, was further removed from the
religious soul than Plato whose teaching had inspired the Alexandrian-Jewish philosophy, and was

the basis of the neo-Platonic speculation of an Ibn Gebirol and a Crescas. His influence, which prevailed from the eleventh till the sixteenth century, tended to formalize Jewish theology and to invest it with a rational severity to which it had hitherto been a stranger. The tendency was to an extent redressed by the mystical movement which derived from the Jewish neo-Platonists, but rationalism remained the dominant tone.[3]

The first Jewish scholar of modern times to attack the rationalizing movement was Samuel David Luzzatto, one of the founders of the new Hebrew school, who flourished in the first half of the nineteenth century. He denounced Maimonides, the chief Jewish Aristotelian, for disloyalty to the Jewish intuitive standpoint, and following the line of ha-Levi, he broadly pointed the contrast between Hebraism and Hellenism—or Atticism, as he called it.[4] All the philosophy derived from the Greeks is for him a root of gall and wormwood. Atticism is progressive, Judaism is stationary. Atticism is constantly assuming new forms, Judaism is immovable and seems old and ugly. But human nature harbors an inextinguishable love of the good which Judaism, or its spirit, alone can satisfy.

351

Its teaching makes people happy, while Greek philosophy renders them pessimistic.

Luzzatto, however, though he impugned the
scholastic Jewish philosophy of the Middle Ages,
paid little heed to the earlier Jewish Hellenistic
literature. But nearly three hundred years before
he wrote, another Italian Jew had made that
literature the subject of study, and tried to show its
relation to Jewish tradition. Azariah dei Rossi is
the pioneer in the " Science of Judaism," and he had
no successors for three centuries. He translated
the Letter of Aristeas into Hebrew under the title
of *Hadrat Zekenim* (" Glory of the Ancients ") ;
and in his *Meor 'Enayim* he dealt with the works of
Philo and Josephus and other Hellenists, and attacked Philo for his allegorical interpretation of
the narrative and legal parts of the Bible, on the
ground that they were false to the spirit of Judaism.

Dei Rossi lived before his time: he was one of
the few Jews of his age to imbibe the spirit of the
European Renaissance that opened up to humanity
the Hellenic treasury. No Jew continued his his-
torical investigations till the time of Luzzatto.
Then, however, Krochmal, the devoted student of
Galicia, basing his work on the researches of the
German scholar Neander, gave a critical account

of the Hellenistic-Jewish development in his *Guide of the Perplexed of the Time,* and restored it to the knowledge of the Jewish scholars. The Essene speculations and the relation of Philo to the Midrash received special consideration. He was dependent on second-hand sources—for he had no Greek—but his work was fruitful in that it formed the foundation of the scientific study of the German school. Bernays, Zunz, Frankel, Graetz, and Jellinek were masters of Greek, and possessed the external equipment necessary for independent judgment. The place of Hellenistic literature in Jewish thought and its influence on the world's history were at last elucidated in their writings from the Jewish point of view. Enough and to spare of Christian divines had searched in it for the source and justification of Christian dogmas, and had loved to contrast for their own purposes its broad universalism and ethical spirit with the narrow legalism of the Talmud—which most could not read. Historical justice began to correct these easy views, and it has not yet completed its part. The work of Zunz and his contemporaries has been continued and amplified by a large band of Jewish scholars, many of them still living and actively prosecuting their researches.

A new relation has been set up between Hebraism and Hellenism in the present age. The Renaissance of the sixteenth century let free on western European society an overpowering stream of Hellenism, not the impure medley of Alexandrian civilization, but the pure inspiration of the Classical Age. " We are all Greeks," exclaimed Maine. Our ideas of law, of politics, of philosophy, of ethics, in short, of life are largely determined, on the one hand, by the ideas of the classical Hellas which form the foundation of our higher education, and, on the other, by the doctrines of the Hellenistic-Jewish syncretism which, as we have traced, formed the basis of the Christian Church. As the centuries went by, the stream of the Renaissance continued to modify the Christian civilization enshrining the ideas of the Alexandrian culture. It could not reach for a time the Jewish community which was cribbed, cabined, and confined in its narrow ghettos, and forcibly isolated from its environment. Its appeal for clearer thought and the search for truth reached a few individuals only, who burst the bonds which fettered them, notably Spinoza, who, by his synthesis of Greek intellect and Jewish intuition, laid the foundation of modern philosophy. But when the French Revolution heralded the dawn of emancipation for the Jews of the West, the influence of outside thought became of commanding importance. The position of the Jews was now in many ways like that which existed when Alexander conquered Palestine and opened to them the Greek world. Only the attraction of the outside culture was more powerful, because the Jews had not now, as they had then, a national centre where their own standard of life and thought flourished in competition with the universal appeal of their environment. The Jewish life in the ghetto was intense, but it was not inspiring as the life of the people was in Judea. The position again was quite different from that which existed in the period of emancipation under the Moors and Arabs. Then, although free, the Jews preserved their national organization amid a friendly population, and the Hellenism which they invoked to the support and progressive development of their religion was not part and parcel of the thought of the people, or organically fused with life, but a philosophical system known to the few, and strictly limited by them to the purpose of providing a rational basis for theology.

During the nineteenth century the isolation of the ghetto in the West was more completely broken down, the mingling with the Gentile population was more thorough, and the assimilation more rapid. The spread of printed books and the facilities for communication increased the force of the external culture. Centuries of persecution also caused Jewish thought to be obsolete in certain of its concepts, and weakened the power of the Jew to resist foreign ideas. His traditions seemed narrow and mediæval by the side of the new civilization in which he could now play a part. They lacked the elegance and the many-sidedness of European thought. Hence it is not surprising that many of the Jews of talent during the century assimilated so fully the outlook of their environment that they rejected altogether the national aspect of Judaism, neglected altogether its literature, and proclaimed abroad the principle that Judaism was simply a matter of religious creed which asked nothing of its followers save assent to certain articles of belief. Not a few were willing and even eager to transform that religious creed with ideas taken from outside; a new form of *Minut* began to flourish, as dangerous to the integrity of Judaism as the old heresies; and the attempt was made again to dissociate the religion from the law and the language. The feeling of race and nationality was indeed reawakened among a few who had at first felt most strongly the attraction of foreign ideas. The most distinguished Jewish Hellenist of the period, Heinrich Heine, could write in his Confessions: " There was a time when I did not like Moses overmuch, probably because the Hellenic spirit predominated in me, and I could not forgive the law-giver of the Jews his hatred of images and of plastic art. I did not see that, in spite of his hostility to the arts, Moses himself was a great artist. My preference for Hellas has since declined: I see now that the Greeks were only beautiful youths, but that the Jews have ever been men— strong, invincible men." The recantation which Heine made may be repeated by his people.

Most of Heine's generation, however, could not perceive what his genius grasped, that, despite the blandishments of Hellenic civilization, the Jewish outlook remained something sublime, distinctive, and worth preserving. The assimilation progressed in the second half of the nineteenth century from principle to principle, until at last it received a shock like that which awakened the nation to full self-consciousness in the Maccabean period. The revival of brutal anti-Semitism in eastern Europe

and of social anti-Semitism in several countries
of the West reminded the Jews, in many cases
against their will, that whatever their assimilation,
other peoples still regarded them as strangers. The
loyal spirits among them at the same time saw with
dismay that the absorption of the people and the
disappearance of their individual outlook were
threatened by an assimilation such as the Hellenizers had sought to force on Palestine two thousand
years earlier. The struggle to preserve Jewry
from destruction by the Hellenism of our day has
its closest parallel in the epoch of Jewish thought
which we have been considering. The nationality
indeed was then in a stronger position, because of
its physical and spiritual centre in Palestine and its
well-knit organization in the diaspora. But if the
outward conditions of the Jews are different, the
inner struggle and the genius of Judaism remain
the same. And the harmony of Hebraic and Hellenic ideas, which was not accomplished in that
epoch because of the debasement of the transplanted Hellenism, may be achieved in the future
by a self-conscious Jewish people which will imbibe
those elements of outside thought that are ennobling, but will transmute them by the dominating

Hebrew spirit. Our civilization, which is based partly on Hellenic, partly on Hebraic creations, is continually progressing to such a harmony, and without it humanity will never be tranquil, and culture will not be complete.

NOTES

CHAPTER I

INTRODUCTION

(pp. 15-50)

[1] Numbers 23.9.

[2] *De Vita Mosis*, II. 124.

[3] Psalms 106. 35.

[4] Isaiah 4. 3.

[5] *Ibid.* 56. 7.

[6] Ezekiel 20. 32.

[7] *Ibid.* 37. 11.

[8] See Margolis, *The Elephantine Documents*, in *Jewish Quarterly Review*, New Series, II, 419.

[9] The Elephantine papyri reveal that the Jews of Syene had their own temple or *Bamah*, and, like the Jews in the Egyptian Delta, had a separate temple; but these were exceptional cases.

[10] Sanhedrin 21b.

[11] Ben Sira 39. 1.

[12] Josephus, *Contra Apionem*, I. 12.

[13] Herodotus II. 1-4.

[14] Aristophanes, *Plutus*, l. 265, and *Birds*, l. 307.

[15] Joel 4. 6.

[16] Butcher, *Harvard Studies*.

[17] Yoma 69a.

[18] Josephus, *Antiquities*, XII. 8. 12.

[19] Josephus, *Contra Apionem*, I. 22.

[20] Josephus, *Bellum Judaicum*, II. 18. 7.

[21] Josephus, *Antiquities*, XII. 1.

[22] *Ibid.*, 2 and 3.

[23] Fragment 6. MS. Diodotum.

²⁴ Comp. Josephus, *Antiquities*, XI. 2. αἱ δὲ δέκα φυλαὶ πέραι εἰσιν Εὐφράτου ἕως δεῦρο, μυριάδες ἄπειροι.

²⁵ *Ibid.*, XVIII. 9.

²⁶ C. Flaccum 8.

²⁷ Menahot 109b.

²⁸ Reinach, *Bulletin de Correspondence Hell.*, XIII.

²⁹ See Mahaffy, *Athenæum*, 3527, p. 712.

³⁰ Strabo 14. 7. 2; comp. Josephus, *Contra Apionem*, 11. 4.

³¹ Isaiah 2. 16.

³² Josephus, *Bellum Judaicum*, VII. 3. 3.

³³ Comp. Pliny, Leg. 33.

³⁴ I Maccabees, 15. 22.

³⁵ Josephus, *Bellum Judaicum*, VI. 9. 7.

³⁶ *De Vita Mosis* II. 104, and *De Legatione*, II. 587.

³⁷ Josephus, *Bellum Judaicum*, II. 18. 7; *Antiquities*, XIV. 10. 24.

³⁸ *Ibid.*, *Antiquities*, XIV. 10; Corinth. 11. 24; Philo, *Legum*, 23; comp. Sanhedrin 32b.

³⁹ Strabo quoted by Josephus, *Antiquities*, XIV. 7. 2.

⁴⁰ Josephus, *Bellum Judaicum*, VII. 2. 3; Acts of Apostles 9. 2.

⁴¹ Cf. Macalister, *Civilization in Palestine*. The Greek version renders the word Philistines in Isaiah 9. (11) 12 by Hellenes.

⁴² Pliny, *Natural History*, V. 18. 74.

⁴³ Isaiah 8. 23.

CHAPTER II

THE HELLENISTIC CULTURE

(pp. 51-84)

¹ Greece is the name which the Romans gave to the conquered land of Hellas, because they first came into contact with a tribe of Graeci; just as Palestine is the name given to the land of Israel, because the conquerors first came into contact with Philistia. But the classical Greeks always called themselves Hellenes, and their culture Hellenism.

² Grote, *History of Greece*, vol. XII.

³ Comp. Lowes-Dickinson, *The Greek View of Life*.

[4] *Ibid.*

[5] Plato, *Republic*, II. 382.

[6] *Natural History*, II. 22.

[7] Gilbert Murray in *The Hibbert Journal*, 1910.

[8] *Nicomachean Ethics*, X.

[9] Psalm 115. 16.

[10] Isaiah 55. 8.

[11] Ben Sira 3. 21.

Chapter III

HELLENISM IN PALESTINE TILL THE DESTRUCTION OF THE TEMPLE

(pp. 85-125)

[1] I Maccabees 1. 8. 9.

[2] Fragment preserved by Diodorus, XL. 3.

[3] See Freudenthal, *Hellenistische Studien.*

[4] I Maccabees 1. 14, and II Maccabees 49.

[5] Ben Sira 24. 3-6.

[6] Daniel 3. 5, 10.

[7] Ben Sira 38. 1, *seq.*

[8] Comp. Mahaffy's *Greek Literature,* vol. I, p. 417.

[9] Comp. Ecclesiastes 4. 9.

[10] Pirke Abot 1. 3.

[11] Comp. Hamburger, *Real-Encyclopædie,* II s. v. *Griechen-thum.*

[12] Daniel 11. 14.

[13] Josephus, *Bellum Judaicum,* I. 1.

[14] *Antiquities,* XVII. 2. 1.

[15] II Maccabees 4. 7.

[16] I Maccabees 1. 13.

[17] II Maccabees 10. 19.

[18] Comp. II Maccabees 6. A remarkable example of religious syncretism of the time has recently come to light at Gezer, a city not far from the village of Modin, which was to play such an important part in the national redemption. A pillar has been

found there, the one side of which is inscribed with a votive offering to Heracles, while the other bears the name of Jehovah in Greek letters. (Macalister, *Side Lights on the Bible*.)

[19] I Maccabees 14. 5.

[20] Testament of Levi XIV. 4.

[21] Gospel according to Matthew 23. 15.

[22] *Antiquities*, XIV. 9. 4, and XV. 1. 1, 1.

[23] *Bellum Judaicum*, V. 1. 3. and IV. 4. 3.

[24] Mishnah Shekalim 1. 3; 3. 2; Gospel According to John 12. 20.

[25] Comp. M. Joël, *Blicke*, II, p. 170.

[26] *Antiquities*, XIII. 10. 8; XVIII. 1. 4.

[27] 1. 16; 11. 22.

[28] Sanhedrin 90b; Mark 12. 12.

[29] Sanhedrin, *loc. cit.*

[30] διαλέκτου Ἑλληνικῆς παρώνυμοι ὁσιότητος (chapter 13).

[31] *Jewish Encyclopedia*, s. v. *Essenes*.

[32] Shekalim 5. 6.

[33] *Antiquities*, XVIII, and *Bellum Judaicum*, II. 8. 5.

[34] *Quod Omnis Probus Liber Sit*, XII.

[35] *Antiquities*, XVIII. 2. 1.

[36] Josephus, *Bellum Judaicum*, II. 8. 7.

[37] Refutation of all Heresies, 9. 20, *seq.*

[38] *Meor 'Enayim*, Cassel's edition, II, p. 32.

[39] Comp. *Historia Ecclesiastica*, 11. 17.

[40] *Moreh Nebuke ha-Zeman*, II. 8.

[41] Ben Sira III. 20.

[42] Apollonius is a typical character of the period, a mixture of religious philosopher and miracle-monger, who travelled over the East collecting all kinds of magical lore. A modern scholar has seen a corruption of his name in the title of the book of " Ben La'anah," which was barred by the Rabbis from public reading. If the conjecture is correct, it would show that Hellenistic apocalypses were studied by Palestinian Jews.

[43] Sotah 7. 3; Megillah 1. 9.

[44] Yerushalmi Megillah 71c.

NOTES

⁴⁵ *Ibid.*

⁴⁶ *Gottesdienstliche Vorträge*, p. 105.

⁴⁷ Sanhedrin 17a.

⁴⁸ Comp. Yerushalmi Megillah 73a.

⁴⁹ Acts 6. 19.

⁵⁰ Yerushalmi Megillah 73d.

⁵¹ Acts 6. 4.

⁵² Comp. Josephus, *Bellum Judaicum*, I. 21.

⁵³ Acts 21.40; 22.2; Josephus, *Bellum Judaicum*, V. 9. 2; VI. 2. 1.

⁵⁴ *Antiquities*, XX. 11. 2.

⁵⁵ Josephus, *Bellum Judaicum*, I. 1.

⁵⁶ *Aspects of the Jewish Genius* (edited by L. Simon).

CHAPTER IV

HELLENISM IN THE DIASPORA

(pp. 126-169)

¹ Soferim 1. 8; Megillah 9a.

² Megillat Ta'amit (Hebrew supplement), Neubauer, *Mediæval Jewish Chronicles*, II, p. 24. See Joël, *Blicke*, I., p. 6, *seq.*

³ Exodus 24. 10.

⁴ *Ibid.* 33. 11.

⁵ Yerushalmi Megillah 71d; comp. also Babli 9a.

⁶ It is suggested that the description of the creation of the world ἐκ μὴ ὄντος (from the non-existent, III Macc. 7. 28) reflects Greek philosophical teaching; and the emphasis laid on the immortality of the soul may also be due to the foreign influence.

⁷ *Corpus Inscriptionum Graecarum* 4838.

⁸ Compare Joël, *op. cit.*, I, p. 80, *seq.*

⁹ *Amos* 8. 11.

¹⁰ Eusebius, *Praeparatio*, 20, *seq.* translated by Gaisford. In Ben Sira there is also a reference to the making of a reservoir for the city of Jerusalem (50. 3).

¹¹ See *Sibylline Oracles*, 1. 811.

[12] Psalm 104. 30.

[13] See later, chapter VI.

[14] *The Decline and Fall of the Roman Empire*, chapter XV.

[15] Comp. Josephus, *Contra Apionem*, II. 37.

[16] Philo, *De Vita Mosis*, II. 28.

[17] Chapter 2. 1-9.

[18] Chapter 4. 1-6.

[19] Chapter 13.

[20] Wisdom of Solomon 15.

[21] Psalm 16. 10, 11.

[22] *Ibid.* 6. 6.

[23] *Ibid.* 17. 15.

[24] Job 14. 14.

[25] Ecclesiastes 2. 14.

[26] Ben Sira 17. 27, 32.

[27] Daniel 12. 2, 3.

[28] See, on this point, Ahad Ha'am's essay on "Flesh and Spirit" (*Selected Essays*, translated by L. Simon, p. 146).

[29] Comp. *Abot de-Rabbi Natan*, edited Schechter, p. 26.

[30] Job 28.

[31] Proverbs 8. 22-30.

[32] Ben Sira 1.

[33] *Ibid.* 24. 1, *seq.*

[34] *Ibid.* 15. 1.

[35] Wisdom 7. 21, *seq.*

[36] Proverbs 9. 1.

[37] Wisdom of Solomon 18. 14.

[38] *Ibid.* 9. 1, 2.

[39] Comp. Bacher's *Wörterbuch der Tannaiten.*

[40] Hosea 12. 4, 5.

[41] Exodus 15. 22.

[42] Isaiah 55. 1.

[43] Exodus 15. 25.

[44] Proverbs 3. 18; comp. Mekilta 53a.

[45] *De Posteritate Caini,* 45.

[46] Comp. *Legum Allegoriae*, II. 21; *De Somniis*, II. 31, 38.

[47] Mekilta de-Rabbi Shim'on 82.

[48] Pirke Abot 6. 2.

[49] Numbers 21. 19.

[50] *Legum Allegoriae*, III. 6.

[51] *De Congressu Eruditorum Causa*, 1. 54.

[52] *De Somniis*, 1. 5.

[53] Comp. *De Migratione Abrahami*, 20. 20; *De Specialibus Legibus*, III. 32.

[54] *Legum Allegoriae*, 1. 135. Philo, quaintly enough, states that Moses received in Egypt this encyclic education from Greek teachers.

[55] *De Congressu Eruditorum Causa*, 34.

[56] Comp. *Quis Rerum Divinarum Heres*, 300; *De Cherubim*, 21-27.

[57] *De Ebrietate*, 33.

[58] *Legum Allegoriae*, I. 102.

[59] *De Migratione Abrahami*, 12.

[60] Deuteronomy 13. 1.

[61] *Ibid.* 19. 14.

[62] *De Justitate*, II. 360.

[63] *Quod Deterius Potiori Insidiatur*, 7.

[64] *De Fuga et Inventione*, 5.

[65] *De Migratione Abrahami*, 5.

[66] *Quis Rerum Divinarum Heres*, 53.

[67] *De Vita Mosis*, II. 260.

[68] *De Mundi Opificio*, 24.

[69] *Quaestiones in Genesis*, III. 45.

[70] *De Somniis*, II. 242.

[71] *De Gigantibus*, 30.

[72] *Legum Allegoriae*, III. 119.

[73] Comp. *De Migratione Abrahami*, 24.

[74] *De Vita Mosis*, I. 2.

[75] Josephus, *Contra Apionem*, II. 16.

[76] Acts of the Apostles 7.

[77] *Ibid.* 11.

[78] Comp. Montefiore, *Judaism and St. Paul*.

[79] *De Monarchia*, II. 2.

[50] Comp. Acts 2. 5.

[51] Comp. Bacon, *The Making of the New Testament.*

[52] Comp. John 3. 14; 6. 3.

[53] Hebrews 7. 15, 24, 25.

[54] Comp. Bacon, *op. cit.*

[55] *Epistola ad Africanum,* II. 3. 13.

CHAPTER V

THE HELLENISTIC JEWISH LITERATURE

(pp. 197-249)

[1] *Historia Ecclesiastica,* I. 23.

[2] This Eupolemus is confused by Polyhistor with the Jewish writer of that name, but is obviously writing from a different standpoint.

[3] Writers like Artapanus were really trying to square the data of world-history known to them with their national prepossessions and traditions. When a modern historian does the same thing, it is called Scientific Research.

[4] Comp. *Jewish Quarterly Review,* vol. XV, p. 337.

[5] Letter of Aristeas 128.

[6] *Ibid.* 142, *seq.*

[7] *Ibid.* 150, *seq.*

[8] *Ibid.* 234.

[9] Das Vierte Makkabäerbuch.

[10] Comp. Eusebius, *Praeparatio Evangelica,* 7. 13; 8. 10; Clem., Strom. V. 14, 97; XIII. 12.

[11] II Maccabees 1. 10; comp. Eusebius, *Praeparatio Evangelica,* 8. 10.

[12] Elter, *De Gnomologia Graecorum Historia,* p. 221; Bréhier, *Philo,* p. 48; comp., too, Joël, *op. cit.* I, p. 74.

[13] See later, p. 225.

[14] *Ueber das Phokylidische Gedicht.*

[15] It is noteworthy that the Rabbis expressly deprecated the deduction of general moralizing lessons from this command. See later, chapter VI, p. 266.

NOTES

[16] *Descriptio Graeciae,* X. 121, 9.

[17] *Sibylline Oracles,* III. 218, *seq.*

[18] Ἔσται καὶ Σάμος ἄμμος: ἐσεῖται Δῆλος ἄδηλος: καὶ ῥώμη ῥύμη.

[19] *Ibid.* 652, *seq.*

[20] Hirsch, *The Jewish Sibylline Oracles.*

[21] Comp. Origen, *Versus Celsum,* V. 61.

[22] It is referred to in the recently discovered Hebrew fragments concerning a Jewish sect, presumably of the first century, as the " Book of the Division of Time by Sabbatical Years and Jubilees." Comp. Schechter, *Fragments of Jewish Sectaries* (*Introduction*).

[23] Genesis 5. 24.

[24] Isaiah 11. 1.

[25] Psalms of Solomon 17.

[26] Enoch 48. 6.

[27] *Ibid.* 62. 5; 69. 29. For the title " Son of Man " comp. Yerushalmi Yoma 42c.

[28] Enoch 51.3.

[29] *Ibid.* 45. 3, 4.

[30] *Ibid.* 8. 1; 69. 9.

[31] *Ibid.* 69. 9, *seq.*

[32] ἀνατολή, δύσις, ἄρκτος, μεσημβρία.

[33] *Ibid.* 30. 13.

[34] *Ibid.* 65. 2; comp. Ben Sira 17. 3.

[35] Like Jubilees this book is referred to in the recently discovered Hebrew document of the supposed Zadokite sect.

[36] Comp. *Revue des Études Juives,* July, 1911.

[37] In the Protestant Apocrypha the book is known as Esdras II.

[38] II Esdras 320, *seq.*

[39] *Ibid.* 6. 60.

[40] *Ibid.* 7. 27.

[41] *Ibid.* 8. 29, *seq.*

[42] *Ibid.* 8. 41.

[43] *Ibid.* 9. 20.

[44] *Ibid.* 9. 33.

[45] *Ibid.* 7. 13.

[46] *Ibid.* 9. 3.

[47] According to an alternative reading, the number of books is two hundred and four.

[48] Josephus, *Vita,* 75.

[49] Josephus, *Contra Apionem,* II. 18.

[50] Josephus, *Bellum Judaicum,* Preface.

[51] Yerushalmi Kiddushin 59c.

[52] Psalm 45. 3. See Yerushalmi Megillah 71c.

[53] Quoted in Schechter's *Studies in Judaism,* Second Series, p. 23.

[54] Hagigah 12a.

[55] Origen, *Epistola ad Africanum,* 2.

[56] Yerushalmi Shabbat 6. 4; Yoma 3. 8; Sukkah 3. 5.

[57] *Jewish Quarterly Review,* VII, p. 275.

[58] *Jewish Quarterly Review,* New Series, IV, p. 9.

CHAPTER VI

THE RABBIS AND HELLENISM

(pp. 250-296)

[1] Genesis 9. 27.

[2] Yerushalmi Megillah 71c; comp. Joël, *Blicke,* I. 5.

[3] Yerushalmi Megillah 71c; Shabbat 115a; comp. Joël, *op. cit.,* pp. 64, 65.

[4] Yerushalmi Megillah 71a.

[5] Gittin 9. 8.

[6] Megillah 1. 8.

[7] Baba Kamma 82b; comp. Joël, *op. cit.*

[8] Josephus, *Antiquities,* XV. 10, 4.

[9] It has been suggested that Abtalion's warning, not to be exiled to a place of evil waters lest those who follow be corrupted, refers to Alexandria, where he had probably lived in exile with Judah, and that he was pointing to dangerous Alexandrian heresies. But "the place of evil waters" is better taken figuratively.

[10] Wayyikra Rabbah 34. 3.

[11] Pirke de-Rabbi Eliezer 18.

[12] Tamid 32a.

[13] Timæus, 8. 40.

[14] Erubin 13b.

[15] Pesikta Rabbati, Friedmann's edition, pp. 84a, 195a.

[16] Neumark, *Geschichte der Jüdishen Philosophie,* vol. 1, p. 70.

[1f] Pesahim 54a.

[16] Bereshit Rabbah 14.

[19] Enoch 4. 4.

[20] Berakot 16b.

[24] Bereshit Rabbah 14.

[28] Sanhedrin 38a; Hagigah 12a.

[23] Bereshit Rabbah 1. 2.

[24] Yalkut 2.

[25] Ben Sira 1. 9; comp. above, chapter IV, p. 154.

[26] It may be noted that one of Philo's treatises, in which he develops his mystical doctrine, is entitled " Cherubim," and starts from the description of the angels stationed at the entrance of the Garden of Eden.

[2f] Comp. Bemidbar Rabbah 9. 39.

[28] See above, chapter IV, p. 159.

[29] Comp. Lauterbach, *Jewish Quarterly Review,* New Series, vol. I, p. 503, *seq.*

[30] Exodus 21. 6.

[31] Kiddushin 22b.

[32] Leviticus 25. 55.

[33] *De Posteritate Caini,* 22.

[34] Tosefta Baba Kamma 7. 6.

[35] Deuteronomy 27. 5.

[36] *Ibid.,* 22. 6, 7.

[37] Galatians 4. 22.

[78] Romans II. 28.

[33] Galatians III. 10-13.

[40] Epistles 9.

[41] Justin, *Dialogue,* 40-46.

[42] Clement, 11. 21.

[43] Sanhedrin 99b.

[44] Hagigah 13a.

[45] Isaiah 14. 14.

[46] Proverbs 25. 16.

[47] Psalm 116.15.

[48] Ecclesiasticus 5. 5.

[49] Song of Songs 1. 4.

[50] Hagigah 14b; Yerushalmi Hagigah 2. 1.

[51] Hagigah 15a.

[52] Yerushalmi Hagigah 2. 1.

[53] Hagigah 14b.

[54] *Ibid.* 15a.

[55] *Ibid.*

[56] *Ibid.*

[57] *Ibid.*

[58] *Ibid.* 14a.

[59] Pirke Abot 3. 19.

[60] Yerushalmi Yadayim 3. 5.

[61] Song of Songs, Homily IV.

[62] Yerushalmi Sotah 24a.

[63] Hullin 60a; Bekorot 8b.

[64] Niddah 69b.

[65] *Historia Ecclesiastica,* IV. 2.   Dio, LXXVII. 32.

[66] Sanhedrin 10. 5.

[67] Berakot 61b.

[68] Deuteronomy 30. 20.

[69] Joshua 1. 8.

[70] Menahot 99b.

[71] Sanhedrin 11. 1.   (Joël, *Blicke,* I, p. 72, *seq.*)

[72] Midrash Kohelet 12. 13.   Joël (*op. cit.,* p. 74) ingeniously suggests, however, that Ben Sira is here a mistake for Ben Satda (Christian books).   Ben Sira belonged to the class of external books which was not for common study, but not to the class which was altogether reprobated.

[73] *Jewish Quarterly Review,* III, 541.

[74] Sanhedrin 100b.

[75] Comp. Schechter, *Jewish Quarterly Review,* III, 682.

[76] Shabbat 30a.

[77] Abot de-Rabbi Natan. (Schechter's edition, pp. 2, 3.)

[78] Shabbat 13b; Menahot 45a.

[79] It is noteworthy that Ben Sira obtained in the Christian Church the name of Ecclesiasticus, just because it was deemed fit for reading in Church (Ecclesia). Together with the other books of the Apocrypha, it was retained in the public ritual as possessing a moral value, though not invested with independent dogmatic authority.

[80] *Contra Apionem,* I. 8.

[81] Yadayim 3. 5.

[82] Hagigah 2. 1.

[83] Yerushalmi Hagigah 2. 1.

[84] Sotah 49a.

[85] *Ibid.*

[86] Tosefta Sotah 5. 8.

[87] Yerushalmi Megillah 71c.

[88] Sotah 49b.

[89] Soferim 1. 7; Megillat Ta'anit (Hebrew supplement), Neubauer, *Mediæval Jewish Chronicles,* II, p. 24.

[90] Hosea 8. 12.

[91] Tanhuma Wayyera.

[92] Pirke Abot 3. 23.

[93] Comp. *Quod Deterius Potiori Insidiatur* 191, 197; *Legum Allegoriae,* I. 102.

[94] Berakot 28b.

[95] Shabbat 116a.

CHAPTER VII

THE AFTERMATH

(pp. 297-330)

[1] Yerushalmi Sanhedrin 29b.

[2] Mekilta 22. 20.

[3] Berakot 10b. Renan deprecates the suggestion of the importance of the Christian version as against the Jewish at this period.

[4] Zechariah 10. 4.

[5] Yerushalmi Sanhedrin 20c.

[6] Psalms 26. 5.

[7] Yerushalmi Berakot 7d.

[8] Bereshit Rabbah 65. 16.

[9] Longinus, chapter 9.

[10] Comp. Origen, *Versus Celsum*, 5. 43.

[11] Bereshit Rabbah 1. 2.

[12] Sukkah 51b.

[13] Megillah 9b.

[14] Genesis Rabbah 16. 7.

[15] See Juster, *Les Juifs dans l'Empire Romain*, vol. I, p. 366.

[16] Joël, *op. cit.*, I, p. 52, seq.

[17] Moed Katon 28b: ὡς σπεῖρα ἐν στόματι ἱστου.

[18] Yerushalmi Rosh ha-Shanah 57a: πρὸ βάσιλεως ὁ νόμος οὐ γραφεὶς.

[19] Yerushalmi Nedarim 38a: πολὺ, κύριε, ἔβρειξας.

[20] Bereshit Rabbah 36. 12.

[21] Yerushalmi Sotah 24c.

[22] *Ibid.* 21b.

[23] Megillah 6a.

[24] Bereshit Rabbah 11. 7.

[25] Comp. *Jewish Quarterly Review*, III, 357.

[26] Hullin 60a.

[27] The words philosopher and *Min* are used almost synonymously for a person who disputed Jewish monotheism.

[28] *Legum Allegoriae* 3. 134.

[29] Berakot 55a.

[30] Yerushalmi Hagigah 77c.

[31] Hagigah 13a.

[32] *Geschichte der Jüdischen Philosophie.*

[33] *Novel* 146.

[34] See Zunz, *Gottesdienstliche Vorträge*, p. 301. Comp. also on this question Juster, *op. cit.*, I, p. 374.

[35] Comp. Epstein, *Revue des Études Juives*, vol. XXI.

NOTES

Comp. Steinschneider, *Jewish Quarterly Review,* vol. XVI, p. 390, *seq.*

Chapter VIII

CONCLUSION

(pp. 331-359)

[1] Comp. James Darmesteter's " Essay on the History of the Jews."

[2] Comp. Horowitz, *Die Stellung des Aristotels bei den Juden des Mittelalter.*

[3] An interesting study of the mediæval Jewish attitude toward Greek philosophy is to be found in an essay on " Maimonides and Halevi," by H. Wolfson, *Jewish Quarterly Review,* New Series, II, p. 297, *seq.*

[4] " Atticism and Judaism " in אוצר נחמד.

375

BIBLIOGRAPHY

I. BOOKS DEALING WITH THE WHOLE SUBJECT

The Apocrypha.

Schürer, E., History of the Jewish People in the Time of Jesus.

Wellhausen, J., Jewish History.

Graetz, H., History of the Jews, vols. II and III.

Renan, E., The Origins of Christianity.

Hamburger, Real-Encyclopädie für Bibel and Talmud.

Juster, Jean, Les Juifs dans l'Empire Romain.

Friedlaender, M., Zur Entstehung-Geschichte des Christenthums.
  Die Jüdische Apologetik.
  Die Religiöse Bewegungen der Juden im Zeitalter Jesus.

Wendland, Die Hellenistisch-Römische Kultur in ihrem Bezug
  zu Judenthum und Christenthum.

Hastings, Dictionary of the Bible, *s. v.* Apocrypha, Diaspora, etc.

Bauer, Von Griechenthum zu Christenthum.

Friedlander, G., Hellenism and Christianity.

II. BOOKS DEALING WITH SPECIAL ASPECTS OF THE SUBJECT

(A) HELLENISTIC CULTURE

Lowes-Dickinson, The Greek View of Life.

Zeller, E., History of Greek Philosophy: Stoics, Epicureans,
  and Sceptics.

Murray, Gilbert, Hellenistic Religion. (*Hibbert Journal,* 1910.)

Bevan, E. A., The First Contact of Hellenism with the East.
  (*Quarterly Review,* 1910.)

Butcher, S. H., Harvard Essays.

377

BIBLIOGRAPHY

(b) Hellenism in Judea

Smith, G. A., Jerusalem.

    The Minor Prophets.

Freudenthal, Hellenistische Studien.

Willrich, Juden und Griechen in der Vor-Makkabäischen Zeit.

Bevan, E. A., The Seleucid Empire.

Kautzsch, E., Pseudepigraphen der Juden.

(c) Hellenism in the Diaspora

Philo, Edited by Cohn and Wendland.

Siegfried, Philon als Ausleger des Alten Testaments.

Bréhier, Les Idées Philosophiques et Religieuses de Philo.

Drummond, The Alexandrian-Jewish Philosophy.

Mahaffy, J. P., The Silver Age of Greece.

Bacon, The Making of the New Testament.

(d) Hellenstic-Jewish Literature

Josephus, Edited by Niese.

Eusebius, Praeparatio Evangelica, edited by Gifford.

Reinach, Th., Textes des auteurs grecs et romains relatifs au Judaïsme.

Bernays, Gesammelte Schriften.

Thackeray, H. St. J., The Letter of Aristeas.

Charles, R. H., The Book of Enoch.

    The Slavonic Book of Enoch.

    The Testaments of the Twelve Patriarchs.

    The Assumption of Moses.

Duff, The Books of Esdras.

Rendel-Harris, The Odes of Solomon.

Hirsch, S. A., Sibylline Oracles (Collected Essays).

Zunz, L., Gottesdienstliche Vorträge der Juden.

BIBLIOGRAPHY

(E) The Rabbis and Hellenism

Graetz, Gnosticism in Judenthum.

Taylor, C., Sayings of the Jewish Fathers.

Bacher, W., Agada der Tannaiten.

Agada der Amoräer.

Wörterbuch der Tannaiten.

Joël, M., Blicke in die Religionsgeschichte zu Anfang des Zweiten christlichen Jahrhunderts.

Krauss, S., Lehnwörter.

Strack, Tractat Aboda Zara.

Krochmal, N., Moreh Nebuke ha-Zeman.

Neumark, D., Geschichte der Jüdischen Philosophie.

Harnack, A., The Expansion of Christianity, vol. I.

Lauterbach, J. Z., The Ancient Jewish Allegorists. (*Jewish Quarterly Review*, New Series, vol. 1.)

Montefiore, C. G., Judaism and St. Paul.

INDEX

Abbahu, amora, 309.

Abtalion, tanna, 100, 254, 370.

Adam Kadmon, 181.

Ahad Ha'am, 366.

Ahasuerus, 23.

Aher, 274; see also Elisha ben Abuyah.

Akiba, tanna, 247, 272, 273, 275, 276, 277, 278, 280, 300, 302, 317.

Alexander the Great, 24, 28, 29, 30, 31, 32, 33, 35, 45, 47, 48, 54, 55, 61, 65, 70, 85, 86, 208, 216, 255, 332, 349, 355.

Alexander Jannæus, 99, 116, 254.

Alexander Polyhistor, 129, 199; *see also* Polyhistor.

'*Am ha-Arez, Galilean*, 114.

Ambrosius, 320.

Ami, amora, 315.

Amos, 135.

Anileus, a Jew of Nehardea, 35.

Antigonus of Soco, tanna, 92.

Antiochus III, 94.

Antiochus Epiphanes, 89, 93, 94, 95, 96, 120, 132.

Antoinette, Marie, 82.

Aphrodite, 57.

Apion, 26.

Apocalypse of Baruch, the, 233.

Apocalypses, the, 198, 223.

Apocalyptic literature, 109-117, 223.

Apocalyptics, the, 224, 225, 227, 229.

Apocrypha, the, 198.

Apollo, 57, 133.

Apollonius of Tyana, 113, 364.

Aquila, 247, 248, 252, 287, 294, 307, 322, 323, 324.

Ares, 57.

Aristeas, 127, 134, 204, 206, 208.

Letter of, 134, 137, 203, 204, 209, 213, 216, 352.

Aristobulus, 134, 312.

Aristobulus, Alexandrian Jewish philosopher, 116, 212, 213, 214.

Aristobulus, " Exegesis " of, 134, 226.

Aristophanes, 25, 59, 361.

Aristotle, 29, 30, 63, 67, 68, 69, 211, 249, 288, 347, 349, 350.

Arnold, Matthew, 51.

Artapanus, a historical romancer, 136, 368.

Artaxerxes I, 20.

Asineus, a Jew of Nehardea, 35.

Assouan, Aramaic papyri found at, 18.

Assumption of the Prophets, the, 284.

Assumption of Moses, the, 235.

Astarte, worship of, 88.

Athene, 57.

Atticus, philosopher of fourth century, 249.

Augustine, 320.

Bacchus, 63, 97.

Bacher, W., 13, 366.

Bacon, 368.

Balaam, blessings of, 15.

Bar Cochba, the rising of, 278.

Bar Kappara, 285, 309, 310, 315.

Barnabas, gnostic, 268.

Ben Azzai, tanna, 272, 273.

Ben La'anah, the book of, 282, 364.

Ben Satda, 372.

381

INDEX

Ben Sira, 22, 68, 89, 90, 112, 116, 148, 197, 262, 282.
Ben Toglah, the book of, 282.
Ben Zoma, tanna, 272, 273, 274, 280.
Bernays, 217, 353.
Boethus, Alexandrian family, 116.
Book of Enoch, 227, 230, 232, 259, 327.
Book of Ezra, the, 235, 245.
Book of Jubilees, 225-227, 328, 329.
Book of Raziel, the, 327.
Bréhier, 368.
Butcher, S. H., 51, 361.

Cæsar, Julius, 251.
Cain, symbol of impious pride, 182.
Cainites, the, 291, 292.
Caird, Professor, 53.
Celsus, pagan impugner of Christianity, 222, 304.
Chance, worship of, 61.
Christian Science, spread of, 62.
Cleanthes, Stoic, 29, 30, 71, 72.
Clement of Alexandria, 213, 268, 270, 312, 349.
Cleodemos, Malchos, 200.
Cleopatra, 115.
Constantine, emperor, 218, 319.
Crescas, 329, 351.
Cynics, the, 72, 75.
Cyril, bishop of Alexandria, 320.
Cyrus, 23, 34.

Darmsteter, James, 375.
dei Rossi, Azariah, 107, 352.
Demetrius, Chronicles of, 132, 199.
Dio Cassius, 278.
Diodorus, Greek historian, 215, 363.
Diogenes, 185.
Dionysus, festival of, 133.
Dionysus, patron deity of Scythopolis, 88.
Dionysus Sabazios, 97.
Divine Presence, doctrine of, 175.

Domninus, Jewish neo-Platonist, 249.
Dorshe Hamurot, 160, 206, 264, 265.
Dorshe Reshumot, 159, 161, 266.
Dositheus, 115.

Ebionites, the, 109, 286.
Eighteen Benedictions, 229, 292.
Eleazar, tanna, 205, 206, 247, 286, 299.
Eleazar Hisma, 290.
Eleazar ben Pedat, 308.
Eliezer ben Hyrcanus, 270, 271.
Eliezer ben José of Galilee, 269.
Eliezer, tanna, 162.
Elijah, teacher of Pythagoras, 79.
Elisha ben Abuyah, 272, 274, 275, 302.
Elter, 368.
Epicureans, the, 70, 144, 146, 150.
Epicureanism, 77, 78.
Epicurus, 77, 78, 81, 185.
Epstein, 374.
Essenes, the, 81, 102, 104, 105, 107, 108, 109, 120, 162, 171, 172, 173, 335, 353.
Euergetes, king of Egypt, 116.
Eupolemus, Hellenistic historian, 92, 200, 368.
Euripides, 59, 138.
Eusebius, 105, 171, 199, 278, 350, 365, 368.
Ezekiel, Jewish Greek writer, 136.
Ezra, reformation of, 19.

Falashas, the, 227.
France, Anatole, 345.
Frankel, Z., 353.
Freudenthal, 200, 203, 209, 363.
Friedlaender, Israel, 14.
Friedlaender, Moritz, 12.
Fortune, worship of, 61.

Gainsford, 365.
Galilean 'Am ha-Arez, 114.

382

INDEX

Gamaliel, 349.
Gamaliel II, 287.
Gersonides, 349.
Gibbon, E., 142.
Graetz, Heinrich, 310, 353.
Greek version, 130, 246, 247; *see also* Septuaguit, the.
Grote, historian, 362.

Hadrian, 301.
Hai Gaon, 276.
Haman, attacks of, 33.
Hananiah ben Hezekiah, 282.
Hanina, amora, 308.
Hasidim, the, 93, 97, 102, 105.
Hassideans, 92, 97.
Hebrew Canon, the, 109, 110, 112, 128, 195, 225, 248, 281, 282, 283, 284.
Hecataeus, Greek historian, 87, 215, 216.
Heine, Heinrich, 357.
Heraclitus, Ionian philosopher, 26, 74, 138.
Heracles, Phoenician origin of, 87, 96, 200.
Hermes, mediation of, 180, 201, 202.
Hermetic writings, 113.
Herod, 116, 120, 251, 310.
Herodotus, 25, 361.
Hesiod, 74, 158.
Hillel, tanna, 101, 124, 254, 255, 256, 267, 316.
Hippolytus, 105, 106.
Hirsch, S. A., 369.
Homer, 73, 74, 91, 158, 220, 221, 304.
Homeric mythology, 60.
Homeros, the books of, 282.
Horowitz, 375.
Horus, 66.
Hosha'ya, amora, 310, 311, 312.
Huna, Rab, amora, 306.
Hypsistanae, the, 291.

Ibn Gebirol, 329, 349, 351.
Ishmael, tanna, 276, 280, 293.
Isis, 63, 64, 66.

Jannes and Jambres, history of, 138.
Jason, 87, 95, 96.
Jason, a Carian Jew, 133.
Jason of Cyrene, 132, 209.
Jellinek, A., 353.
Jerome, church father, 40, 286.
Jesus, 189, 192, 193.
Joël, M., 307, 364, 368, 370, 374.
Johanan, amora, 309.
Johanan bar Nappaha, 308.
Johanan ben Zaccai, tanna, 263, 264, 265, 270, 271, 316.
Johanan of Eleutheropolis, 306.
John the Baptist, 109.
John Hyrcanus, 99.
Johnson, Samuel, 63.
Jonathan, 98.
José of Galilee, 275.
Josephus, 24, 26, 29, 33, 34, 41, 86, 94, 101, 103, 105, 106, 107, 121, 122, 127, 143, 187, 209, 241-245, 283, 352, 361, 362, 364, 365, 366, 367, 370.
Joshua, amora, 313.
Joshua ben Hananiah, 247, 273, 277.
Joshua ben Levi, 311, 312; Mystery of, 326.
Judah, amora, 313.
Judah ben Ilai, 305, 315.
Judah ben Pazzi, 273.
Judah ben Tabbai, 287.
Judah ha-Nasi, 285, 298, 308, 309.
Judah ha-Levi, 329, 350, 351.
Judas Maccabeus, 98, 200.
Julian, emperor, 319.
Juster, Jean, 374.
Justinian, anti-Jewish legislation of, 321.
Justus of Tiberias, 241.
Juvenal, 291.

383

Kabbalah, the, 327.
Karaites, the, 324.
Krauss, S., 249.
Krochmal, N., 111, 352.

Lauterbach, J. Z., 371.
Levi bar Haita, 310.
Libertini, the, 118.
Luther, Martin, 310.
Luzzatto, Samuel David, 351, 352.
Lysimachus, son of Ptolemy, 115.

Ma'aseh Bereshit, 257, 285.
Ma'aseh Merkabah, 257, 263.
Macalister, 362, 364.
Macaulay, 177.
Maccabees, Second Book of, 209, 212; Fourth Book of, 209, 213.
Mahaffy, 362, 363.
Maimonides, 329, 349, 351.
Maine, 354.
Manetho, Egyptian historian, 131.
Marcion, gnostic, 268.
Marcus Aurelius, 301.
Margolis, M. L., 361.
Mazzol-Tov, the Jewish goodwish, 63.
Meir, tanna, 302, 303, 305.
Meleager, 48.
Men of the Great Synagogue, 20, 23, 59.
Menander, comedies of, 139.
Menelaus, 96.
Metatron, angel, 273, 274, 327.
Midrash Konen, the, 328.
Midrash Tadshe, the, 328.
Minim, the, 284, 290, 291, 292, 312, 374.
Minut, 291, 292, 303, 356.
Mommsen, Th., 191.
Montefiore, C. G., 367.
Moses, 20, 130, 184, 185, 200.
Müller, Max, 179.
Murray, Gilbert, 363.
Musæus, verses on, 138; identified with Moses, 202.

Neander, 352.
Nehunyah ben ha-Kanah, 302.
Neo-Platonists, the, 79.
Neo-Pythagorean brotherhood, 63.
Neo-Pythagorean school, 79, 81, 107, 139, 144, 150, 158.
Neumark, David, 316, 371.
Nicholas of Damascus, 241.
Numbers, veneration of, 225.
Numenius of Apamea, 303.

Odes of Solomon, the, 234.
Oenomaus of Gadata, 303.
Olympian gods, 58, 87.
Olympian hierarchy, 56, 73.
Onias, 36.
Onias, family of, 94.
Onias III, 94, 95, 96.
Onias IV, 116, 132.
Ophites, the, 291.
Origen, church father, 195, 270, 275, 310, 311, 312, 369, 370, 374.
Orpheus, verses on, 138, 202, 203.
Orphism, Hellenic mystical teaching, 63.
Osiris, 64, 66.
Ossian, 140.

Pan, patron deity of Panios, 88.
Pan, temple of, 133.
Paul, apostle, 40, 121, 267, 280, 292.
Pauline Epistles, 267.
Pausanias, 218.
Perseus and Andromeda, story of, 87.
Persius, 291.
Perushim, the, 93.
Pharisees, the, 100, 102, 104, 105, 113, 116, 120, 150, 336.
Philemon, Greek comic poet, 216.
Philip the Macedonian, 28, 54.
Philo-Judæus, 15, 34, 36, 41, 43, 127, 143, 157-187, 190, 191, 192, 193, 197, 212, 213, 214,

226, 231, 232, 235, 240, 244,
249, 260, 261, 263, 264, 265,
270, 275, 291, 293, 303, 311,
312, 314, 317, 328, 329, 339,
340, 341, 352, 353, 370.
"Philo," 105, 106.
Philo, author of a narrative poem
in Greek, 137.
Philocrates, 204.
Philodemus, 47.
Phineas ben Jair, 328.
Phocylides, 138, 217, 219.
Photius, 241.
Plato, 26, 59, 68, 69, 74, 177, 249,
255, 288, 351, 363.
Platonists, the, 139.
Pliny, 61, 362.
Plutarch, 29.
Pollion, 101; see Abtalion.
Polyhistor, 368.
Pompeius, 119, 250, 251, 253.
Porch, school of the, 178.
Psalms of Solomon, 228, 234.
Pseudo-Aristeas, 92.
Pseudo-Artapanus, 201, 202.
Pseudo-Eupolemus.
Pseudo-Hecatæus, 216.
Pseudo-Phocylides, 218.
Pseudo-Solomon, 151.
Pseudepigraphic literature, 109-
117, 203.
Ptolemy, 32, 37, 86, 92, 115.
Ptolemy Philadelphus, 127, 128,
130, 204, 205.
Ptolemy Soter, 215.
Ptolemies, the, 45, 65, 94, 115, 131,
132, 205, 212, 214, 336.
Pythagoras, 79, 81, 107, 108, 185.
Pythagorean school, 80, 81.
Pythagoreans, the, 80.

Quietus, 287.

Rab, amora, 261.
Rabbah, amora, 313, 314.
Reinach, 362.

Renan, Ernest, 41, 373.
Reuben, amora, 313.

Saadya, 329, 347.
Sadducees, the 102, 103, 104, 109,
150, 324; see also Zadokites.
Sameas, 100; see Shemaiah.
Scaliger, 204, 217.
Sceptics, the, 79.
Schechter, Solomon, 14, 366, 369,
373.
Schürer, E., 13, 100, 199.
Scriptures, Greek translation of,
115, 127, 128, 129; see also
Septuagint Version.
Sefer ha-Yashar, 327.
Sefer Hekalot, 326, 327.
Sefer Yezirah, 327.
Sefirot, doctrine of, 328.
Seleucus I, 33.
Seleucids, the, 65, 86, 94, 132.
Seneca, Roman philosopher, 188.
Septuagint Version, 92, 115, 129,
130, 132, 138, 195, 197, 198,
199, 200, 203, 246, 247, 289,
294, 322, 323, 324, 337.
Sethites, the, 291.
Severus, 278, 319.
Shammai, 254, 255, 256, 257
Shekinah, doctrine of, 175.
Shemaiah, tanna, 100, 254.
Sibyl, the, 140, 203.
Sibyl, verses on the, 138, 218.
Sibylline oracles, the, 141, 215, 218,
223.
Sibyllistae, the, 222.
Sicimos, son of Hermes, 201.
Simon the Just, 92, 349.
Simon ben Gamaliel, 253, 287.
Simon ben Judah, 265.
Simon ben Lakish, 308.
Simon ben Shetah, 254.
Simon ben Yohai, 298.
Simon, L., 365, 366.
Socrates, 67, 68, 74, 185.
Socratic system, 80.

Sophocles, 138, 203, **216**.
Spinoza, Baruch, 354.
Steinschneider, M., 375.
Stephen, one of the "Grecian Jews," 189.
Stoics, the, 70, 71, 73, 74, 75, 76, 78, 79, 81, 82, 104, 107, 144, 150, 158, 178, 186, 208, 211.
Stoicism, 71, 77, 211.
Strabo, 33, 37, 43, 362.

Targum, the, 115, 118, 128.
Targum Onkelos, 252.
Tarphon, tanna, 293.
Tatian, 286.
Testaments of Twelve Patriarchs, the, 234, 284.
Theocritus, idylls of, 91.
Theodosius, anti-Jewish legislation of, 321.
Theodotion, 248.
Theodotus, 201.
Theophrastus, 30.
Therapeutae, the, 164, **171**, **173**.

Titus, 121, 191.
Tobiades, the, 94.
Trojan, 287, 301.

Vespasian, 122.
Voltaire, 319.

Wisdom of Solomon, 145-147, 151, 152, 154, 197, 233, 245, 249, 259, 283.

Xenophanes, Ionian philosopher, 26.

Yabneh, the vineyard of, 263.

Zadokites, the, 103; *see also* Sadducees.
Zarathustra, 23.
Zeno, Stoic, 71.
Zerubbabel, 34.
Zeus, 72, 97.
Zeus Olympios, 96.
Zeus Xenios, 96.

𝕿𝖍𝖊 𝕷𝖔𝖗𝖉 𝕭𝖆𝖑𝖙𝖎𝖒𝖔𝖗𝖊 𝕻𝖗𝖊𝖘𝖘
BALTIMORE, MD., U. S. A.

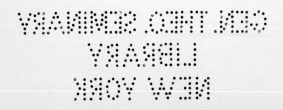